THE CATTLE GUARD

JAMES F. HOY

THE
CATTLE GUARD

Its History and Lore

FOREWORD BY JIMMY M. SKAGGS

UNIVERSITY PRESS OF KANSAS

© Copyright 1982 by the University Press of Kansas
Printed in the United States of America

Published by the University Press of Kansas (Lawrence, Kansas 66045), which was organized by
the Kansas Board of Regents and is operated and funded by Emporia State University, Fort Hays
State University, Kansas State University, Pittsburg State University, the University of Kansas,
and Wichita State University.

Library of Congress Cataloging in Publication Data

Hoy, James F.
The cattle guard.

Bibliography: p.
Includes index.
1. Cattle guards — History.   2. Cattle guards — Folklore.   I. Title.
SF206.H68   1982   636.2'01   82-9055
ISBN 0-7006-0226-7   AACR2

For my parents

CONTENTS

LIST OF ILLUSTRATIONS

FOREWORD

In *Pecos Tales* (1967), Texas folklorist Paul Patterson recalled when his father reluctantly gave up his horses and wagon for newfangled automotive power, about 1920:

> Although the label on the radiator said "Ford," it was of the mongrel breed. Like the team we had traded off, it was no thoroughbred but was kin to all of them—Buick rear, Chevrolet universal, etc., with strains of Hupmobile, Apperson Jack Rabbit, and Cole Eight blood in evidence here and there. In deference to Henry Ford, and since we'd gotten the majority of it from Dr. McDonald, we called it Mack.
>
> So here we are rattling down the road. [Brother] Ralph had relinquished the steering wheel to Papa, because of the latter's desperate need to become attuned to the machine age. What with Ralph in close attendance, and deep ruts to simplify steering, Papa ought to make it all right. Even so, Ralph had his misgivings. And rightly so, for when a big wooden gate loomed up it took all of Papa's strength and Ralph's ingenuity to get Old Mack to "whoa."
>
> [Brother] John jumped out, or rather off, to open the gate. Just as he had gotten it pointed directly at us, Old Mack cold-jawed, or something, on Papa and lunged into the one-by-four that served as a latch, gave a coughing, gurgling sound and died. But the gurgling sound continued. The gate latch had stabbed open Old Mack's bladder.

"What's it look like?" Papa asked, his tone three-quarters in anger, one-quarter in shame, since he felt some blame for Old Mack's lurching. John's reply was one to bring joy to any Westerner that ever lived, if the inquiry pertained to a brand new well and windmill on his property. But on this occasion it fell on unappreciative ears.

"Oh, Papa, it's throwin' a fine stream."

Had Patterson continued his story, he might have told how Papa so thereafter installed a cattle guard to replace the obsolete gate, which h wounded Old Mack. Undoubtedly the West Texan had seen the devices the Kokernot Ranch near Alpine or on Joseph Tweedy's spread at Knick bocker or on the vast Noelke Ranch, which fanned out west of San Angelo, on all three. Cattle guards were appearing in every place where barbed wi roads, and automobiles converged, and each one of them was a bit differe from the one before.

The cattle guard is a folk innovation, a bit of practical technology th literally traces its origins to antiquity. Unlike barbed wire, which also h many would-be inventors, the cattle guard ultimately saw no one design b come standard in the way that Joseph Glidden's double-twist barbed wire l its industry. Glidden's 1874 patents on the wire—and on the machine th economically produced it—enabled the Washburn & Moen Manufacturi Co. of Massachusetts to monopolize the barbed-wire market. When John ("Bet-you-a-million") Gates acquired the Washburn-Moen interest, parlayed it into American Steel and Wire, an important component of t U.S. Steel merger in 1901, then the largest in history.

Though fence owners had to buy their wire from U.S. Steel because of patent monopoly, they could (and did) construct their own cattle guards fro logs, upturned two-by-fours, or pipes. Patterson's cattle guard probably w like his hybrid truck, Old Mack, a bit of every functioning device he had ev seen—Kokernot, Tweedy, and Noelke. Prettier versions were available mail-order catalogs, but they were no more effective than homemade one which, for the most part, were cheaper. Because the cattle guard ultimate was an innovation rather than an invention, no one ever cornered the mark on its manufacture and sale. No "cattle guard trust" emerged. Consequentl no systematic body of information about the cattle guard has ever existed, u til now.

The highway cattle guard logically appeared first where it was mo needed—on the Great Plains after the turn of the century as automobiles r placed slow, plodding draft animals. That fact inevitably will draw this wo into the ongoing Webb-Shannon debate about the significance of geograph cal determinism. Walter Prescott Webb, in *The Great Plains* (1931), hypot esized that settlers modified tools and institutions to fit environmental nece sity, as in the adaptation of windmills on the plains, or, more pertinently to this story, as in Glidden's invention of barbed wire, which was so eagerly embraced by plainsmen. Fred A. Shannon's *Appraisal of Walter Prescott Webb's "The Great Plains"* (1940) refuted Webb's thesis by pointing to the origin of the Colt revolver, one of Webb's own examples, which was developed in Connecticut without any apparent reference to the possibility of its eventually being used on the Great Plains. Shannon, an easterner, said that Webb, a westerner, used selective documentation (which was true) to buttress an indefensible argument — namely, that environment modifies institutions, instead of the other way around. In reality, the debate is between unorthodox methodology (Webb's) and tradition (Shannon's). While there is merit in both positions, I side with Webb, perhaps in part because I studied with several of his disciples, but also because I see logic in his "institutional fault" view of human development. The highway cattle guard did appear first where it was most needed — where fences, open-range roads, and automobiles converged most frequently: namely, on the Great Plains.

If cattle guards were products of geographical determinism — and surely they were — they must therefore also have been manifestations of economic determinism, crass necessity. It is no mere coincidence that Hoy discovered the greatest concentration of cattle guards to be in the oil fields of the American Great Plains and the Southwest. Time is money. Cattle guards are infinitely more efficient than creaky gates, which in the words of Paul Patterson "loom up" at unwary traffic. Because the highway cattle guard has worked so well, use of it has spread worldwide, wherever fences, roads, automobiles, and economic necessity have come together.

The folk-device reality of the cattle guard has necessitated an unorthodox methodology in this book, a blending of traditional history and folklore that reveals much, I think, about the American character — our common quest for a better design, a more practical and cheaper way. Anyone who has driven over a cattle guard at any speed will vividly recall that teeth-chattering, pipe-clanging experience and no doubt will appreciate the evolutionary adaptation of painted stripes on western highways, which somehow deter livestock. Shannon no doubt would argue that those painted stripes are proof that mankind modifies the environment, while Webb would point to the location of those surrealistic caricatures of jarring reality — in the West, along paved roadways where people regularly drive fast. Somehow I am reminded of a roadrunner cartoon.

This book by James Hoy, fortunately for the reader, is largely devoid of historiographical posturing. When I first read the manuscript, I remembered J. Frank Dobie's treatment of *The Longhorns* (1941), a rough-hewn blend of folklore and history that simultaneously served both disciplines. Hoy's informal style suits William Curry Holden, who appears as a source in the text.

Warm, insightful, leathery Curry Holden is an unequaled raconteur, who, unfortunately, is known mostly as a scholarly historian, author of such works as *Alkali Trails* (1930), one of those works cited by Webb in *The Great Plains*. Hoy's Holden is the personal, informal version whom I enjoyed knowing one winter in Lubbock. He is but one of many interesting, vivid folk who are encountered on the pages that follow.

Wichita State University   JIMMY M. SKAGGS

PREFACE

Cattle guards are associated with two of my favorite childhood memories: shipping cattle and Wilbur Countryman's yearly rodeo. I grew up on a small ranch in the Flint Hills near Cassoday, Kansas. From the time we started school, my sister, Rita, and I were helping to drive three- and four-year-old Texas steers from summer grass in Western Greenwood County to the Santa Fe stockyards at Cassoday. Our father would wake us at 3:00 A.M. to do chores and load horses, then we would drive fifteen miles east to Frank Klasser's ranch. I would usually doze during the first half of the trip, but the cattle guard at Harsh's Hill Pasture, where the flats gave way to the open-range roads of the Flint Hills proper, always jarred me awake, and the other guards, into and out of the Turney and Mosby pastures, kept me awake.

We would be in the pastures by daylight, rounding up the steers and holding the cut for Jake Jordan or Olin Weaver; then we would head the selected fat cattle back toward Cassoday, driving them through the gates at the sides of the cattle guards that we had bounced across only a few hours earlier.

We drove cattle almost every weekend from late June through September, but Countryman's Rodeo came only on the Fourth of July. Wilbur Countryman lived in the middle of a section pasture a few miles south of Cassoday, and he and his family staged a genuine ranch rodeo, one of the last in the nation. He had his own string of brahma bulls and bucking horses, and his herd of Herefords provided some salty times for calf ropers and wild-cow milkers. The large arena was covered with buffalo grass, except for a little natural

xvii

gravel near the chutes, where bulls and broncs had worn the grass away. At each end of the pasture, north and south, was a cattle guard. My sister and I would enter the pasture at the gate at the side of the cattle guard, having left home at dawn to ride to Countryman's in time to help round up the stock. Our parents were secretaries for the rodeo, so we always stayed late; usually it was after dark before we loaded our horses into the truck to go home. Driving across the cattle guard on the way out signaled the end of an annual event that was surpassed in our young lives only by Christmas.

Thus, in my mind, cattle guards have always been linked with ranches and cowboys. Most people have given little thought to cattle guards. I hope that this book will help others to see the cattle guard as I see it, as a symbol of the modern West.

Footnotes can be exasperating; so can lack of them. Because of the nontraditional nature of much of the research for this book and because most of my information has come from oral sources, I have decided to use a nontraditional method of documentation. I have chosen to list, chapter by chapter, both the published and the unpublished sources, along with appropriate commentary, in a section called Sources of Information. This section should allow those who might be interested in doing so to trace my exact use of published material and my general use of unpublished material while simultaneously presenting to the reader an uncluttered text, one free from the distractions of numerous footnotes to oral sources. More complete information about the people listed in the Sources of Information can be found in the List of Contributors.

No author writes alone, although authors are often alone when they write. My first and greatest debt is to my wife, Cathy, my daughter, Farrell, and my son, Josh, for their help as planners, researchers, travel companions, and critics. I could have written this book without their help, but I would not have had as much fun doing it.

Because no previous scholarship on the cattle guard exists, I have had to seek out nontraditional sources of information. Many people have helped in this search, more than six hundred of whom are named in the List of Contributors. Many others, I fear, must share the anonymity of the inventor of the cattle guard, for it is impossible to name all who deserve mention. I do, however, want to note certain areas of assistance and give credit to those whose help was especially timely or whose suggestions proved especially fruitful.

Finding potential informants for this study was greatly facilitated by cooperative members of the media. I sent a letter of inquiry to every county-seat newspaper in the seventeen western states, as well as to dozens of farm and ranch magazines, petroleum and railroad publications, and scholarly journals. I am grateful to the many editors who published this query. I am also grateful to the following individuals for their early publicizing of my search for information about cattle guards: Don Coldsmith, syndicated columnist, Emporia, Kans.; James J. Fisher, *Kansas City Star* and *Times;* Al Gustin, KFYR Radio, Bismarck, N.Dak.; Roger Hartsook, KVOE Radio, Emporia, Kans.; Paul Omondsun, KROP Radio, Brawley, Calif.; Rick Plumlee, *Wichita Eagle-Beacon;* and Ralph Titus, KSAC Radio, Manhattan, Kans.

A scholar cannot work without libraries and archives. I want to thank the personnel of the many historical societies, museums, and libraries who helped me gather information. The following people deserve special mention: John Creasey, of the Museum of English Rural Life, University of Reading, England, who first told me about Cornish stiles; Mae Andrews, of the William Allen White Library at Emporia State University, and William Longenecker, of the National Agricultural Library, Beltsville, Maryland, who conducted computer searches of relevant bibliographies; Vicki Phillips, of the Oklahoma State University Library, for her help in searching patent records; Larry Remele, of the North Dakota State Historical Society, who first told me about Andrew Johnston's cattle guard; Steve Hanschu, Nannette Martin, and Kathy Mitchum, of the William Allen White Library; and cooperative interlibrary-loan librarians everywhere for tracking down and making available scores of obscure books and articles.

I am grateful to Marge Jeffrey, secretary for the Department of English at Emporia State University, for help in the clerical work of this study. Student secretaries who helped include Karen Huber, Laurie Morris, Eileen Probst, and Regina Terick. For help in obtaining photographic reproductions, I am indebted to Les Marks, Kay Shireman, and the staff of the Emporia State University Instructional Media Center.

Institutional support from Emporia State University came in the form of grants from the Faculty Research and Creativity Committee, from a sabbatical leave, and from the personal and professional support of Charles E. Walton, former chairman of the Department of English; from John E. Peterson, dean of Liberal Arts and Sciences; and from Patrick O'Brien, director of the Center for Great Plains Studies. Encouragement for this study was also provided by the editors of *The Cattleman, Kanhistique, Kansas Quarterly,* and *North Dakota History,* who published portions of chapters 3, 4, and 7 in their respective journals; I thank them for allowing that material to be reprinted here. Encouragement of another sort has come from my students. Their expectations and demands have, over the years, been a source of continuing inspiration.

My special thanks go to Ace Reid for permitting me to use his cartoon from the June 1981 edition of the Cowpokes calendar.

Finally, I want to thank Mel Storm, Dick Keller, and Tom Isern, friends and colleagues, whose frank criticism and good judgment kept me honest and whose tolerance and good humor kept me human during this five-year under-taking.

THE CATTLE GUARD

Yet a barful strife!

Shakespeare, *Twelfth Night*

1

THE CATTLE GUARD:
AN OVERVIEW

In 1905 Theodore Roosevelt was in the middle of his presidency, and America's big stick was being felt both at home and around the world. During the previous year, Roosevelt had "busted" his first trust, and during the following year he had become the first American to win the Nobel Prize for Peace. America's self-image was taking shape, as was its self-awareness: St. Louis had played host to the third modern Olympic Games in 1904; Devil's Tower had been designated as the first national monument in 1905; and Upton Sinclair had published *The Jungle* in 1906, with resultant shock waves that surpassed even those of the San Francisco earthquake of the same year. By this time the land frontier had disappeared (Oklahoma had become the forty-sixth state in 1906), but other frontiers were rapidly emerging: Einstein published his Theory of Relativity in 1905; and two years before that, the Wright Brothers had conquered gravity at Kittyhawk. Above all, that decade marked the triumph of the automobile. The first National Auto Show was held in New York City in 1900, the same year that the *Saturday Evening Post* published its first automobile advertisements. Three years later a Winton crossed America coast to coast; the trip took sixty-three days. In 1908 Henry Ford introduced the Model T, perhaps the most far-reaching automotive event of all time.

In the midst of this tumultous decade — probably in 1905 — someone on the Great Plains of the United States built and installed the world's first automotive cattle guard. It was a relatively minor invention, an element of rural folk life that directly touched the lives of only a limited number of people; on those lives, however, it had immediate and definite consequences. Those who were most immediately affected were—and are—ranchers and farmers, but indirectly the cattle guard has benefited many more. Virtually everyone who has ever driven the roads of cattle country, for instance, has crossed cattle guards. Unless these guards were exceptionally rough and bumpy, however, few travelers will have given them a second, or even a first, thought. When the cattle guard is placed among the other inventions of its decade, its obscure position in the popular mind is understandable and not undeserved. Yet it has some claims to importance, not the least of which is that the cattle guard is a symbol of range country, an emblem that evokes the contemporary West in much the same way that the Winchester rifle or longhorn cattle call to mind images of the Old West. When you cross a cattle guard, you look for livestock and you look for cowboys.

The immediate predecessor of the automotive (or highway) cattle guard was the railroad cattle guard, which functions primarily as an extension of the right-of-way fence. Between 1837 and 1934, patents were issued on at least 409 railroad cattle guards. American railroads used cattle guards at least as early as 1836, and they are still using them.

Automotive cattle guards, which function primarily as gates, have taken several forms since they began to be used on American roads during the early 1900s. The dominant type is the pit-and-pole (or bar-grid) cattle guard, which consists of a series of bars (usually of pipe or rail) laid parallel across the road over a pit in the roadway. Automotive traffic can pass over the grid freely, if somewhat bumpily, but livestock is deterred. During the first quarter of the century, three other major types of cattle guard were also developed. (1) The trough cattle guard took the shape of two parallel wheel troughs passing lengthwise of the road at ground level through a gap in the fence, usually over an open pit. (2) The ladder cattle guard used a series of spaced bars (which replaced the board floors of the troughs) held between a wooden framework, again with an open pit in the middle. (3) The arched-crossover cattle guard had the troughs going up and over a fence, like an overpass. None of these variations, however, could handle either two-way or speedy traffic, thus accounting for the ultimate triumph of the pit-and-pole cattle guard. The first of at least thirty-eight patents for highway cattle guards was issued in 1915; the latest, in 1975.

Highway cattle guards are both a labor-saving convenience and an economic necessity. A well-placed cattle guard on the average farm or ranch, for instance, can save as much as a week of work time over the course of a year; in that same year a farmer will walk more than ten miles while simply opening and closing a sixteen foot gate once a day. Such industries as logging and petroleum benefit economically as much or more from cattle guards as does

4

A cattle guard in the
Gypsum Hills of Barber
County, Kansas

A cattle guard in the
Flint Hills of Greenwood
County, Kansas

A cattle guard at the
entrance to the YMCA
ranch near Camp
Verde, Arizona. This
ranch was formerly
owned by Gene Autry.
(Courtesy of Ted Baehr)

agriculture. Still the chief attraction of a cattle guard is its convenience, a point that is graphically made in this story told to me by Glenn Ohrlin:

> In the summer of 1943 I was working for the Rabbit Ears brand (Mullins and Dozier) at Kingman, Arizona. We were hauling fence posts about 100 miles from some mountains southwest of Seligman. There were several gates to open on one route home and no brakes on the truck. I rode the running board while the driver, Jack Mullins, slowed down the best he could in second gear. I'd jump off and run like hell to the gate and open it. (All down hill this way.) We finally wrecked one gate and eventually the truck. We sure could have used some cattle guards on that road.

Today that road, if it is still in open-range country, probably does have cattle guards, for literally hundreds of thousands have been installed on American roads in the past forty years. My field study of the use of cattle guards in the Kansas Flint Hills shows that cattle guards are most numerous in areas where oil leases and pasture land coincide. The second most common use of cattle guards is on open-range public roads running through some of the big pastures of the Flint Hills. The third major use is at entrances to private driveways on individual ranches and farms. Finally, many cattle guards are used at miscellaneous sites: entrances to watershed dams, stone quarries, construction sites, cemeteries, and radio relay towers. In other areas of the country, the relationship among uses may vary, but travel through some twenty states and provinces in search of cattle guards has convinced me that the ranking found in the Flint Hills can be considered typical: the heaviest concentration will be on oil (or other mineral) leases, numerous guards will be found on open-range roads and on private ranch and farm roads, and fewer will be scattered among a variety of miscellaneous sites.

Cattle guards can be found throughout the nation and beyond, and I have been able to document their use in every state of the union except the small, urbanized eastern states of Rhode Island and Massachusetts. Not surprisingly, cattle guards are most often found in the western states, but they are also used extensively in southern, eastern, and midwestern states such as Virginia, Mississippi, Delaware, Illinois, and Missouri. Hawaii, with its large ranching industry, has many cattle guards. Some have been used in Alaska.

Cattle guards often turn up in interesting, famous, or unusual places. Visitors to the LBJ Ranch in Texas or to the Custer Battlefield in Montana or to Yellowstone National Park, to name only a few such places, will have driven over cattle guards. Moviegoers can see Robert Mitchum driving over an English cattle guard in *The Big Sleep*. Children can see Snoopy bounce across a cattle guard in *Run for Your Life, Charlie Brown*. Watchers of the evening news during the summer of 1980 may have noticed a cattle guard at the entrance to the site of the Titan missile that exploded in Arkansas.

A cattle guard near Crazy Woman Canyon in the Big Horn Mountains of Wyoming

A cattle guard at the entrance to the Tom Case farm near Platte City, Missouri

Today, cattle guards can be found from the shadows of Windsor Castle to the Outback of Australia, from the Swiss Alps to the Argentine pampas. From its obscure beginnings on the Great Plains of the United States seventy-five years ago to now, when hundreds of thousands are found throughout the world, the cattle guard has become a permanent part of livestock country.

If for no other reason than that it is an emblem of twentieth-century ranching, the cattle guard deserves to be rescued from the scholarly obscurity which it has suffered till now. Moreover, an understanding of the early history of the cattle guard can help to illuminate some of the important changes that were occurring in American ranching during the early part of the twentieth century, just as a study of its lore can add to our understanding of the stockman himself. Historians and folklorists have lavished attention on other innovations that have become symbols of range country—such as the six-shooter, the trail drive, the sod house, the windmill, and barbed wire—but cattle guards have been as ignored by scholars as they have been taken for granted by the people who have built them and used them. This book seeks to put an end to this neglect.

2
THE NEED
FOR CATTLE GUARDS

Originally, cattle guards were needed primarily because of two developments: (1) the widespread fencing of livestock range country, particularly in the plains region, and (2) the introduction and the rapid spread of automobiles into this same area. Fences require gates, and motorists want gates that can be operated without having to leave their cars, a need that is well met by cattle guards. This chapter will provide, not a thorough discourse into the history of fences, gates, and automobiles, but a backdrop against which, in chapter 3, the development of the cattle guard can be described.

The prototype of fencing is undoubtedly to be found in the branches of the thorn trees that prehistoric man used in order to protect himself from lions and other predators. In early historic times a more durable form of fencing was devised, whose purpose was to hinder human traffic; for by this time, man's major predators were other men. The Great Wall of China and Hadrian's Wall in England come to mind as perhaps atypical but certainly impressive examples.

Today, fencing is commonly associated with agricultural use, particularly the need to control or restrict the movement of livestock. This need, though, is of relatively recent origin. Early nomadic herding cultures such as that of the Mongols had no need for fences, and even today some nonnomadic pastoral peoples find them to be of little value. The Bokkos Fulani of Nigeria, for instance, instead of using fences, use children to herd and tend cattle. Joe Hickey, an anthropologist at Emporia State University, who lived with the Fulani for a year, told me that cattle are considered to be part of a Fulani family. Runaway livestock are rare, because cattle, each head of which is named, never leave the company of humans; they even sleep within a few feet of the family's hut each night. Thus, fences—and therefore gates—are not necessary.

When Robert Frost wrote his well-known lament about his wall-mending neighbor's belief that good fences make good neighbors, he was protesting an urge that has long been cherished in the Anglo-American heritage. Enclosures for livestock or for crops can be found all over the world and in every period of history, but the English seem to have been more inclined to fence than any other nationality has been before the Americans.

The English attitude toward animals and fences is quite different from that of the Fulani and from that of other Western nations as well. Thus, even today, cattle guards are common in England, where livestock is put out to pasture and left there for relatively long periods of time. But cattle guards are extremely rare in Germany, for instance, where cattle are often taken to pasture during the daytime and then are driven into barns and lots for the night. While Europe historically has tended toward open-field husbandry, with cattle being either herded or kept penned up (the French government hired human cattle guards to patrol public roads), the English, as early as 1463, were stressing the importance of fencing not only in fields but also in grazing areas. An agricultural manual of 1532 states that a fence increases the value of farmland by one-third. The chief impetus toward fencing began during the reign of Charles II with the passage of the first of the Enclosure Acts. By 1805, some 2,591 acts had been passed, enclosing 4,817,056 acres.

Miles and miles of stone wall can be seen in Britain, but the main form of fencing there was hedge, a form that was not overly popular in America and that was not without its critics in England also. One estimate, made in 1846, suggested that 1,280,000 acres could be reclaimed for cultivation if the hedge were replaced with board or iron fencing. Not only did hedge take farmland out of production; it also served as a haven for insect and bird pests.

In Colonial America, fencing, or the lack of it, played a role in the development of our representative form of government. In Boston on 14 May 1634 a group of delegates met (the first such meeting on this continent and the forerunner of the Massachusetts Senate) in order to determine what to do about a straying hog. Ten years later, one of the earliest laws enacted in America concerned fences, as Henry M. Smith noted in the 1882 edition of *New Hampshire Agriculture:*

> It is therefore ordered that all fences generall and particular at
> the first setting up be mayde so sufficient as to keep out all manner
> of swyne and other cattle large and small, and at whose fence and
> part of fence any swyne and other cattle shall break through, the

party owning the fence shall not only beare and suffer all damages but shall further pay for each rod so insufficient the somme of two shillings. It is likewise ordered that the owners of such cattle as the town shall declare unruly or excessively different from all other cattle shall pay all the damages that the unruly cattle shall doe in breaking through fences.

One of the key questions in fence law concerns whether it is the duty of the owner of the livestock to fence his stock in or of the crop grower to fence the cattle out — a question that is still being disputed in some areas. Although the tendency has been toward the rule of the open range — namely, that cattle must be fenced *out* not *in* — still, as seen in the 1644 law, the precedent obligating the owner to restrain his stock or pay the damages was established early.

In the mid nineteenth century there was a strong movement for doing away with fences. In 1871 the commissioner of agriculture cited statistics showing that fences were so expensive as to threaten the economic base of agriculture: Fencing cost as much to build and maintain as did the livestock that it kept either in or out. The commissioner noted a tendency among farmers to reduce fencing, to move toward a sort of fencing-in-common such as that used at Greeley, Colorado, which had fenced the entire perimeter of the town in order to keep unwanted livestock from destroying gardens and truck farms.

In 1872 Kansas had a herd law that worked by county option. This herd law was a form of the movement against fences, so that farmers would not have to fence in order to protect their crops. If two-thirds of the voters of a county petitioned, then cattle would be prohibited from running at large, and the owner of damaged crops would be awarded payment for them, no matter what the state of the fences. In other words, it became the duty of the livestock owner to herd or fence his animals, thus saving crop farmers untold expense. This law was favored by the commissioner of agriculture, who had noted that a homestead worth only $200 often required $1,000 for even a minimal fence. Thus it could have cost a community of twenty farmers $20,000 to fence out cattle that were worth only a fraction of that sum.

One reason for the great expense of fences, especially on the Great Plains, was that no cheap yet effective fencing material existed, for barbed wire had not yet been invented. Living hedges had disadvantages: they harbored pests and drew water and nutrients from crops, and it was difficult to get an even stand of shrubs or trees to grow, especially in drier climates. Also, a hedge could not be easily altered or moved if ownership of the land happened to change. The most immediate problem, however, was the expense. In 1871, boards that cost $9.80 per thousand in Maine cost $53.50 in Nevada. Rails, worth $8.12 per thousand in Florida, brought $120 in Nevada. In Kansas, boards cost $28.95 and rails cost $67.91 per thousand. Of fences reported in Kansas at this time, worm fences (made of rails) constituted 18 percent;

board fences, 12 percent; and post and rail, 9 percent. The remaining 61 percent included a large variety of types, including stone walls, Shanghai (a type of rail fence), and Osage orange. Cherokee County, according to the report of the commissioner of agriculture, reported "fences with names hitherto unheard of, the eccentricity of whose construction language very feebly conveys." Fencing in all the Trans-Mississippi West was similar to that of Kansas—a hodgepodge of whatever was both available and affordable. Wooden fences required an annual upkeep expense of 15 percent of their replacement value, and, even if kept in good repair, they still had to be replaced every dozen or so years.

Into this primed and ready situation in 1873, only two years after the commissioner of agriculture had issued his report deploring the unreasonable burden placed upon farmers by fencing (the greatest single expense in the farm economy), came barbed wire, which in many ways was as important a factor as the railroad in the settling of the American West. So effective, so economical, and so appropriate for the Great Plains was barbed wire that within seven years of its first commercial production (1874, when ten miles of wire were sold), nearly 450,000 miles of barbed-wire fence had been built in the United States and Canada. Between 1850 and 1865, more than 150,000 miles of plain-wire fencing had been put up, much of it in Kansas, but it was notably ineffective at turning livestock. The barbs in the new wire made the difference, and the market was ready; in 1875 some sixty companies were selling a total of nearly 90 miles of barbed wire per day.

The story of barbed wire and the fencing of the West is well known, particularly because of such fencing feats as the enclosure of the XIT Ranch in the Texas Panhandle. Soon after barbed wire was invented, its effects on the life style and landholding system of range country were foreseen. By the beginning of the 1880s, not only quarter-section homesteads but also huge ranches, such as the 700,000 acre Maxwell Ranch in New Mexico, were being fenced. In all, some 401 patents have been granted for barbed wire, and over 1,600 variants have been catalogued. The names of Joseph Glidden, Jacob Haish, I. L. Ellwood, and John Warne ("Bet-you-a-million") Gates are not so well known as are those of J. B. Stetson, Samuel Colt, and Levi Strauss, but the physical and sociological effects of their contributions are every bit as significant.

A fence, however, is not complete, not really usable, without a gate. Therefore, as the miles of barbed wire shot forth in the 1880s and 1890s, so did attempts to devise a gate that would be effective, durable, and easy to operate. These attempts were inevitably affected by the introduction of the automobile onto the Great Plains.

The automobile industry in the United States began in the 1890s. In 1893 Charles E. and J. Frank Duryea made the first gasoline-powered car to be built in America, and two years later they organized the first American company to manufacture gasoline-powered cars. Steam-driven and electric automobiles were also being experimented with at this time. By 1900 there were some eight thousand cars in America, a figure that jumped to 3.5 million by 1916. Henry Ford built his first automobile in 1896, and in 1908 he was selling his first Model T Fords for $850, a hefty sum at that time. Eight years later, his streamlined manufacturing techniques had reduced the cost to $345. From 1907 through 1927, Ford sold some 15 million of these cars, over half of the automobiles sold in America during that period. Even with this growing number of cars on the road, as late as 1914 only two roads in the entire country were intended exclusively for automobile traffic—one at Asheville, North Carolina, and the other at Pelham Parkway in New York. Thus, although automobiles had been in use before the turn of the century, it is safe to assume that the automobile had its first real impact on the rural areas of America no earlier than, say, 1905 and that the automobile did not become a definite factor in agriculture until around 1910.

The first references to automobiles in the *Breeder's Gazette* (probably the leading agricultural journal of the time), for instance, appeared in volumes 42 and 43 (published late in 1902 and early in 1903), with a single unimportant reference in each volume. In volumes 46 and 47 (late 1904 and early 1905), several references occurred. Not until 24 November 1909 did the *Breeder's Gazette* carry an article ("Influence of the Auto on Farm Life," by Hayden Eames) suggesting that the automobile was becoming an important factor in rural America.

Evidence from government documents reinforces that of the *Breeder's Gazette*. In the annual reports of the U.S. Department of Agriculture, the *Yearbook for 1907* was the first to take note of the automobile. In a report on roads (pp. 257-58), the compiler commented on the disruptive effect (particularly in the eastern United States) of rubber tires and high speed (up to 40 miles per hour) on macadam gravel roads that had been built for iron-tired horse-drawn vehicles. The 1916 *Yearbook* contained some comments about the effect of engine-powered vehicles on the horse trade: "Slowly but surely the auto-truck is driving horses off the country roads." The writer went on to support the claim of tractor manufacturers that small tractors would someday displace draft horses.

In the 1920 *Yearbook*, H. S. Fairbank, senior highway engineer of the Bureau of Public Roads (who opened his report with a quotation from Milton—how many bureaucrats could do so today?), stated that motor trucks were a major factor in tearing up roads because they carried twice the load of horses at three times the speed (i.e., at fifteen miles per hour).

The 1920 *Yearbook* also contained some interesting statistics concerning the use of automobiles throughout the United States for the year 1919. The relevant information for the seventeen western states, for instance, showed that in this area there were 924,000 miles of public rural roads upon which to travel and that 2,265,302 cars had been registered in those states. Thus, there were 2.32 cars per mile of public rural road and an average of 11.35 persons per car, not all of whom, of course, lived on farms—many lived in the cities and towns of the western states. Figures from the 1920 United States Census show that the seventeen western states had a population of 19,943,531, or 18.9 percent of the national total of 105,710,620. In the same year, over 35 percent of the automobiles in the United States were registered in these seventeen states. In other words, not quite one-fifth of the population was operating over one-third of the cars and trucks in the entire country, a circumstance that clearly shows the commercial and social importance of the automobile in the great distances of the West.

From 1906 until 1913, some 3,924,000 cars had been registered in the United States. This number, according to the *Yearbook* report, probably represents a reasonably accurate estimate of the total number of automobiles in the country at the time. From 1906 through 1919 the total was 30,319,800, although included in this figure were many cars that were being reregistered each year. Obviously, the automobile was rapidly becoming an accepted part of American life, both urban and rural.

The figures for 1920, contained in the 1921 *Yearbook,* provide even more evidence of the growing need for cattle guards in the western range country. Of all farms in the seventeen western states, for example, 44.21 percent had automobiles, 7.14 percent had tractors, and 3.31 percent had trucks. During the teens, five of the leading states in the installation of cattle guards were Texas, North Dakota, Kansas, Nebraska, and New Mexico. The 1920 *Yearbook* figures showed that, with the exception of New Mexico, these states were among the leaders in the use of automobiles. Texas, for example, ranked second among the western states in terms of the total number of automobiles registered; Kansas, third; Nebraska, fourth; North Dakota, tenth; and New Mexico, sixteenth. In total miles of public rural roads, Texas was first (127,000); Kansas, third (109,000); Nebraska, fifth (80,000); North Dakota, sixth (64,000); and New Mexico, eighth (45,000). Population per car showed Nebraska tied for least (7); Kansas, next lowest (8); North Dakota tied for fourth (10); Texas, fifteenth (14); and New Mexico with the most people per car of the western states (25). The surprising factor here is that New Mexico, with the next-to-smallest number of cars, with the most people per car, and with only a middling amount of mileage in public rural road, was a leader in the installation of cattle guards on public highways, not just on private roads.

The figures and statistics cited above show that the use of the automobile had pervaded the plains states during the early part of the twentieth century,

TABLE 2.1
MOTOR VEHICLES REGISTERED IN 1919 AND 1920

STATE	NUMBER OF AUTOMOBILES REGISTERED IN 1919	PERCENTAGE OF FARMS WITH AUTOMOBILES IN 1920	PERCENTAGE OF FARMS WITH TRUCKS IN 1920	PERCENTAGE OF FARMS WITH TRACTORS IN 1920
Arizona	28,919	45.5	5.3	8.2
California	477,450	53.1	5.0	10.3
Colorado	104,865	47.3	4.8	7.6
Idaho	42,220	39.6	1.9	3.5
Kansas	228,600	62.0	2.3	9.8
Montana	59,324	36.0	2.0	12.0
Nebraska	200,000	75.6	5.1	8.3
Nevada	9,305	45.4	5.1	5.8
New Mexico	18,082	18.6	1.9	1.5
North Dakota	82,885	56.7	1.0	15.2
Oklahoma	144,500	25.5	1.1	3.0
Oregon	83,332	41.0	3.4	5.8
South Dakota	104,628	69.4	5.7	16.3
Texas	331,310	22.9	1.2	1.9
Utah	35,236	32.1	2.1	2.2
Washington	148,775	41.7	4.8	3.7
Wyoming	21,371	39.2	3.5	6.2
Average	124,753	44.2	3.3	7.1

SOURCE: Based on figures in the *Yearbook* of the United States Department of Agriculture for the years 1920 and 1921.

as had the use of barbed wire at the end of the nineteenth. Together, these two instruments of change had created the need for a trouble-free gate.

Unquestionably, fences and gates are troublesome to travelers — and they were so even before the days of the automobile. Several important types of gates have been devised and used with American fencing. In this country, fence builders quite early became aware of the need for ease of mobility. Pehr Kalm, a Swedish visitor to the Colonies in 1748, had noted that fences in Pennsylvania were made very low so that men could easily step over them. Pigs were kept from doing so by being fitted with triangular wooden yokes. Horses wore a forked stick hanging from their halters so that the stick would catch on the fence if the horse should jump over it. Sometimes a hobble was made by fastening a stick to the front and back feet of the same side of the horse so that it could not jump the low fence. In rail fences the "settler's gate," a gap where two sets of rails overshot each other, let people walk through while it turned away animals.

The problem of gates arose early in our history, as G. B. Smith noted in the *Cultivator* in 1844:

> As long ago as in 1820, the writer of this travelled through several counties in the middle states, where nothing but boundary fences were thought of, and the public roads were crossed on the line between every two farms by gates, which the traveller was obliged to open and close in passing. These gates were permitted by law, owing to the deficiency of timber for fencing the fields bordering on the roads. It is believed the same state of thing still exists in that part of the country.

The problem was still current several decades later and several hundred miles farther west, where, in 1883, Coloradans were complaining that fences were forcing people to go miles out of their way in order to reach post offices and that even main highways were reduced to the level of third-rate trails by the necessity of opening and closing numerous gates.

So, both before and after the invention of barbed wire, gates were a problem, not just for farmers in their barnyards but also for travelers on public roads. Smith's account noted that gates on public highways were legal because of the expense of fencing materials. Even after barbed wire had made border fences economically feasible, gates were still occasionally built across public roads. In March 1877, for example, George T. Ergenbright and J. A. Coffey built such a gate between their properties in Montgomery County, Kansas, although a special act of the legislature was required before they could do so. Carl Rauch sent me a newspaper account of section 2 of this legislative act:

> Such gate shall be constructed and arranged so as to be readily opened and closed by persons traveling that way, and such gate shall not be so kept and maintained for a longer period than five years from the taking effect of this act; and any person or persons willfully leaving said gate open, or injuring or removing the same, on conviction thereof shall be adjudged guilty of a misdemeanor and punished as in other cases; and he shall also be liable to the party injured for all of the damages resulting from such leaving open or removal of said gate, the damages to be recovered in a civil action.

It is not clear why this gate was necessary or why it was allowed to exist only for five years. Three years later a Quaker, Daniel Votaw, established on the Ergenbright land a colony where former slaves could raise cotton on eight-acre tracts. Frequent flooding and the vicissitudes of raising cotton in Kansas, however, caused the colony to be abandoned by 1900.

The simplest gates, those made of the same material as the fence, were not always the most efficient. In a rail fence, for instance, a gate of wooden

A step stile in a stone wall in Cornwall, England

George Altland, Vici, Oklahoma, with a model of a pull gate made by his grandfather in 1906. (Courtesy of George Altland)

An automatic gate near Eden, Texas

17

bars was quite easy to construct but frustrating to use. C. W. Wimberley has described such a gate, used by his great-grandfather, Bill Adare, in Texas during the middle years of the nineteenth century, as an "antiquated contraption of inconvenience." The gate was made by boring a line of holes in large gateposts standing on each side of the road and by then placing small poles in these holes. Anyone who passed through the gate had to remove each of these poles one at a time, lay them aside, then carefully put each one back in place after having driven his team through—a very tedious procedure. Wimberley noted that "by the time he had replaced each of these poles to its proper position and had regained his seat in the wagon, the traveller was certain to feel that he had had his dose of self-control for the day." Frederick Remington's painting *The Fall of the Cowboy* shows two cowboys taking down the poles of a wooden-bar gate between two pastures that are separated by a barbed-wire fence.

Wire gates used with barbed-wire fences, though an improvement over gates made with poles, still had some serious disadvantages. If these gates (sometimes called wire gaps, saddle gaps, or Texas gaps) were not stretched tightly enough, livestock could rub them down. Yet if they were stretched too tightly, they were almost impossible to open, especially by women or children. Often a "cheater," a lever made of a stick or an old harness hame, was (and is today) wired to the gate post, but even with such help, a horseman, a teamster, or an automobile driver must dismount or leave his vehicle in order to open and close such a wire gate.

An even more time-consuming method, similar in a way to taking poles out singly, was the slip gap, described by C. G. Wood of Floresville, Texas. In places where a wire fence crossed an old trail, cowboys would sometimes construct a slip gap by loosening the staples on several adjacent posts. They would then drive in two staples where one had been, one staple just above the other, their loops parallel to the wire and to the ground, and just wide enough for the wire to fit between them. After taking down the fence and walking his horse across, the rider would then place each wire between the slot formed by each set of staples and put a third staple in the loops in order to hold the wire in place. After that, the wires could be taken down and crossed with relative ease.

A system of gates that required only one exit from the car was used in Wyoming in the 1960s, according to Roy D. Mockamer. This system required a chutelike lane of fencing with a gate on either end, one of which was kept closed at any one time. A driver could, for instance, enter the chute through an open gate, stop, shut the gate behind him, open the gate in front of him, get in, and drive on. Thus, one gate was always open, and one was always closed. The driver had to walk no farther with this arrangement than if he were opening and closing only one gate, and he was saved one time of getting into and out of his car.

Most ranchers and travelers wanted something that was less time-consuming and easier to open than any of the gates described thus far. As a result, scores of wooden and metal gates were invented, which were built so that a person could operate them without having to leave his horse, wagon, or automobile. Many of these gates worked by a system of weights, levers, pulleys, and pull ropes, as did the one in the western film classic *Duel in the Sun*. Several of these gates were described in *Scientific American* during the 1890s. On some gates the pull ropes caused the gate to swing open; then a pull on the other side, after one had passed through, would cause the gate to swing closed. My father-in-law, Wilbur R. Thompson, remembers that as a boy growing up on an Illinois farm, he would try to pull the gate open, but he was too young and lightweight to be able to operate it.

In some pull-type gates, the gate stood straight up and back along a track. Elvis Riggs of Stephenville, Texas, remembers a "jump gate" that was built by his grandfather and great-uncles (T. E., J. M., and M. M. Riggs) about 1910. The jump gate was a wooden panel that sat, not in line with, but alongside, the corral fence. From the middle a T-shaped frame stuck straight up, with the crossbars placed perpendicular to the fence line. A pull rope dangled from the end of each crossbar. A horseback rider or a buggy driver would give one rope a strong pull, and the gate would be pulled up and would jump back alongside the fence, guided by a track made of two-by-fours. After one had passed through, he would pull the second rope, and the gate would jump back into place.

Most of these gates required both a relatively heavy framework and rather precise adjustment in order to work properly. Sometimes the pull ropes were equipped with a weight to keep them from blowing out of reach, but these weights had the adverse effect of being able to break a windshield if the driver was not careful. These gates had one major advantage, however, which tended to outweigh all the disadvantages: they had a remote mechanism that was easily worked by men but not easily triggered by livestock.

George W. Carpenter, a wheelwright-carpenter-blacksmith of Woodward, Oklahoma, after he had seen a picture of a pull gate in the *Kansas City Star* sometime around 1905 or 1906, made one which he installed on the south edge of town. Carpenter had moved to Sterling, Kansas, after the Civil War, then took a homestead in Woodward County in 1901. A scale model of the gate (one inch per foot) has been built by his grandson George Altland of Vici, Oklahoma, who told me that his grandfather was Pennsylvania Dutch and extremely handy with tools. The gate, Altland said, could be used by drivers of either teams or automobiles.

A similar gate was built a few years earlier on what is now known as the

Birdhead Ranch near Watford City, North Dakota. This ranch was originally part of the Morning Star Cattle Company, which was established in 1893 by J. M. Uhlman and the Jaynes brothers. In order to keep their saddle horses close to headquarters, they built a drift fence that happened to cross a road that was used twice a week by the mail wagon and later by a chain-driven, solid-tired motorized truck. Not only the truckdrivers but also the teamsters who drove newly broken horses complained about having to open and shut the wire gate. So, in 1904 or a bit earlier, Cornelius Jaynes built a gate that could be opened and closed from the driver's seat of either a truck or a wagon. The exact design of this gate is not known, but Fred Shafer of Watford City, who as a child had accompanied his father many times through the gate, remembers that ropes dangled from each side. A pull on one rope caused the gate to stand up on end. This was made possible by two homemade weights, which were made of bull's hide filled with stone and had a hole in the bottom of the hide to let rainwater drain out easily. After one had gone through, a pull on the rope from the other side would return the gate to its closed position. As with most modern-day cattle guards, a wire gate was provided at the side. Because the Patent Gate, as it was known locally, did not work well in snow, the wire gate was often used in winter. The gate itself has long since disappeared; it is preserved, however, not only in local folklore and history but also in the local political structure as well: it gave its name to the township in which it once stood — Patent Gate Township.

In 1893 Silas Portis of Monrovia, Indiana, patented a gate-opening device that did not even require the buggy driver to pull a rope. All he had to do was steer his buggy wheels over a square-U-shaped rod on either side of the gate. This rod was connected to a mechanism consisting of a gate latch and a chain. After passing through, the driver could shut the gate by making sure that his wheels again crossed the trigger device on the other side of the gate.

Once the automobile had come into use, inventors tried to devise a gate that did not require a rope pull. One such gate, a metal frame with wire mesh and hinges at the bottom, was made that could be pushed down with a car bumper and then could be pulled upright by springs after the car had passed over it. This gate was in use in Nebraska around 1915. Other bump-type gates parted in the middle so that the car could drive through. A major problem was that the gate panels of this type of gate often scratched and dented the sides of the car. One farmer in Baca County, Colorado, who used one of these gates as late as the 1940s, attempted to counter the problem by affixing an inflated bicycle tire to each panel, so that the bicycle wheel would roll along the sides of the car. After World War II, however, automobiles became less uniform in height, and they began to be produced in colors other than black. The black marks made by the tires therefore marred the car's surface, thus making the device unacceptable.

A more successful gate requiring a nudge from the automobile was called the bump (or bumper) gate. This gate seems to have been most popular in the Southwest, particularly Texas, although at least one was used in Kansas (just east of Virgil in Greenwood County). The bump gate was once widely distributed throughout Texas, but today not many remain. Some are to be found on the King Ranch, which is said to prefer them to cattle guards because the bump gate deters sight-seers and joy riders much more effectively than does the cattle guard. According to Dudley Dobie, among others, the bump gate was in use before cattle guards were invented. John R. Shaw of Dallas has described bump gates:

> Bump gates were used [in the 1920s] on the road that went through ranches from San Angelo through Eldorado, Sonora, to Del Rio. A double opening wider than the width of two cars was made in the fence. A tall post was placed in the center of this space. One gate of heavy lumber was made to span this space, overlapping at each end. The center of a steel cable was attached to the top of the tall post. One end was wrapped part way round the post and to one end of the gate. Likewise the other half of the cable was wrapped part way around the post in the opposite direction to the other end of the gate. The gate was suspended a few inches above the ground. You would drive through the right half of the gate. The overlap of this end of the gate rested against the other side of the fence post. The left end of the gate overlapped against its fence post on this side.
>
> To go through this gate you would ease your car to a stop. Then you would put the car in low gear and pour the coal to it to force the heavy gate to pivot around the pole enough to allow your car to clear before the gate swung shut. You could get the back end of your car banged up as the gate swung around if your timing was off. The key to the gate's operation was the twist of the cable around the pole so the gate would return to a closed position. They had to be heavy on account of the high winds or cattle nudging them open.

Dr. W. Curry Holden, professor emeritus of history at Texas Tech University, agrees that using a bump gate required more than a little skill: "You eased up to the gate, put your car bumper against the two-by-twelve bumper board, and accelerated. The gate swung around at a right angle. You drove through before it could swing back." That is, you tried to. Several correspondents have reported that if one accelerated too rapidly, the car would move ahead too quickly, and the bump gate would scrape along its side. If one went too slowly, on the other hand, the gate would swing back and hit the side of the car. It is called a bump (or, depending upon local usage, bumper) gate because one bumps the gate with the car bumper to open it; but many people think that the name could just as easily have come from the bumping that the gate does to the car. Mrs. Corwin Trosper of Higgins, Texas, said not only that she banged up a new Oldsmobile on their bump gate but also that one can always find an assortment of red, amber, and clear glass scattered along the crossing area.

Some ranchers have had special metal bars welded to the bumpers and sides of their cars so that they can work their bump gates without doing excessive damage. In earlier days one could spot a western-Texas Cadillac by the bump-gate guards welded to it. In fact, the bump gate is so much a part of Texas lore, so much a symbol of the area, that Mason Crocker of Brady had a furniture maker in San Antonio construct a bed, the head of which was a wagon wheel and the foot a replica of a bump gate.

Dr. Holden has recalled an experience with bump gates in the late 1920s when he was traveling in the vast ranch country of the Big Bend: "All day I had encountered bumper gates, the first I had ever seen. In the late afternoon I came to an ordinary plank gate. On it was a big sign: DON'T BUMP! It was well placed; otherwise, I would have whammed it." Undoubtedly the gate had been whammed a few times before, thus accounting for the sign.

The bump gate has many advantages. It is no more expensive than a cattle guard, and if the tension on the cable and the fifteen-to-twenty-foot-tall center pole is adjusted properly, it is a sure and humane way to restrain livestock. If struck properly, it lets automobiles go through unscathed. Unfortunately, it is often struck improperly. On a private ranch road that is not heavily traveled, the bump gate works well. But for a highway or a road with even moderate traffic, a bump gate (or a series of them) is simply not practical. Nor is it practical for the long trailers used in hauling livestock today.

The search for an ideal gate continues. Sometimes, modern gates are based on principles that were in use at the turn of the century. Mason Crocker, for instance, has seen a gate in southern Texas that seems to be a combination of the pull-rope and the U-rod gates. The automobile wheel is driven over a treadle, which activates a mechanism of weights that sinks down into a pit and thus tips the gate on end. Crossing the treadle on the other side causes the gate to move back into a closed position. Often, however, modern gates are based on modern principles, particularly electricity. Electrically controlled gates, like those used on garage doors or estate entrances, are not economically feasible for most livestock owners, but the Farnum Company has for nearly a decade marketed its "Drive Thru" gate, a pair of fiberglass hinged arms that extend across the driveway. These arms, which look something like buggy whips or radio antennas, support some two dozen long electrified streamers. These streamers are attached to a standard electric fencing unit and will, according to Farnum's brochures, turn anything from bulls to turkeys. The gate is impervious to weather, easy to install, and flexible enough to protect vehicles from scratches. By early 1980 the company had sold seventy thousand units, 95 percent of which were still in operation. Another ingenious automatic gate, marketed under the name "Horn Gate," is made by the Acme Manufacturing Company of Filer, Idaho. It is designed to open in response to a single blast from an automobile horn or to a two-blast code. A battery-operated electrical system provides an electric charge to the slender bar that extends across the roadway; it also initiates the action of the pneumatic system that raises the arm on signal. According to promotional material from Acme, the air tank will open and close the gate 250 times before it has to be recharged. The battery will operate from three to six months on a single charge, which can be supplied by an automobile's cigarette lighter.

Ivan Hatch of Meriden, Kansas, has invented a less complex but no less effective electric gate of his own. His horse was accustomed to an electric fence, so in June of 1978, in order to spare himself and his guests the necessity of opening and closing two gates between his house and the highway, Hatch put in two high poles at each gate site, ran a hot wire over the top, and fastened a number of small wires to this top cross wire. These dangling wires reached to within a couple of feet of the ground. At the top each dangling wire is "braced" by triangular wiring in order to keep the wind from wrapping it around the poles. Hatch thinks that, with a 110-volt unit, this type of electric gate would turn cattle, if they were already acquainted with an electric fencing system; his horse, he told me, will not bother the wires even when the battery-powered fence charger is turned off.

The search for a perfect gate will undoubtedly go on indefinitely, for no one gate will suit every purpose. In the first few years of this century, gate innovators were working at an almost feverish pitch, yet they had not met the special needs of the automotive traveler, needs that would be met only with the invention of the cattle guard. Barbed-wire fencing and the automobile formed a singular set of circumstances: the point at which convenience and necessity merged and the cattle guard was born.

Many informants have said that the development of the cattle guard was primarily a matter of convenience, a way of avoiding that bane of fencing — the opening and closing of gates; but the automobile posed special problems beyond inconvenience. With a horse and buggy, a driver could get down, open a gate, cluck to his team to get them moving, call whoa to stop them when the wagon had cleared the gate, then close the gate, get back in the buggy, and go on down the road. A lone teamster driving a pair of green horses had special problems, but the automobile driver faced an even more complicated situation. More than once a proud first-time car owner has been known to have cried "whoa" to his new vehicle, pulled back on the steering wheel, and gone crashing right on through the end of the buggy shed or through the barbed-wire gate at the end of the lane.

Life in the days of the horse-drawn buggy was inherently slow paced.

An electric gate of hanging wires made by
Ivan Hatch of Meriden, Kansas

A drive-through electric gate near Ashland,
Kansas

The automobile brought with it not only speed but also impatience: "A man
was never in a hurry until he bought a car," one old-time Texas cowman has
said. The inconvenience that gates caused for horsemen sometimes turned
into outright problems for motorists. The situation was not so bad for a man
traveling with his family, for his wife or one of the kids could open and close
the gate; but the driver traveling alone must have had a rough time of it. Consider an extreme but not improbable example: A lone driver would have to
stop his car, set the brake, get out of the car, and open the gate. In the meantime the car's engine might have died, the brake might have slipped, and the
car could have rolled forward, pinning him to the gate and causing a torn
shirt and some wire scratches. But the Model T was a lightweight car, so the
driver could shove it back easily enough and then try to find a rock with which
to block a wheel. Once the gate was open, he had to crank the car, remove the
rock, get in, drive through, reset the brake, get out, replace the rock, shut the
gate, recrank, kick aside the rock, get in, release the brake, and drive on. Although automobiles were faster than horses on the road, they were certainly
frustrating at gates. James Herriot, the famous Yorkshire veterinarian, spoke
for many besides his own fellow professionals when he wrote in *The Lord God
Made Them All:* "Gates are one of the curses of a country vet's life."

Among these curses a driver could include such things as having to chase
back into the pasture some of the milk cows or saddle horses that might have
gotten out while he was driving through, or being chased by a cow that had
chosen that area in which to have a new calf. Certainly it would take only a
few such experiences either to make one sure that he would never drive without a companion to open gates—or to set one's creative wheels turning.

Dallas W. Perry of Kimball, Nebraska, was the "gate-hop" for his family

24

when his father bought a new Hupmobile in Omaha in 1913 and drove it home across the ruts. It was not always possible to take along a gate opener, and even if it had been, the loss of time meant a loss of money, even in that slower era. But money wasn't everything. According to Ira ("Ike") Osteen of Springfield, Colorado, after the old JJ cattle range had been closed off by homesteaders about 1910, "they just had so many gates you couldn't get to the country dance until after the first jugs were empty."

The cattle guard benefited others besides dancers. Elderly cattlemen (for whom the opening of gates could be a genuine threat to health), haulers of livestock and grain, and rural extension workers were among those who were well served by cattle guards. Extension workers have been among the most enthusiastic promoters of cattle guards. For example, Fred B. Curry was working as an extension agent in Lee County, Texas, in the 1950s in an area where most of the farmhouses were set back from the road, often two or three gates back from the road. Curry encouraged — and often helped — the farmers to install cattle guards, even if they were only made of poles cut from trees from their own pastures. Oilmen also were quick to recognize the time- and money-saving potential of the cattle guard. Nowhere is the cattle guard used more extensively than in oil fields. If rain had followed the plow as surely as cattle guards have followed oil wells, then the Great Plains today would be a rain forest.

Sometime, then, after the turn of the century, when the ranges had been crisscrossed with barbed wire and the farmer was trading in his buggy for a Ford, the cattle guard was born. C. W. Wimberley gives a colorful summary of that birth:

> Stopping and getting out to open and close a gate has always been a fretful chore to the country traveler. Today it's an impossible task. Nowadays when you can bank, eat, see a movie, or go to church without leaving the car seat, who the devil is going to open a gate? That's how cattle-guards were born. Using the wreckage from several gates, an Edison-inclined owner devised a contraption a car could run over with only minor damage and a cow would have better sense than to walk into, and he called the thing a cattle-guard.

These "things" and the range-country Edisons who devised them are fully explored in the next chapter.

3
CATTLE-GUARD INNOVATORS,
1900 TO 1920

While giving a marvelous account of building three cattle guards in southwestern Texas in the mid teens, William M. Jolly of Clifton, Texas, said: "There is one thing for sure. You will never find out who built the first one." In studying folklore, one is conditioned to expect obscurity of origins. Yet that does not mean that an inquiry into origins will necessarily prove fruitless. On the contrary, the search for the first cattle guard has unearthed some fascinating information about its history and about life and times in range country in the early twentieth century, information that might otherwise have been lost.

Printed references to early-day automotive cattle guards are rare; I have found only a half-dozen that predate 1920. Patent records suggest that only four highway cattle guards (three automotive, one for horse traffic) were patented before 1920. Because of the paucity of documentary evidence, most of the information about cattle guards from this period has come from oral history and thus ultimately is dependent upon the frailties — and strengths — of human memory and recollection. As a consequence I have had to be very careful in sifting evidence from the stories and accounts that I have collected. I do not think that anyone has deliberately tried to mislead me, but more than once I have been reminded of the fragility of human memory when informants have placed automotive cattle guards on roads a dozen years before automobiles existed on those same roads. For the most part, though, the recollections that have been passed on to me seem to be reasonable and of honest intent, and many have been corroborated by other evidence as well.

The dates most often given for the introduction of the first cattle guards into any given locale range from 1912 to 1915, or, as most respondents put it, just after automobiles began to be used with some frequency in their areas. In some places this date would be later—well after 1920—while in others it would have been earlier. The earliest cattle guard that I know about was in place at least by 1907, perhaps as much as two years earlier; but accounts of pre-1912 cattle guards are rare. I believe that 1905 is the likeliest date for the first automotive cattle guard.

Another valid conclusion from this study is that the Great Plains is the home of the automotive cattle guard. The special conditions on the plains— the mix of small and large ranches and farms, of oil, of wheat, of cattle—and the advent of barbed wire and cars served as a catalyst to produce the cattle guard. Conditions in other rural regions of the country failed to result in the production—or reproduction—of cattle guards until some years later. Of the forty-odd references to and accounts of pre-1920 cattle guards in my collection, only four lie beyond the boundaries of the plains—two to the west, one to the southeast, one to the east. Even if it were to be proven that the first automotive cattle guard had been invented outside the boundaries of the Great Plains (as were, for example, barbed wire, the sod house, and the six-shooter), still its major initial development is so clearly and firmly associated with the plains and its special technological properties are so appropriate and adaptable to conditions on the plains that the cattle guard must be considered an aspect of Great Plains folk life, an essential part of the Great Plains cultural milieu.

The urge to avoid gates began early on the Great Plains. During the late nineteenth century at least three attempts were made to design highway cattle guards for horse-drawn traffic. The least successful of these cattle guards, which was made entirely of earth, has been described by C. W. Wimberley of San Marcos, Texas, based upon an account given him by his father, Rufus Wimberley:

> The first attempt to devise a cattle-guard in this area took place at a site some two miles from San Marcos on the Old Wimberley Road during the late, late 1890's. As is often the case, the name of this creative genius has been lost to time and it is just as well.
>
> From logic that only he could fathom, he figured that a steep barrier in the middle of the road would serve to stop and turn livestock. So, he set about to fill one side of the road with a long slope gradually rising from ground level to the height of three or four feet, then dropping back to ground level within a distance of about four feet. Parallel to and at opposite hand, he filled the other side of the road with another slope.

28

Needless to say, cattle paid no heed to this cattle-guard, but a short-fused teamster did. One run through this cattle-guard and on his return trip, he skirted it, and cut a hole in the fence to create a new bend in the Wimberley road that remained intact long after the reason for its existence had been forgotten.

The logic behind this early attempt to turn cattle without using gates is valid, for livestock will try to avoid a pit or a sharp-walled ravine. Moreover, it is similar to the open-pit cattle guard used by the early railroad builders. Unfortunately, a man-made pit that would be effective against cattle would also be a barrier to either motorized or animal-drawn vehicles.

A more successful type of highway cattle guard was used in the Gypsum Hills between Medicine Lodge and Coldwater, Kansas, in the 1890s and early 1900s. Three of these guards were on the ranch where W. C. Mills has lived since his birth in 1897, and others have been found on the stagecoach road that connected Coldwater, Deerhead, Sun City, Lake City, and Medicine Lodge. According to Mills, these guards were made by sawing three two-by-twelve-inch-by-six-foot boards into a gentle curve, placing them on edge straight side down, and nailing two-by-sixes onto them in order to make a kind of bridge. These cross boards were then placed on the frame so that there was a space of about one and one-half or two inches between them. This guard would turn cattle and range horses, but it could be driven over with a horse and buggy or ridden over on horseback. A loaded wagon was too heavy for the structure and had to be driven through a gate at the side where cattle could also pass through the fence. According to Mills, much of the old stagecoach road had been fenced in with barbed wire by the time the wooden guards had rotted out; thus there had been no need to replace them. The places that did require gates were fitted out with automotive cattle guards during the teens. Most of the older guards were gone by the time the first cars were introduced into the Gypsum Hills, but at least one of these stagecoach cattle guards had been adapted to automotive traffic and was being used as late as 1918, according to Thomas W. Winkler.

The earliest known of the preautomotive highway cattle guards was one built in 1881 in Archer County, Texas. The Henrietta and Archer City Stagecoach Line was established in that year, and in its run from Henrietta to Archer City it encountered, on the Ikards' 75,000-acre O Circle Ranch, the first barbed-wire fence built in the county. Instead of by gate, the stagecoaches crossed the fence by a wooden-plank bridge that arched over the fence. Because of the height, this guard would have been even more forbidding to cattle than were the ones on the stage route from Medicine Lodge to Coldwater, and probably the teams crossing the guard found it equally forbidding. As Jack Loftin noted in his book *Trails through Archer*, "This must have been quite a chore to get horses and mules to travel up and over this cattleguard-bridge." The stage line and the cattle guard were abandoned in 1908 when the Henrietta and Southwest Railroad was completed.

A wooden bridge, especially if it is arched, is a structure that range livestock seem to avoid instinctively, a circumstance that observant stock handlers have been quick to notice. Green D. Wyrick, for instance, who was reared in southwestern Missouri, has said that wooden bridges over Ozark ravines that were built for either foot or automotive traffic had the extra advantage of keeping cattle at home, although they were not intended for that purpose. In western Texas this principle was also used in some of the earliest crossover highway cattle guards, some of which were modeled after a bridge near Knickerbocker. William Jolly has told this story about the prominent pioneer Texas sheepman Joseph Tweedy:

> In about 1908 there was a man [who] bought a bunch of land about 30 miles southwest of San Angelo on a draw called Dove Creek. He put up a store there and as the talk went at that time, gave Mexicans all they could make or raise on a piece of that creek land, provided they did all of their trading at his store. He got a post office there and called it Knickerbocker.
>
> There was a road ran right by the store, and big herds of cattle came right through there in the fall going to San Angelo for shipping. So Mr. Tweedy (I believe that was his name) had to lane the road through his part of that road to protect his farmers.
>
> Then he had a lot of land left above the road with no water on it. So he built a bridge over and across these two little side draws high enough for cattle to cross under and go to the creek for water. He pulled his lane fences in at the ends of the bridge and tied them to the bridge. That forced all cattle herds to cross this little wooden bridge just wide enough for two wagons to pass each other. Now you drive about seven to nine hundred range cattle up to a bridge like that and all you do is after the cattle tear the fence down on both sides of the lane is to get them back together on the other end of the bridge.
>
> In the early trials of cattle guard designs there were a few people who put up a kind of cross-over much like the cross-over at Knickerbocker. They would simply bridge over the fence and stock just didn't like to walk up and over.

The first patent for a highway cattle guard was filed by William W. Brian of Woodsboro, Texas, on 21 December 1915. This guard, which was intended for horse-drawn traffic, was modeled after the wooden-plank bridge, but was flat rather than arched. Instead of crossing over a fence, it was designed to double as an actual bridge, spanning a stream or a ditch. It was made of six movable planks (about two-by-six inches in size) that stood on edge in order to turn aside cattle. The planks were hinged to the base of the bridge and were all connected to rods that extended several feet down the road in each direction. These rods were connected to handles that could be pulled by the approaching traveler in order to lay the planks flat, thus forming a solid surface. Once the traveler had crossed, he could pull the rod on the other side, and the planks would return to their vertical position.

Well before this patent for a horse-traffic cattle guard was filed, however, the first automotive cattle guards were being used throughout the Great Plains. Information about them is sparse before 1912, the year when reports become relatively common. Bill King, now of Kim, Colorado, was a member of the well-known family of rodeo producers and contestants who helped start Garden City's Cattlemen's Carnival, one of the nation's largest professional rodeos, in 1912. In 1909, when he was five years old, his family moved from Plains to Garden City, Kansas. One thing that impressed young King at the time of the move was a homemade trough-type cattle guard, which he reports having seen near Garden City: "They were just two wooden troughs spaced the width of a car with a hole in the middle. Then they would put an old dried cow hide in the center, and the cattle wouldn't jump it." King now estimates that there were probably no more than a dozen cars in Finney County at the time, two of them owned by their neighbor, a real-estate man named Charley Zirkly. "He had two two-cylinder Buicks that cranked on the side, and he had a full time mechanic by the name of Case Vanscoit hired to keep those things running."

King has also told me another story about a grid-type cattle guard on the Sugar Company cattle ranch just outside of Garden City. This cattle guard was about six by eight feet in size and was made of two-by-sixes turned on edge. In 1916 King and a neighbor boy "used to run our horses and make them jump it, which sends a chill down my spine to think about it now. It was lots of fun but we could have got killed."

The trough guards seen by Bill King in 1909 or 1910 were contemporaneous with some pit-and-pole guards built by Robert Crane in Barber County, Kansas, in 1909. In 1908 Crane had been elected clerk of the district court, so the next spring he built six cattle guards on the pasture roads from his ranch to the highway in order to be able to travel more easily to his job in Medicine Lodge. Crane poured a concrete foundation, which formed a pit roughly six by eight feet by three feet deep and had a center wall running with the road for extra support. Into the wet concrete he placed a number of bars made of two-inch lumber. Crane used these guards for two or three years before he moved to Medicine Lodge and leased out his ranch.

The earliest printed reference to cattle guards, a brief notice about a type of cattle guard that may be termed an arched crossover, appeared in "Bridging a Fence for an Automobile," in the May 1909 issue of *Popular Mechanics:*

31

An Indiana farmer solved the problem of passing in and out of his yard with his automobile without using a gate. The illustration shows how he goes over the fence instead of through a gate. The main channels for the wheels of the automobile are 6 in. wide at the top and broaden out at the foot on each side of the fence. The wide part of the channels resting on the ground guides the wheels as the approach is made. The channels are supported by timbers of sufficient size to carry the weight of the automobile.

A drawing of the troughs arching over the fence, with an automobile halfway across, accompanies the article. Its caption, "Roadway over a Fence," shows that the device was thought of, not as a gate or as a cattle guard, but as part of the road.

From interviews with old-timers the earliest firm date I have been able to establish for an automotive cattle guard is 1907. E. S. Sutton of Benkelman, Nebraska, believes that this particular guard was in use at least as early as 1905. The builder, a German bachelor who was farming on the high plains near Barr Lake, Colorado (where Sutton's father was a station agent for the Burlington Railroad), employed Sutton to work in his hayfields during the summer of 1908. Sutton is positive that the guard was in place by then, because he left home to travel during the summer of 1909. The Sutton family had moved to Barr Lake in 1905 when Sutton was twelve years old, and he is fairly certain that he saw this guard while he was chopping weeds on a neighboring beet farm that year. He is even more certain that he rode across the cattle guard on his bicycle during the summer of 1907.

Sutton has furnished some background on the German bachelor, who seems to have been quite inventive:

> Neitchez [Sutton's spelling of the man's name] was the Dutchman who built the cattle guard. He spiked lodgepole pine about three inches thick over a drain ditch, three or four feet wide, spanned by three or four railroad ties, about six to eight feet wide. He had been in the Russian army. He made a model steam engine for pumping purposes. When I knew him he had rigged a motor to a buggy — rather it was what we called a "Democrat" and was unpredictable in operation. Coming to a wire gate, if shut down, it was very apt to refuse to restart. It just chugged and died while closing a gate. The country road coming to town crossed the railroad and there were railroad guards on both sides, so that is probably where he got his idea. He had an Old Brush auto, rounded up dashboard, motor under the seat, when I was peddling out to work at odd times for him. He was good at blacksmithing, and blacksmiths were the first garagemen. He soon left for Denver and left that farm.

The automotive cattle guard made by this German-Russian immigrant may not have been the first one ever built, but it is the earliest one for which I have been able to collect an account.

As stated earlier, 1912 seems to be the watershed year for accounts of automotive cattle guards. Cattle guards have been reported in 1912 on the oil leases between Independence, Kansas, and Copan, Oklahoma. Jim McEndree had traveled with his family in a covered wagon from Osborne, Kansas, to Buffalo, Oklahoma, in 1910, and he remembers that cars and cattle guards both appeared near Buffalo two years later. In 1915 he moved to Springfield, Colorado, where he also saw cattle guards. Richard Robbins, Jr., of Pratt, Kansas, remembers having seen an old cattle guard on a pasture trail between camps on the Anchor D Ranch in Texas County, Oklahoma. This guard was made of railroad rails set in concrete, and the date 1912 had been marked into the wet concrete when the guard was made. An oil company replaced this old guard in the middle 1950s. Cattle guards were also being used on the Goodnight Ranch (owned by my great-uncle Frank Goodnight) near Englewood, Kansas, in 1912 or 1913.

There were cattle guards in Texas in 1913, according to the late John R. Shaw, who has recounted an episode that also illustrates the hazards of automotive travel in western Texas in 1913:

> With the advent of the automobile another type of guard appeared [in addition to the railroad cattle guard]. It was made of slats of steel turned on edge in a steel or wood frame. This was set in the opening in the fence over a shallow pit. The first of these I saw were in 1913 on a trip from Colorado City to Odessa. The road went through Big Spring and Midland. At times it just took off across the ranches as two ruts. I imagine they were old wagon trails. You followed the most travelled and hoped that you were on the right road. Highway signs were local projects then. Sometimes a prairie dog would dig his hole in one of the paths. They were quite a hazard to the tires and springs of autos in those days.
>
> I made this trip with my aunt, uncle, and cousin. My uncle, Judge Charlie Earnest, had to be in court at Odessa by 4:00 P.M. His car was a six-cylinder Chandler touring car. The tires were smooth tread. You could not let your wheels get out of the ruts or you might encounter some cactus which could easily damage a tire.
>
> Between Midland and Odessa the road crossed a small buffalo wallow, really a shallow lake. We slipped and skidded through it and arrived at the court house at 3:45. (He won his case.) On the return trip we were not so lucky crossing the wallow. The smooth tires would just spin. Trying to push the car was to no avail. Out of nowhere appeared a cowboy. He tied one end of his lariat to the front axle of the car and wrapped the other end around the saddle horn. With the wheels spinning he worked his horse and pulled the car free.

L. P. Wakefield standing at the site of a cattle guard built by Riggs and Hurley near Stephenville, Texas, in 1913. The piece of oak stringer near Wakefield's foot is from the original structure; the pipe grid was added some years later.

Andrew Johnston, who invented a cattle guard near Watford City, North Dakota, in 1914. (Courtesy of Larry Adams, North Dakota Stockmen's Association)

Shaw next saw cattle guards during the summer of 1924, when he made a trip around Texas in a 1923 Ford roadster.

Shaw was not the only person to report that he had seen cattle guards in Texas in 1913. L. P. Wakefield of Stephenville was sixteen years old that year, when his uncle Hugh Hurley and T. E. Riggs built three cattle guards on Hurley's place and on the W. W. Jarvis Ranch. Riggs was a machinist, a farmer, and a technological innovator, who, along with his brothers, built a jump gate described in chapter 2. Hurley, a blacksmith and a jack-of-all-trades, was also a progressive-minded innovator. His grandfather, Henry Hurley, was a Texas Ranger who had come to Erath County for a six-month tour of duty in 1834, then had been recalled to Hunt County. Immediately after the Civil War, Texas granted Hurley a quarter section of land (measured in the old Spanish varas), a portion of which is now owned by the fifth generation of the Hurley family. Henry Hurley was also a Baptist minister, and he built the first Trinity Baptist Church in Erath County shortly after moving onto his land in 1865. He also built the first house in the county to be made of boards, not of logs. Much of this house, its timbers hewn from native oak, is still standing, and the notches, pegs, and square nails are plainly visible.

It would seem, then that Hugh Hurley came by his progressiveness naturally. He had the first horse-powered cotton gin in the area, then the first horse-powered thresher. He operated the first steam thresher and hired a crew to do custom threshing. In 1925 he bought the first gasoline-powered tractor in the area, an Aultman-Taylor that now rests on Elvis Riggs's farm. In the winter, when he was not using the tractor for farming, Hurley would move houses with it. Wakefield has said that although his Uncle Hugh may not have been a millionaire, since few millionaires existed then, he was well off and always had lots of projects under way.

When I went to Stephenville in the fall of 1979 to visit the site of the cattle guards built by Riggs and Hurley, Wakefield took me to the Jarvis Ranch, which is now abandoned but has a nice-looking set of native stone buildings still standing. At the southwestern corner of the corrals was an unused pipe cattle guard next to a barbed-wire gate across a little-used lane that was once a public road but had long since been closed. Along the north edge of the pipe grid was a piece of very old oak planking, originally a three-by-twelve cut from native wood, Wakefield said, that had been used as a sill or base for the 1913 cattle guard.

When I asked Wakefield if he was sure that the guards had been built in 1913, he replied: "Let's go talk to Elvis Riggs. He was with his grandfather when they put them in." On the way to the Riggs place, Wakefield pointed out the sites of the other two guards built in 1913. Elvis Riggs still remembers that in the fall of 1913, when he was six years old, he went with his grandfather and his Great-Uncle Hugh when they built three cattle guards, all within three-quarters of a mile of one another. He told me how each guard had been built. Two of them were made entirely of native oak. For each of these, two stringers (or sills) approximately three inches by twelve inches were hewn out to form a base that ran about twelve feet across the roadway. (Wakefield had shown me the remains of one of these stringers earlier.) About four more of these stringers, each around five or six feet long, were run with the road between the two longer pieces, thus forming a framework on which the pole grid could be placed. This grid was made of seven or eight round oak poles, each placed in notches that had been cut into the shorter sills. Because these poles, naturally enough, were larger around at one end than at the other, the notches varied in size so that the poles would lie level and smooth. The poles were then wired into place. No pit was dug for these two cattle guards. Instead, dirt was used to build the road up to the top of the twelve-inch sills.

The third cattle guard built by Riggs and Hurley also used native oak for the sills that crossed the road, but the shorter frame pieces that went with the road were made by nailing a pair of two-by-sixes together, then notching out half circles to hold the twelve to fifteen crossbars. These crossbars were made from metal flues taken from a steam threshing machine. Wakefield remembers that the cattle guards were built in the fall, because the flues had not been removed from the steam separator until after the August threshing season had ended. These pipes were about two inches in diameter, and they were spaced about four inches apart, as had been the oak poles on the wooden cattle guards. They were wired down to the notches in the frame, and they were also held in place by strips of thin strap iron, hammered around the flues and nailed to the two-by-sixes. A pit two and one-half feet deep was dug for this cattle guard.

As far as Wakefield and Elvis Riggs know, the idea for building these cattle guards was original with the builders. Given their inventiveness and their technological aptitude, they may well have conceived the idea on their own. If they had not seen other automotive cattle guards, then they probably derived the idea from railroad cattle guards.

A pile of rocks was all that remained of one of the wooden guards, which a prairie fire had burned many years ago. Most of the other wooden cattle guard had gone to pieces quite some time back, and a pipe grid had been installed on top of what was left. A rather sizable chunk of the three-by-twelve-inch oak base was still lying alongside the edge of the pipe grid. I asked, "Is this part of the original 1913 framework?" Wakefield nodded in affirmation, then reached down and broke off a two-foot chunk and handed it to me: "You might want to have this. It's not doing any good here." I did want to have it, for this piece of oak was part of one of the earliest automotive cattle guards and perhaps the oldest extant cattle guard.

Evidence of a roadway and pit still mark the spot where the metal cattle guard stood, even though the gate and the road were moved several yards farther up the hill some years back. The flues had been nearly worn through before they were used to form the grid of the cattle guard. Had they not already been worn thin, they would never have been replaced to begin with, and thus they would not have been available to Riggs and Hurley, who would then undoubtedly have made three wooden cattle guards. Because of their weakened condition, the flues rusted out rather more quickly than the pipes in a modern cattle guard would, and the cattle guard that they formed was scrapped some forty years ago.

Of all the people who were independently installing cattle guards during the first two decades of the century, only one of them fully realized the significance of what he had done. The late Andrew Johnston of Watford City, North Dakota, is the only person ever to have claimed that he had invented the automotive cattle guard. By doing so, which he did in all good faith, he acknowledged in effect that he understood what an important labor- and time-saving device he had built, one that would become a hallmark of range country, a symbol of ranching. His story deserves extensive treament, for Johnston, an extraordinary man, can at the same time be considered typical of many of the people who built the early cattle guards.

Andrew Johnston, son of Peter and Brita Paul Johnston, was born in Dakota Territory near what is now Taylor, North Dakota, on 25 March 1885. At the age of ten he was herding, by himself, some four hundred of his father's cattle; two years later he was burning the VVV brand on his own stock. In his late teens he moved to Watford City, where, in 1907, he formed a partnership with August Jens and began operations on Wild Cow Creek about fifteen miles north of Watford City. At its peak, this partnership ran thirteen hundred Herefords and five hundred horses (four hundred draft and one hundred saddle). In the drouth years, Johnston sold out, formed a new partnership with Nels Langdon, and moved to Alpha, where he ran his VVV Ranch from 1937 to 1943. From there he went to Red Rock, Arizona, for six years and served as foreman on the Kenny Ranch until he returned to North Dakota in 1949 and bought the Western Trading Post in Dickinson. He made saddles and sold western goods until a fire destroyed the building in 1966. From then until his death he spent summers with friends in North Dakota and winters in Tucson. He died in a Dickinson hospital on 3 March 1970, just three weeks before his eighty-fifth birthday. Johnston never married, but his nephew Ben and his great-nephew Carroll today own and operate the Watford City ranch where he built his cattle guard in 1914.

Johnston, an active rancher most of his life, was instrumental in developing and initiating many reforms and aids to ranching. One of the earliest manifestations of his industry-wide concern culminated in the Packers and Stockyards Act of 1921, for which he had organized rancher support. Further, until 1940, North Dakota had not had any statewide livestock organization. Johnston himself had joined the South Dakota Stock Growers in 1907 and had been made a director of that group in 1914, a post he held for thirty years. His work there reinforced his belief that North Dakota needed an organization of livestock producers of its own, so in 1928 he proposed to a group of eighteen ranchers who pastured cattle on the Fort Berthold Reservation that they institute a reward fund to discourage rustlers. From this action the Western North Dakota Stockmen's Association emerged in 1930, with John Leakey as president and Johnston as secretary-treasurer, a position he filled for the next six years. He served as president from 1939 to 1941, the period during which the organization became the North Dakota Stockmen's Association. Among his accomplishments was having this organization authorized in 1949 as the official brand-inspecting agency of the state. This authorization completed an effort that had had its first concrete results some twelve years earlier when Johnston had compiled and published the first complete North Dakota brand registry. He was a member of the American National Cattlemen's Association for fifty-five years, attended fifty-two of its conventions, and was made an honorary vice-president of the organization. In 1955 he was honored with the G. F. Swift Centennial Founders Award for his outstanding contributions to the beef industry.

Johnston's interest in history and in the cultural heritage of the West is illustrated by two major actions. First, Johnston was a founding member of the National Cowboy Hall of Fame and Western Heritage Center in Oklahoma City; his $200 contribution was among the first to fund its establishment. Second, he was a cofounder of the Fifty Years in the Saddle club, formed in Sanish, North Dakota, in the 1940s. Besides giving old-time ranchers and cowboys a reason to get together, this group also published two volumes of reminiscences: *Looking Back down the Trail* (1963) and *Another Look at the Trail* (1966). Johnston had a prominent hand in this venture: he not only compiled and edited the volumes; he also did much of the writing and supplied many of the stories.

From the foregoing brief biographical sketch, one can see that Andrew Johnston had the intelligence, the initiative, and the perceptivity required by an innovator. He seems to have been capable of conceiving unusual but practical ideas, then of putting his plans into action. One of his close friends, C. J. Goddard of Watford City, remembers that Johnston was "quite ingenious and something of an engineer as well as a cowman." Indeed, by his own testimony, Johnston did "serve as McKenzie County surveyor . . . in addition to studying a great deal at the college and university level." Evidence of his innovativeness is seen in his work in organizing livestock associations, but his inventiveness also showed itself in physical, about-the-ranch improvements such as the gravity-action grain elevator he built on a hillside on the Watford City ranch. This large building is now many decades old but is still functioning. At harvest time, loads of grain are dumped into the upper level; when the grain is to be removed, a truck or wagon is driven under the spouts at the bottom, a lever is pulled,and the grain is loaded, all without a shovel being lifted. Thus, Johnston's assertion that he invented the labor-saving cattle guard gains plausibility.

This assertion appears in print twice: once in Johnston's own published account and once in a newspaper interview. In addition, his fame as the builder of the first cattle guard lives on among the people of western North Dakota; several residents of the area told me about Johnston's cattle guard. This is Johnston's own printed version from *Looking Back down the Trail*:

In the spring of 1914 I bought this beautiful automobile, a Model T Ford.

38

Plaque marking the site of Andrew Johnston's original cattle guard

Arched crossover cattle guard built in the teens by John Applegate, Wood Lake, Nebraska. (Courtesy of Albert Lawlis)

1,185,072. ARCHED CROSSOVER-TRACKWAY. ALBER'
NEWTON DURBIN, North Platte, Nebr. Filed Feb. 18
1916. Serial No. 79,163. (Cl. 104—14.)

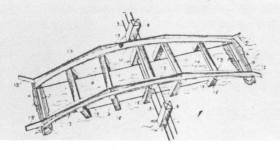

The first patent on an automotive cattle guard. (Photo from *U.S. Patent Gazette*)

In going to town from the VVV Ranch that was in one of the ranch pastures, the gate was on a level place so the Ford would stay, while opening and shutting the gate. But the gate going out the other way to the ranches of Grantiers, Keoghs, Goodalls and others as well as to the reservation was on a steep side hill and we soon found the Ford brakes would not hold it if you weren't there stepping on them. So it took two men to go out this way.

I got the idea of a quite deep hole and troughs across it for the wheel to travel in. I made two troughs fourteen feet long, eight inches wide with a two by four on each side. We planned to have this trough lower than the level of the ground so it would be handy for the driver to get the wheels in the troughs to cross.

We went on one side of the gate and dug two holes one on each side of the fence lengthways of the fence about thirteen feet long, three feet deep and three feet wide. There was about three feet of ground between them in the center for about seven feet (little more than road width). We put two logs across the hole, car wheel width, burying them below the ground enough so the troughs on top of them would still be below the level.

When we got to deciding how many poles to put under those troughs to carry the cars and also to keep the stock from stepping in the hole and crossing, we discovered by using a few more we could cross the car without troughs—on the poles and not near enough together so stock could walk across.

We hauled the troughs back to the ranch and got more poles and nailed them on. Thus the cattle pass or guard was invented.

The two holes on each side of the fence made it look quite bad and we never had any stock attempt to cross it.

Many cattle guards have been put in too careless so they will not fill the place but when put in more careful will in most cases do the job.

Johnston's second account of the invention of the cattle guard appeared in an interview in the *Bismarck Tribune* in 1967:

Flood, Drought of '36 Didn't Faze Johnston

"I invented the first cattle pass," Johnston said, "and if anyone doubts it, I can prove it."

The events leading up to the cattle pass, now manufactured out of metal and so constructed that cattle will refuse to cross, involved a Model T Ford with faulty brakes and the creek into which it rolled.

"The hired man and I," he said, "decided to prevent the car from rolling into the creek again. We dug a ditch and while in the process of putting in small logs, the idea came to me that if we'd use smaller saplings that not only would it serve to hold the Model T back when it was parked there, but it'd keep cattle from leaving the pasture."

Plans are now underway, said Johnston, to erect a plaque at the site of the first cattle pass, now located on the Ben Johnston ranch 10 miles north of Watford City. "It'll be there for anyone who doubts my claim to see," he said, "as well as to mark the spot of this inspiration which has done so much to serve my fellow cattlemen in all of the years since 1914."

There are differences other than length between these two accounts. Johnston's, for instance, is more complex; the newspaper version mentions a hired man whose presence is only implicit in the "we" of the first; in the second account the installation of logs seems to be only to prevent the car from rolling; and the creek of the second version is absent from the first. My own judgment, having visited the site of Johnston's original cattle guard in the summer of 1978, is that the newspaper account is somewhat oversimplified and sensationalized. For example, the creek mentioned in it is far below the site of the pits dug by Johnston. If by chance the car had rolled even once from the gate down the steep hill to the stream, it is most unlikely that it would have stayed on the curving road, and it is most likely that it would have suffered serious damage by the time it had come to rest on the rocks and the stream banks below. Thus, Johnston's own version is, I believe, the more accurate.

His version, however, is admittedly difficult to envision. As I decipher his plan, he and the hired man dug a rectangular pit, leaving in the middle an island of dirt as wide as the road. The troughs for the car wheels were to be placed across this pit, resting on poles, and the idea of adding more poles while dispensing with the troughs resulted in the pit-and-pole design of the cattle guard, the design most commonly favored today.

As we have already seen, however, Johnston's was not the first cattle guard, despite his claim. Even his close friend C. J. Goddard concedes that "as cars came into use, someone else someplace must have had the same idea," while Robert Cory of the *Minot Daily News,* who wrote several articles about Johnston, states:

Frankly I never had time to investigate his claim that he "invented" the cattle guard, and was somewhat disbelieving that there were not cattle guards anywhere on the Great Plains until he made one. It seemed to me that inventing a cattle guard would be like inventing a pasture gate made of boards. But I never doubted Andrew's sincerity in making that claim, and he had traveled more in the plains country than I, by far.

It is hard to doubt Johnston's truthfulness, since both Goddard ("However, Andrew's was the first cattle guard in our area that I saw or knew about") and Cory ("Johnston was highly respected by the ranchers of western North Dakota") attest to his reputation. I am convinced that Andrew Johnston did invent the cattle guard at Watford City, North Dakota, in 1914. On the other hand, as Goddard and Cory suspected, he was not the only one at this time who was inventing cattle guards. Johnston must have been influenced by the railroad cattle guard, for if he had not been aware of these devices and their name, then he surely would have gone into greater detail concerning how he came to call his invention a cattle guard.

Yet Andrew Johnston is unique in that he was the only inventor of the cattle guard with the foresight to recognize the importance of what he had done. Thus, his is the name on the only plaque that commemorates the invention of the cattle guard.

In the years following Johnston's innovation, cattle guards were being installed all over the plains. In Kansas, for instance, when Vern Kysar, who grew up in Goodland, drove his new Model T across Greeley County from north to south in 1915, he had to cross several wooden-plank cattle guards in the process. In 1917 a cattle guard was built on the Bert Lovett Ranch on Homer Creek in Greenwood County. The guard still stands, although it has been almost totally rebuilt over the years. In 1917 cattle guards were also being used on the Shumway Oil Lease near El Dorado in central Butler County. In 1918 Earl E. Perkins of Howard built a pipe-grid cattle guard as a bridge across a drainage ditch into his feedlot when he replaced his team-driven feed wagon with a truck. Also in 1918 Peter Meier of Quinter placed some wooden planks on edge over a pit to make a cattle guard on a newly opened road into his ranch. This was two years before Albert Tuttle installed one on his family's ranch near Quinter.

At the same time that Andrew Johnston was inventing his cattle guard, another guard was beginning to make its appearance on roads in the Nebraska Sandhills. This guard, an arched crossover similar to the Indiana guard of 1909, was widely used in Nebraska and parts of Texas during the teens and even into the twenties, despite some inherent disadvantages. Albert Lawlis of Broken Bow, Nebraska, sent me a photograph that shows an arched crossover built by John Applegate on his brother Lee Applegate's ranch a few miles south of Wood Lake, Nebraska. Mabel Hickman Pearson of Valentine, a niece of the Applegate brothers, wrote in a letter: "I think that was the one and only guard of that type ever made. Uncle John was given to the unusual." In 1918 Applegate sold the ranch to Elmer Reddick, whose widow, Ella, reported that the crossover worked very well and that driving over it was no problem if one approached it slowly. This particular guard remained in use until 1921, when Reddick replaced it with one of standard design, using two-by-fours placed edgewise as bars. This guard lasted until it was replaced by a pipe guard in 1941.

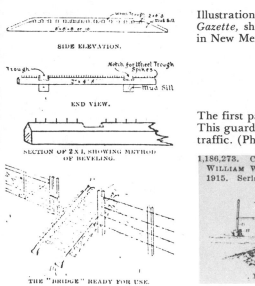

SIDE ELEVATION.

END VIEW.

SECTION OF 2 X 1, SHOWING METHOD OF BEVELING.

THE "BRIDGE" READY FOR USE.

Illustrations from the 29 June 1916 *Breeder's Gazette,* showing plans for a cattle guard used in New Mexico as early as 1915

The first patent on a highway cattle guard. This guard was intended for horse-drawn traffic. (Photo from *U.S. Patent Gazette*)

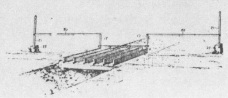

1,186,273. COMBINED BRIDGE AND CATTLE-GUARD WILLIAM W. BRIAN, Woodsboro, Tex. Filed Dec. 21 1915. Serial No. 67,982. (Cl. 39—6.)

Mrs. Pearson was wrong in thinking that Applegate's guard was unique, for arched crossovers were fairly common. Another Nebraskan, Albert Durbin of North Platte, took out what seems to have been the first patent on an automotive cattle guard in February 1916. Undoubtedly he had built arched crossovers several months before that date, although I do not know if there is a connection between Durbin and the Applegates (none of my correspondents was aware of any link between them). Durbin's guard may even be older than that of the Applegates. It is also possible that neither party was aware of the other's efforts.

The first lengthy published reference to an automotive cattle guard was in an article by Will C. Barnes, "Crossings in Fences for Autos," on pages 1349-50 of the *Breeder's Gazette* for 29 June 1916. A regular service of that trade journal was to print replies to readers' queries. As the first known full-scale description of a cattle guard, it is important enough to quote in full:

Replying to D.S., Middlewater, Tex., who asks for plans, specifications and the cost of cattle guards in a fence which will permit autos to go over and still turn the cattle, one of the simplest and most satisfactory plans for auto crossings through wire or other fences is used in New Mexico, where there are many fences across public roads, and some sort of opening that will save getting out to open gates and at the same time keep stock from escaping from pastures, is an absolute necessity. I regret my failure to take pictures of some of them, when there last summer, but they can be described, so that any one can understand their construction. The design is of course similar to the ordinary cattle guards used on railroads, but without any pit. Take two heavy timbers 8 by 8 inches square and 9 or 10 feet long for mudsills or foundations. A common railroad tie answers the purpose admirably. Lay these on the ground through the cut in the fence, so as to rest on each side equally. Space them on the ground to lie parallel and 56 inches apart, measured from center to center. Slope each end with an axe from a point about 12 inches back from the ends. Have enough 2 by 4-inch scantlings 6 feet long to lay across these mudsills not more than 3 or 4 inches apart; these are crossties. Take a hatchet and bevel off the tops of the crossties, trimming them to an edge on top of about ½ of an inch. Cut a mortise in each end of the crossties 10 inches wide and 1 inch deep, measured so that the center of the mortise will space exactly 56 inches from center to center. Spike the crossties to the mudsills, getting the center of the mortise exactly over the center of the mudsills. Spike a light strip of 1-inch stuff along the ends of the crossties, to steady them and keep them from warping. Into the tops of the crossties drive 20-penny spikes deep enough so that they will stand up about 2 inches. Space them about 2 inches apart. Make two wheel troughs 8 inches wide in the clear, of either inch or 1½-inch stuff for the bottom, and the sides of inch stuff. These should be the same length as the mudsills, less the sloping ends, which should be built up with boards level with the floor of the wheel trough on top and short sections of trough run down to the ground. Flare the troughs at the ground end, so that wheels will readily enter. Place these troughs in the mortises at each end of the ties and spike them firmly down, being careful that they space the necessary 56 inches from center to center.

The cut in the fence should be 10 feet in the clear, and the crossties 6 feet, so that one will have a space of 2 feet on each side between the ends of the crossties and the fence post. Spike a piece of 2 by 4 stuff on the fence post about level with the crossties and long enough to almost touch them; then run another piece from the top of the post to the outer end of this lower piece which will close the gap between the posts and the guard, and the natural slope will furnish plenty of clearance at the height where it is needed to allow for the overhanging sides of the cars. Stock will never get through such guards, unless under unusual conditions; the cost is small, and the benefit to the autoist great. If the builder has the necessary timber on his place, the stuff for the mudsills can easily be hewn from the tree, which reduces the cost. Such a guard should be furnished at the side of every gate where autos use the road. I have seen special auto roads in several parts of the west, where, by the use of such crossings at the fences, and trough bridges across the arroyos and washes, autos could have a road to themselves, ordinary traffic being unable to use it on account of lack of bridges, culverts and fence crossings. An auto stage company in the Pecos country in southeastern New Mexico has such a road for more than 100 miles across the prairies, and through pastures, and by using these appliances teams are unable to trespass upon it, and it is always in good shape, and not cut up by wagon wheels.

Barnes makes several comments that are particularly interesting and one that is disappointing—I regret far more than did Barnes his failure to take photographs. First, these guards were in service at least as early as the summer of 1915, maybe much earlier. Second, this cattle guard had troughs, as does the arched crossover guard, but it was built at ground level in a gap in the fence, not over it, and it had no pit. In order to provide the grid of a modern cattle guard, one would only have to double the number of two-by-four spike-studded "crossties," which are spaced about ten inches apart and placed over a pit, and to remove the spikes. (Andrew Johnston's account seems to indicate that his original intention was to build a trough-type guard and that his innovation was to recognize that the support poles themselves would turn cattle and allow cars to pass.) Third, Barnes's observation about the similarity between railroad and automotive cattle guards reinforces the theory that the highway cattle guard was suggested, consciously or otherwise, by that of the railroad. Fourth, Barnes notes the necessity for, and describes how to construct, rudimentary wings to connect the edge of the cattle guard with the fence, and thus allow plenty of clearance along each side. Wing fences had been used for years with railroad cattle guards, but this is the first documented occurrence with highway cattle guards. Finally, the comments about the competition for roads between horses and automobiles provides a brief but interesting historical perspective on a major sociological change in our culture. It is intriguing that as late as 1916 Barnes can refer to horse-drawn traffic as ordinary traffic.

The building of a trough cattle guard has been described by Everett Anderson of Torrington, Wyoming, who grew up in Henry, Nebraska, on the Wyoming border. In 1919 the foreman of the PF Ranch bought a Ford roadster to use around the ranch. He then built a box on the back of it so that he could use it as a pickup. This industrious man soon felt the need for a cattle guard, so he set two heavy posts in the fence, about twelve feet apart, then dug a trench, about four feet wide and equally deep, from one post to the other. Next he took two two-by-twelve planks, ten feet long, and nailed two-by-sixes on the sides of each plank in order to form troughs. These troughs, which extended three feet beyond the pit on both sides, were laid out precisely to accommodate the wheels of his Ford. Anderson watched this cattle guard take shape as he drove the family's milk cow back and forth to pasture that summer.

The cattle guards seen by Will Barnes may have been of the trough type, but pit-and-pole cattle guards were also in use in New Mexico around 1915.

Sometime between 1914 and 1916 a photograph was taken of a grid-style cattle guard on a New Mexico state highway in Guadalupe County (Santa Rosa). This photograph was published in the *Second Biennial Report* (1914–16) of the New Mexico state engineer, a copy of which is in the New Mexico State Archives in Santa Fe. Dr. Myra Ellen Jenkins, head of the Historical Services Division, has sent me a copy of the photograph. Unfortunately, the photographer stood some distance from the cattle guard when he took the picture; nevertheless, one can discern that the guard is at ground level and apparently does not have troughs. Wooden wings, slanting at about a 45° angle, are also plainly visible, as is a gate at the side for livestock to use. This seems to be the earliest surviving photograph of an automotive cattle guard.

The third report of the state highway engineer, published in 1917, shows that the New Mexico Highway Department built fifteen cattle guards that year, all of them in Chaves County (Roswell). Grant County (Silver City) also installed, at its own expense, a cattle guard on a state road.

In 1916 Ray Purinton of WaKeeney, Kansas, built a pit-and-pole cattle guard at the entrance to his family's ranch, located twelve miles south of Collyer. In an interview at his home in 1979, Purinton said that his paternal grandfather, Albert, suggested the design of the cattle guard to him. Albert Purinton had come to Kansas from Vermont in 1878, and he could, according to his grandson, "make anything and everything out of wood or timber." Albert had settled a ranch and built a store halfway between the Union Pacific and the Missouri Pacific railroads, which went through WaKeeney and Utica respectively. It was here that Purinton, who had just bought a new Dodge, dug a pit and spaced some ash poles over it. Perhaps the elder Purinton had seen a dry moat (a yard gate for foot traffic, made by spacing small logs over a ditch—see chapter 6) in use back in the eastern woodlands; his idea for an automotive cattle guard may have been suggested by that early memory. If this were the case, it would be the only instance that I am aware of when a dry moat has served as a direct model for a cattle guard. Whatever the case may be, Ray Purinton's cattle guard exhibits the spontaneity of an independent invention. He cannot remember having seen or read about any other cattle guard before he built his own, yet many guards had already been built in other parts of the plains.

Purinton reported that the ash poles lasted about a year and that they worked fine for cloven-hoofed cows but not so well for horses. He replaced this guard with a very solid one: for stringers he used twelve-foot-long U-iron beams from an old set of wagon scales, and for the grid he used eight-foot flues out of a steam thresher, just as Riggs and Hurley had done in Texas a few years earlier. The pit was lined with stone and could be walked through by some of his horses. The pipes had been spaced far enough apart so that his draft horses could not step on two bars at once and just walk out, but some of

The earliest known photograph of a cattle guard, from the New Mexico Highway Engineer's Report published in 1916. (Courtesy of Myra Ellen Jenkins)

Spencer Allen and his cattle guard, invented in 1917 and patented ten years later. (Courtesy of Pollie Allen Fitch)

A ladder-type cattle guard, with open-pit middle, in Llano County, Texas. Concrete wings are common in this region of Texas.

the smaller horses could step between the bars and escape unless the pit was cleaned regularly. One of their ponies once got caught, all four legs down between the bars, but it was extracted without injury. This guard was well constructed and would probably be in place today, Purinton said, if it had not been torn out when the entrance to the ranch was changed several years ago.

A short article in the November 1916 issue of *Popular Mechanics* described an arched crossover in western Texas. The article also contained a photograph of a car, pulling a trailer, in the middle of the crossover. The caption read: "An Incline on a Road in Western Texas Which Enables the Motorist to Dispense with Opening and Closing a Gate." This is the text:

> In many parts of the West and Southwest where automobiles are numerous it is becoming common to drive one's car over a fence instead of stopping to open a gate, drive through, and then shut it. The new and quicker method is made possible by the construction of inclines which make it an easy matter to mount to the top of the barrier and then descend on the other side. The inclines are usually composed of two tracks, set the proper distance apart for automobile wheels and supported by posts. The tracks are equipped with a guard at one side, which prevents a car from running off, although accidents happen occasionally in spite of this provision. Cattle will not walk up these inclines, since ordinarily no floor is laid between the tracks.

The most detailed account of the building of an early-day cattle guard has come from William M. Jolly, who was born on 7 November 1890 and during his twenties worked on a ranch near Ozona, Texas:

> In 1916 or 1917, before I went to the war in 1918, I helped build three cattle guards. This was on a ranch owned by Charles F. Davidson who had two sons, a Mexican, and myself working for him. We built the guards at spare times on the ranch.
>
> Among the things to do on a cattle ranch is to go over to a neighboring ranch and drive three or four cattle that had gotten out of the pasture where two bulls had torn the fence down. Then you check all of your watering places two or three times a week. If a windmill has quit pumping you get someone on the ranch to help you fix it. Someone comes by the ranch and leaves word that they saw a cow of yours over at a certain windmill with a very new calf and the cow's teats were so large and full the calf couldn't suck them. On and on like that the year round.
>
> Back in those days not most but all ranchers did all the work that was done. And a ranch owner didn't turn loose a nickel that he didn't have to. Now this Mr. Davidson had a law office in Ozona, about seven or eight miles to the north. He and his family lived at the ranch house. The whole ranch force stayed there. Mr. Davidson

at that time still used a buggy and team to go places. I don't believe I ever saw him on a horse.

Now to the three cattle guards. There was a public road that came out of Ozona and went south down a big wide draw. The road went through his pasture out west of the house. Mr.Davidson had started up a herd of registered hereford cattle. The pasture he kept them in was west of the ranch. A Mr. Couch owned the ranch between Davidson and Ozona. The pasture below this registered pasture, as it was known, was Mr. Davidson's also. There was a gate out of Mr. Couch's pasture on this public road into Mr. Davidson's registered pasture, also another gate out of the registered pasture. Now if the gate into Mr. Couch's pasture was left open and one of his bulls got into the registered herd, there was a bad mixup on the registration. Same way on the other gate.

There was getting to be a lot of traffic on that road since quite a few cars were coming into the country. Mr. Davidson had a car but I don't remember what it was. But he didn't drive it around on the ranch. For ranch work everything was wagon or his buggy.

Most all ranch people would close the gates behind them, but a lot of just travelling people would say that fellow behind me will close the gate, so Mr. Davidson was almost compelled to either make a cattle guard of some kind or move over and fence off a registered pasture to the east of his house or go out of the registered cow business.

These gates were right on the road so as I was only breaking horses there by the head he would use me a lot of the time as help there on the ranch.

He went over to one of these gates in his buggy. He had a pick and shovel that stayed in that buggy all the time. I came on over horse back. We took a piece of rope and measured off a pit for the cattle guard.

Mr. Davidson had a Mexican there that just helped do any and all things. When this Mexican wasn't busy with feeding cattle or something else, he dug on this pit. One day he said he had it finished. Now the material. Mr. Davidson had a windmill with a wooden tower. It was getting in bad shape, so he got a man from Ozona that made windmill towers to come out there and put a new one up. So he just let this old tower down and left it lay there.

We took the wagon over there, took the tower apart, then when one of us was loose, maybe two of us would go over to where the cattle guard had been dug out and work on it sometimes three hours, sometimes half a day.

We all knew about what we were going to do, so whoever was there working was the boss.

We took two of these tower legs, cut out 14 feet of the best part of them, lay them across the pit the way the traffic went. We sunk the ends in about 12 inch trenches so when the two by six cross beams were set on them, it would bring the top of the cattle guard floor up even with the road level. We spaced these up-edged boards about five inches apart, then sawed a block just as wide as the space was and nailed it in to keep the distance even and to prevent them from turning over or to one side.

After we finished this first one we could see how to improve on the next one. After we fixed the fence up to each end to keep the cattle from walking around the ends, we turned the traffic loose on it. Mr. Davidson drove his car across it back and forth several times and everything worked just fine.

As well as I can remember we dug the next hole for the guard, but we got busy at other ranch work and it was a month or more before we got back to it. During that time we had run out of feed for some young registered bulls we were feeding there. A freighter was to bring the feed out to the ranch, but didn't show up. Mr. Davidson had gone into Ozona on some office work. Someone phoned in and asked him to bring out enough feed for that night for the bulls. So he put about eight sacks of feed in the back seat of his car and when he got the hind wheels out to about the center of the cattle guard, one of those 6 by 6 supports broke in two, let that side of his car down, and he was stuck. He had to walk about two miles to the ranch.

The work horse team was out in a pasture but they wanted the feed for those bulls that night, so we got the horses in, hitched the team of work horses up to the wagon and pulled the car out of this place. We just pulled it on over to the ranch and fed the bulls and got to bed. We went to improving that cattle guard in our minds.

The easiest way to make the next one hold up with the least amount of work using what we had there on the ranch to work with, for that was all we had and we all knew there would not be any new material from town, was to jack the broken beam up and nail some boards on each side to hold it straight, then put a big flat rock under it to hold up the weight. Then we also put a big flat rock under the other beam (which we should have done the first thing.) That is where you learn by doing.

I refer here as we. That meant that any one or all 5 of us. Charley, the youngest boy, was going to school, but he worked on the ranch every morning and evening, Saturday, and Sunday just like he was drawing wages.

A lot of this informaton may seem useless to you, but I put it in here so you can understand how ranchers worked and also why there were so many kinds of cattle guards built. There simply was no one pattern.

After we got the car unloaded there was a man that worked on cars some came down to the ranch and he and Charley after school straightened up some brake rods, hammered out a pan dent, and the car was back good as new.

Now I believe that takes care of the first cattle guard I ever helped to build. On the second guard we built it the same way, but at the ends of these 2 by 6 cross boards we put another 6 by 6 under each end of them. That made four beams under that one. We also put a big rock in the center of each support beam. That cattle guard would hold up just about anything. I guess we had been two or two and ½ months on those two guards.

Then we got a slack spell on the ranch work, and from 2 to 4 of us worked on the third guard. It was about five miles south of the ranch house, where the road went into another man's ranch, a Mr. Bagget. Mr. Bagget said as we had built two guards, he would furnish the material if we would build the guard between the two ranches. He said he had the material there at his ranch house.

This material turned out just like ours had been. It was an old windmill tower and some one by six corral lumber. We only found enough of this old tower posts to make three beams underneath. Then we had to nail two of these corral planks together to make our 2 by 6s for the top. But we put a big rock in the middle of each beam.

Now you can see the way we made our three cattle guards, and the rest of the ranches in the country all made their own cattle guards the same way—out of whatever old scrap material they could find.

This account provides not only a thorough description of the building of early cattle guards but also a fascinating glimpse of day-to-day ranch life in the early years of the century.

Arched crossover guards were widely used in southern Texas in 1917, according to C. G. Wood of Floresville, who, when he was sixteen years old, saw them on a road along the Nueces River that ran southeast from Cotulla through LaSalle and Duval counties. Each guard consisted of a wooden trough for each wheel, flared at each end to facilitate the entry of car wheels. Livestock and horse-drawn traffic could pass through gates at each crossing. According to Wood, "Cars could cross from either side of the fence, and cross over the top of the fence, but of course very slowly and cautiously. Brahma cattle from India had just been introduced into Texas at that time, and it was quite a relief to be able to cross over the fences where the strange cattle roamed, without having to get out and open the gates."

Wood, whose working career was spent with the Texas State Highway Department, also remembers having seen at about the same time (1917) pit-and-pole cattle guards on the farm-to-market roads in the hill country near Kerrville, where many sheep and goats were raised. Wood assumed that these grid-type cattle guards would work better with goats, which soon learned to walk over the troughs of an arched crossover.

Trough cattle guards were still being used in Texas in 1920 when Jim Roberts built one on his ranch near Wimberley. Ten years later he replaced it with one of a conventional grid design. Also in 1920 near Wimberley, Jim Dobie had installed a bar-grid guard using cedar poles for bars. C. W. Wimberley has said that the cedar-pole guards would have been much more durable if the builders had used bolts instead of nails in putting them together. They worked well under moderate or light traffic, but as cars got heavier and faster, the guards "began to award the speedsters with busted tires and loose mufflers for their driving manners."

An interesting analogue to the development of cattle guards on the Great Plains was taking place in California in 1914. There, according to an article in *Popular Mechanics* ("Grooved Tracks Are Used as Automobile Bridge," September 1914, p. 398), an automobile club had constructed troughs of structural iron and wood and had mounted them on concrete piers in order to form bridges across small streams on roads where traffic was too light to warrant a regular bridge. The open middle between the two troughs, as noted in the article, made it impossible for these bridges to be used by horse-drawn vehicles. Only a small step was necessary in order to adapt this type of bridge to use as a cattle guard.

Although his inspiration came from different sources, Raymond Lauppe of Arbuckle, California, took this step in 1916, his last year in high school. With help from his father, Lauppe built the second cattle guard constructed outside the Great Plains, so far as I have been able to learn. The elder Lauppe had a positive attitude toward agricultural efficiency; as early as 1904 or 1905 he had installed a remote-control gate operated by rope pulls. Raymond Lauppe told me that sometime after 1913 he and his father had seen a picture and description of an arched crossover cattle guard from Texas in a newspaper or a farm or mechanics magazine, but he is not sure of the name or date of the publication. (Nor have I been able to locate this reference. It could possibly be the one from the *Breeder's Gazette,* discussed earlier in this chapter, although that guard was a trough type without a pit, not an arched crossover. The *Popular Mechanics* article about the Indiana guard in 1909 seems too early; on the other hand, the November 1916 article about western-Texas inclines seems a bit late. Of the three, however, this last-named one seems the most likely for Lauppe to have read.) In any case, Raymond Lauppe did build an arched crossover, but it did not work satisfactorily. The guard was so close to the road that it was rather difficult to line up the car to cross the guard. So, he immediately tore down the arched crossover, dug into the fence line a pit that was three feet deep and just wide enough for a car to pass through, and put the troughs from the crossover down at ground level. The result was a trough cattle guard with an open pit in the middle.

About a year later, Lauppe realized that the railroad cattle guards he had been seeing for years could be adapted to highway use. "I don't know why it took me so long to think about the railroad cattle guard," he told me. Once he did think of it, however, he removed the troughs from the pit, put in some stringers, and placed two-by-sixes on edge, spaced four inches apart, as bars,

This guard worked fine, except that the Lauppes' car rolled over it so fast that the boards soon became worn. In 1918, this time with some help from his father, Raymond Lauppe spaced two-inch pipe bars on some four-by-six inch stringers. The result was a cattle guard that stood on the farm until World War II.

A second cattle guard west of the Rocky Mountains was built by Spencer F. Allen of Ridgedale, Idaho. His daughter, Pollie Allen Fitch of Rexburg, has explained the circumstances that led to his invention:

> He had recently bought a Ford car which delighted him until he had to stop at the end of our land to open the gate. He pondered over this; he thought of building an incline over the fence [i.e., an arched crossover]. My mother assured him she would never ride with him ascending into the air. So he devised a cattle guard. According to his diary this was in January 1917 and first used in March 1917. Later he added wooden side sections which were laid down over the guard for horse drawn vehicles. Years later after his friends had told him many times, "You should get a patent on that gate," he applied for a patent.

In 1927, ten years after he had first built his cattle guard, he was granted a patent on it, but he did not try to market it, and he never made much money from it. He did, however, build and install cattle guards at the entrances to cemeteries in Wellsville and Hyrum, Utah, and in Malad City, Idaho. Moreover, he became locally famous, as had Andrew Johnston in North Dakota, for having invented a cattle guard. Several letters from people in the Nevada-Utah-Idaho region testify to the Allen Cattle Guard.

Pollie Fitch did not know where Allen got the idea for the cattle guard, but she thought the idea may have been original with him. "There surely were no cattle guards around our area at the time he devised this solution to the problem." Allen may well have developed a cattle guard independently, as had many others east of the Rockies a few years earlier. I find it especially interesting that his experiments encompassed both the grid cattle guard and the arched crossover.

On 29 March 1919 Edwin H. Underwood of Bainbridge, Georgia, filed a patent on another cattle guard developed outside the Great Plains during this period. This appears to have been a classic pit-and-pole cattle guard, with seven or more metal or wooden bars secured to a metal base, and the whole arrangement placed into a pit in the roadway.

Also in 1919 (on 13 October) two New Mexicans, Emory Hickok of Engle and Albert H. Hollenbeck of Fair View, filed for a patent on an automotive cattle guard. This guard was somewhat complicated to operate, and its design incorporated elements of the trough and the pit-and-pole guards, for the entire surface was supported in the middle by a heavy vertical bolt fixed in such a way that the grid would swing both lengthwise and crosswise. Thus, a cow that attempted to cross it would be frightened off by the quivering and shaking of the trough. As illustrated in the *Patent Gazette,* this guard required a substantial framework, which, instead of being placed in a pit, was placed on the road, with dirt being mounded up to it in order to make approach ramps. This guard, like many of the more complicated railroad cattle guards, undoubtedly turned cattle, but it was much too complicated to be either work effective or cost efficient.

So far in this chapter, three major types of cattle guards have been described: the bar-grid (or pit-and-pole) style, the arched crossover, and the ground-level trough guard. There was one other major experiment in cattle-guard design during this decade of experimentation—the ladder cattle guard. This design incorporated elements both of the trough and of the pit-and-pole guards. Victor H. Merrihew of Ashby, Nebraska, has described how one of these guards was built. A pit was first dug, but instead of regular troughs with solid plank floors, a "ladder" was made for each wheel by inserting numerous pieces of two-inch pipe several inches apart into two three-by-eight-inch bridge planks turned on edge. Holes were bored into (but not through) these planks for the pipe to fit into, and long one-half-inch bolts were run through each end of the ladders to clamp them securely together. The tracks were about twenty-two inches wide, with the bridge plank surrounding them thus forming troughs for the wheels. Local blacksmiths sometimes used steel mine rails instead of bridge planks for the edge pieces and old boiler flues for the bars. The chief disadvantage of this type of guard, especially where the edges did not stick up far enough to form a trough, was that cars often ran off the track and into the open pit in the middle.

Some of these old ladder guards were still to be found on back roads near Hulett, Wyoming, when Melvin Storm was growing up there during the 1950s. A modified form of the ladder guard, which incorporates ladders for troughs and also has three or four bars over the pit, is still being used in the Llano County, Texas, area. These guards are used, not on heavily traveled roads, but on ranch roads where they enter onto a highway or county road.

Interestingly enough, a guard nearly identical to the ladder guard, called a Combermere Ladder, was invented in England in the 1920s by Sir Kenneth Crossley of Crossley Motors, who lived at Combermere Abbey, Shropshire. According to Lady Ruth K. Lowther of Lightwood-on-Green, Wales, he had a rather long driveway on his estate. At some of the gates dividing the fields, he dug pits several feet deep and put in metal-runged "ladders," over which the car wheels could pass, leaving the open pit in the middle to frighten livestock.

Lady Lowther's father installed a Combermere Ladder at the back of his property, a few miles from Combermere Abbey, sometime before 1931. Keeping the car wheels on the ladder could also be a problem there. Lady Lowther wrote that for her twenty-first birthday her father gave her an Austin Mini and this advice for driving her new car over the Combermere ladder: "He told me there were two inches inside before I fell in and two inches outside for the lorry and his car had the middle. I never did fall in." Several years later her father put in a bar-grid guard at the front gate of his estate in order to keep horses from wandering. Steel H-bars were used for the grid, and it was, according to Lady Lowther, "strong enough to hold up the Bertram Mills Circus."

These English cattle guards are actually from the twenties, the subject of chapter 4, but the similarity to the ladder guards from Nebraska makes it appropriate to include them here. After the experimentation during the first two decades of the twentieth century, when the automotive cattle guard underwent its initial development, the time was now ready for a decade of cattle-guard dispersion.

4
THE SPREAD OF CATTLE
GUARDS, 1920 TO 1930

The influence of the cattle-guard innovators of the first two decades of the century was felt both directly and indirectly during the twenties, a decade when the use of cattle guards increased along with the number of automobiles on the roads. The growing number of rural mail carriers, most of whom had switched to automobiles during the late teens, also accentuated the need for cattle guards. During the twenties also, the pit-and-pole guard became the standard design. Some ladder guards and trough guards were installed during the twenties, especially in Texas, Oklahoma, and Nebraska, but heavier vehicles (particularly grain trucks and oil-field equipment) moving at faster speeds soon proved the superiority of a guard that, if properly constructed, could stand up under extremely heavy loads and could handle two-way traffic.

Only in some of the sparsely populated non-oil-producing regions of Texas and Nebraska could the trough cattle guard be found after the twenties. I have been told, although I have not been fortunate enough to find any, that the decaying remains of a few old-style auto gates, long fallen into disuse, can still be seen in some remote areas of the Nebraska Sandhills. The first attempts, some of them successful, to manufacture cattle guards commercially were also made during the twenties.

Possibly because of Andrew Johnston's active role in livestock organizations, his wooden-pole cattle guard quickly spread throughout the western Dakotas and eastern Montana. Old-time cowboy "Slim" Zimmerman of Afton, Wyoming, for instance, remembers a pine-pole cattle guard in 1928 on a ranch seventy miles from Miles City, Montana. The poles were kept apart by spacers, but they were placed loose on the stringers so that they would move underfoot and thus deter livestock more effectively.

Sheila Robinson of Coleharbor, North Dakota, cites an example of a more direct influence of the Johnston guard. Her father, Matt Crowley of Hebron, North Dakota, was a friend of Johnston's and "no doubt heard about this idea not long afterwards [i.e., after Johnston built his first guard], probably at a meeting of the Western North Dakota Stockmen's Association." Mrs. Robinson, who was born in 1920, remembers many cattle guards on their ranch. She frequently crossed one in particular that was located between the main county road and the pasture where their cattle were summered. This guard was made of ash poles, some of them not too straight, placed over a hole with dirt piled on either side. The poles were about four or five inches in diameter and were spaced nearly one foot apart. The guard was about seven or eight feet across, and Mrs. Robinson remembers that one had to drive *up* to cross and that the car occasionally scraped on the bottom. If the pits were not deep enough on these wooden-pole guards, according to Mrs. Robinson, livestock would step between poles and walk across, and some of Crowley's horses would jump over the narrower guards. Mrs. Robinson regrets that they never took a photograph of one of these old cattle guards: "They were just a labor-saving device, and rather crude—not worth a picture back then."

Another early inventor whose guards had a direct influence was Spencer Allen of Idaho. Mrs. R. Wilkinson of Henderson, Nevada, remembers that in the late twenties her father, I. E. Bradley of Malad City, Idaho, installed a metal Allen Cattle Guard in their driveway. I have not been able to trace any direct influence from individual inventors other than Allen and Johnston. Instead, in typical folk fashion, the cattle guard and its lore have generally spread anonymously.

By the twenties the use of cattle guards was widespread in the plains states and was making steady headway into many other regions as well. For instance, in the Far West a pipe-grid cattle guard was being used in Lake County, California, by mid decade. Guards in this area usually had pipe bars that were spaced and boxed in on the ends. These bars were attached to loose rollers so that they would roll under the feet of livestock (much like a railroad cattle guard that was being marketed at the same time). According to one informant, David E. Smith of Olathe, Kansas, if a Model T stopped on one of these grids, it would often spin the loose pipes when the driver attempted to go forward. Because the cars were so light, they did not have enough traction to avoid getting stuck.

There were also cattle guards in Washington State in the twenties, at least one of which was built by Emil Lindgren on his farm in Wahkiakum

A wooden-pole cattle guard near the Wagon Box Ranch, Story, Wyoming. (Courtesy of Anthony James Strain)

Cattle guards just west of the abandoned townsite of Teterville, Kansas. The guard in the concrete pit was built in the early 1920s.

County near the mouth of Deep River. Lindgren dug a shallow pit six feet long and ten feet wide and put in two logs for a base. On these stringers he nailed tough spruce limbs for bars. This guard lasted, in spite of the rainy climate of coastal Washington, until 1945, when Lindgren's daughter and her husband, Mildred and Ivan Jones, who had bought the farm, replaced the old guard with new supports and with bars of four-by-four lumber tapered to about an inch in width on top. This type of bar was being used in the central plains during the twenties, and it is possible that Jones, who had moved to Washington from Beloit, Kansas, may have seen some of these tapered bars before moving west.

During this decade, cattle guards were also moving eastward. The Ozarks of Missouri had large areas of open range where cattle and razorback hogs ran free, and it was the landowner's responsibility to fence animals out of his fields, not the stockowner's to fence them in. Cattle guards were used to help with this fencing in Missouri, as well as in Arkansas. As late as the 1940s in Eminence, Missouri, cattle guards were used between the front yards of houses and the street. Because the open range extended into the town, cattle guards (sometimes called razorback guards in the Ozarks) were the most effective way to keep hogs and cows out of yards. In fact, according to Ralph Ricketts, when the courthouse doors were kept open for ventilation on hot summer days, "there was nothing to keep the hogs and cattle from getting into the courthouse if they really wanted to get in."

I was surprised to discover that one of my great-uncles had built the first cattle guards in Cheyenne County, Colorado. Essie Alexander of Riverton, Nebraska, a second cousin whom I had never met, wrote to tell me that her father, Clark Wright, had built some cattle guards in the late teens and early twenties on his ranch between Kit Carson and Wildhorse. As a boy I visited

Uncle Clark and was fascinated with his collecton of arrowheads, buffalo guns, branding irons, and all sorts of other historical items, but I was too young to pay any special attention to the cattle guards. The original cattle guards he built used railroad ties turned on edge for bars, although these were later replaced with pipe grids, according to his daughter.

In western Kansas, pipe-grid cattle guards were being used in the early 1920s. Elmer W. Sass of Nevada, Missouri, was six years old when his father bought a farm near Kendall, Kansas, on the border between Hamilton and Kearny counties. The father had built a dugout where his family lived for several years. The son remembers that there was much open prairie at the time, and if people wanted to keep stock out of their fields or within a certain distance of home, they had to fence. A cattle guard was already in place on the northwestern corner of their quarter section when the Sass family moved. The guard had stringers of heavy timber, notched to hold three-inch pipe bars set over a pit two to three feet deep. The guard was built for light traffic, and Sass says that he cannot remember any trucks at that time.

Farther east and north, in Trego County, two pit-and-pole cattle guards were being used on the Lynd Ranch in 1925. Three years earlier, even farther east, E. T. Anderson had installed a pit-and-pole cattle guard at the entrance to his ranch in Morris County, north of Hymer. Anderson's ranch was located on the western edge of the Flint Hills, and during the twenties this major grassland became filled with cattle guards, particularly in oil-lease areas such as Teterville in northwest Greenwood County. Conwy Rees of Emporia had some steers on pasture at the head of Fall River during the early twenties; he remembers seeing his first cattle guard then in that area. Mary Etta Funk Davidson saw her first cattle guards in the Flint Hills of Chase County near Shaw Creek in 1927.

Many of the early Flint Hills cattle guards are gone, but evidence of their former existence can still be seen. The first cattle guard that my father, Kenneth Hoy of Cassoday, can remember was north of town, across the Butler County line into Chase County on Kansas highway 13 (now K-177), which was at that time (and continued so well into my memory) a graded sand road. This cattle guard was made of pipe bars and was used for several years before the roadway was completely fenced. Today only a concrete post remains beside the road to mark the spot where this cattle guard, built in the early 1920s, once stood.

Occasionally, while driving the back roads of the Flint Hills, one will drive over the remains of a concrete foundation. Although most people would not notice these concrete outcroppings, unless they jutted above the surface of the road far enough to cause a bump that was more severe than usual, these foundations almost invariably mark the pit where a cattle guard once was. One of these pits, located near the Satchel Creek Ranch in eastern Butler

County, is the earliest cattle guard remembered by Lowell Scribner, a ranch worker and lifelong resident of this area. This cattle guard was built in the mid twenties, and Scribner thinks that the pipe bars, or what is left of them, might still be buried in the dirt and gravel of the road.

No trace at all remains of the first cattle guard remembered by David and Alfred Mercer, lifelong ranchers in the Cedar Point–Matfield Green area of southern Chase County. In the early 1920s the Mercer family lived in the sparsely settled bluestem pastures west of Matfield Green, and the road that led to the town, several miles away, went through the Dean pasture and its two wire gates, which David and Alfred's older sisters, Bessie and Ruth, had to open and shut each time the family went to town. During the school year, this opening and closing became more than a little tiresome. Not only that; their father's large-scale ranching and farming operation required several hired men, and William Mercer did not particularly like the length of time it took some of them to open a gate, drive through, then shut it and start driving again. Whether for the convenience of his family or for the economy of his ranching operation, he decided to put in cattle guards. Neither of the Mercer brothers knows just where his father got the idea, but sometime in the early twenties, William Mercer cut down ten hardwood poles and two hedge posts, then he dug a small pit in the road, put the posts down running with the road, and placed the poles over them, crosswise to the road, thus forming a grid of spaced bars. The cattle guard he made was rather narrow, so in order to keep cattle from attempting to jump over it, he tied some black rags to it that would flap in the wind. The gate that the guard replaced was rebuilt at the side of the pit. This entire process was then repeated at the second gate on that road.

Unfortunately, Mercer had neglected to inform county road officials of his industriousness, and when the drivers of the mule-drawn road graders came upon the cattle guards, rags flapping in the breeze, they were less than enthusiastic about the innovation. Despite the unhappiness of the county officials, these homemade cattle guards remained in use for three years, at which time the county replaced them with pipe cattle guards, charging all the expense to Mercer's taxes. Cattle guards still stand on the open-range road that runs through the Dean pasture, but the pits are now lined with concrete and the bars are made of lengths of railroad rail.

William Mercer's idea for a pit-and-pole cattle guard may have been original, or he may have derived it from some trough cattle guards that had been installed earlier on the Farrington pastures a few miles southeast of his ranch. These pastures were run by the Crocker brothers, Ed and Arthur, whose father first moved to Matfield Green in 1867. Later, his sons had large-scale ranching interests in both Texas and Arizona, as well as in Kansas. In December 1979, when Mason Crocker, Ed's son, had just sold the home place

61

and half of his Flint Hills pasture acreage and was getting ready to move to his Texas home, he gave me an old issue of *Kansas Farmer-Stockman* magazine (15 September 1920). It contained an article about his father and uncle, "Where Cattle Graze on a Thousand Hills," one of the earliest printed accounts of cattle guards:

> In our drive back to the ranch house, after spending nearly a half day in the pastures my attention was drawn to a new and mighty convenient scheme the Crockers have adopted to get away from pasture gates. They have replaced their gates with an arrangement similar to the cattle guards used at railroad crossings. A pit is dug where the gate swings open with a guard at either side. Small poles are placed across the pit, about a foot apart. Across these poles ten or twelve inch boards are laid to form a track for automobiles to cross, thus eliminating the necessity for gates.

Crocker said that there were five or six of these modified trough-type cattle guards at various places on their property. They were replaced with gates in the 1930s because the poles had weakened and because the tenant house on the Farrington place had been torn down and there was no longer a need for the guards.

Although neither the Mercer nor the Crocker guards have survived, one built at about the same time in central Lyon County can still be seen. It is located at the entrance to Frank Arndt's farm, just south of Emporia, but the pit has been filled in and only a few of the original bars are still visible. This cattle guard was quite narrow and lightweight, having been built in the days of Model T traffic, so the Arndts have installed a newer guard made of pipe next to the old one.

The original guard was located several yards to the north of its present site, according to Ruth Lynn, who lived on the farm when the cattle guard was first built by her father, Dan James. He had seen several cattle guards in the oil leases near Teterville, so in 1927 he dug a pit, ran a rectangular concrete foundation approximately eight and one-half feet by six feet with five-inch walls, then ran two concrete cross walls in the pit just where the wheels of his Allen car would go. He next put down a series of iron T-bars, flat side up and three and one-half inches apart, into the wet cement in order to form the grid. Thus, he had a cattle guard, probably the first in the Emporia vicinity.

Five years later the road was widened, so James decided to move his cattle guard to its present location in order to obtain better ditch drainage. Those were depression times, so when a young man came by and offered, for ten dollars, to dig up the old foundation and move it to the new hole that had already been dug, thereby saving the cost of new concrete, he was given the job. First he dug all around the walls, then he cut some skid poles in the timber nearby. After jacking up the concrete pit and sliding it onto the skids, he started pulling it to the new hole. Unfortunately, the concrete had not been reinforced, and the vibrations caused by the dragging skids caused the walls to break apart completely. So James had to buy and pour new concrete after all, although he was able to use the same T-bars for the grid.

So far, I have found only one original Flint Hills cattle guard from this period still in use, and even that one has been supplemented with a second guard. These dual guards are at the entrance to the Morris pasture immediately west of the abandoned townsite of Teterville in northwestern Greenwood County; a concrete pit marks the earlier one. Walt Arnett, a lifelong cowboy in the Matfield Green area, is of the opinion that this cattle guard is the oldest one extant in the area and that it was built in the early twenties.

According to C. E. Dauman, who lived near Hamilton, Kansas, for many years, the Teterville oil field contained some of the earliest cattle guards in Greenwood County. This belief is supported by A. G. ("Jim") Young of Cassoday, who was reared and still lives just a few miles south of Teterville. He especially remembers two early-day cattle guards in that area, one of which was on the road running east toward Eureka along the south side of the Mosby pasture. This cattle guard, built either by the county or by oil-field workers, was made of small pipe interspaced by stringers made of strips of metal nailed onto used oil-field timbers. The second cattle guard was on the trail from Young's place to Cassoday, some dozen miles north and west. No real road into the town existed at that time—the Youngs had to travel along the ridges of the hills until they came to the flats a couple of miles east of the Watkins Ranch. There the trail met the township road at the corner of a pasture, and at that entry point there was a cattle guard made of two-by-tens turned on edge. Both of these cattle guards, built during the early twenties, have long since rotted away.

In Texas during the twenties, cattle guards of all types were being used, although, particularly in oil country, the pit-and-pole guard was becoming dominant. John Shaw, who reported that he saw cattle guards in 1913 in southwestern Texas, also saw many of the metal-bar type on a trip from Laredo to Hebbronville in 1924. O. E. ("Whitey") Cowsar worked most of his life as a carpenter in the oil fields. He first saw cattle guards, with bars of two-by-sixes laid edgewise, near Wink, Texas, in 1917. He remembers welders making cattle guards of pipe in the leases near Breckenridge and Graham in the twenties. Cowsar thinks that the availability of welders contributed greatly to the increased use of cattle guards. He also remembers more than once when welders had to be called in to cut pipe from a cattle guard in order to free horses that were caught, but he does not remember any cows in similar predicaments. He also says that people sometimes made money by charging motorists a quarter to drive through their property in order to avoid a mudhole on the road or by charging them fifty cents to pull them out if they got stuck trying to drive through the mud. As a young man, Cowsar was once hired to haul water to a mudhole in order to keep it good and sticky.

Roy ("Cap") Carpenter of San Angelo recalls a cattle guard that his father had built in Limestone County, Texas. The elder Carpenter, who had arrived there in 1908 as a demonstrator for the Reeves steam tractor, later became manager of the Riley Ranch. In 1923, two years after their Reeves tractor had quit running, Carpenter used the boiler flues for the bars on a cattle guard, the same grid material used by Riggs and Hurley on the cattle guard they had built in Erath County in 1913. The flues were about eight feet long, wide enough for the automobiles of the time and strong enough for all but heavy truck traffic. "Cap" Carpenter said that the bars were spaced about four inches apart, "and I never saw any cattle, horses, or mules try to cross. As the guard was about 100 yards from our house, we had ample time to observe the stock's behavior." Instead of digging a pit, Carpenter simply put the bars on a frame about a foot high and graded an approach ramp from each side.

While many cattle guards were being built in the twenties for oil workers, many were also being built for rural mail carriers. Rural free delivery had been established by law in 1896, and in 1916 the postmaster general noted that the automobile had come into widespread use for mail service. My research has not uncovered any postal-service directives about the duties of mail carriers regarding the problem of opening and closing gates. W. C. Mills of Lake City, Kansas, relates an anecdote about a mail carrier who was not scrupulous about shutting the gates on the Mills Ranch:

> Mailmen didn't like to mess with gates, and one we had was particularly bad, so I laid up for him one day just below the mailbox in a draw where he couldn't see me. The mail carrier had a guy with him who used to work for us, and he told this guy just to throw the gate open. "But what if Toke was watching? Would you still leave the gate open?" Toke was my dad's nickname. The mail carrier said, "I don't care who's watching. I'd throw it open." He didn't know I was laid up where I could hear him.
>
> When they left I followed (I was on horseback), and I let them get far enough that I knew they weren't going to close the gate, then I tried to catch up with them. It took a while, but I caught them at the next mailbox. There was an auto gate [i.e., a cattle guard] there, so he hadn't thrown any gate down. When I rode up I told them to get out of the car and for Frankie, the guy who had worked for us, to get out of the way. He asked what I was going to do, and I said I was going to whip the hell out of that mail carrier if he didn't close our gate.
>
> Well, they drove back to the gate and I followed along and saw him close it. Later that day I had driven the team in for a load of cake and I went into the post office and there he was, looking

through the book of regulations. I guess he couldn't find anything that proved I was wrong, because he always closed our gate after that.

I remember that later this same mailman told one of our neighbors that he'd have to move his mailbox because there was a big mud hole beside it and he had trouble leaving mail there. But the neighbor said he could move the mailman easier than he could the box, and he started to circulate petitions to get him removed. Well, the mail carrier started some petitions of his own to keep his job and he asked me to sign one. I said sure, he'd always closed the gate after I asked him to that time, so I signed his petition.

The problem of the mailman and the gate was resolved in the area around the Mills Ranch by the installation of cattle guards, a solution that was also widely used in the Sandhills of Nebraska.

Lewis E. Phillips of Kimball and his brother, William Henry, built two cattle guards for their mail carrier, Andy Batterton, in 1924. Phillips thinks that 1920 was about the year that mail carriers switched from teams to cars in all of western Nebraska. The Phillips brothers had fenced a section pasture through which the mail route ran on their private ranch road. They built, on this road, trough cattle guards over pits three feet deep and five feet wide, using railroad ties for stringers. Troughs of two-by-sixes were spiked to the ties. The sides of the troughs were sloped out, so that both cars and trucks could move across easily. Lewis Phillips explains how he got the idea for building the guard: "We felt horses and cattle would not attempt to jump a pit with obstructions over it. We just used material we had available at the time."

Phillips also said that Kimball County did not start grading roads until 1919. In 1920 he bought the first pneumatic-tired commercial truck in the area, and he hauled wheat over roads with some very deep ruts. As late as 1928 he used to drive from Kimball to Crawford, opening and shutting gates all the way, for not a single cattle guard had been installed on that particular road. After the county began to grade roads, a few of the wealthier ranchers obtained permission to install pit-and-pole cattle guards, using pipe for bars, concrete for pit walls, and steel I-beams for stringers.

Ralph R. Robinson, who ranched in Cherry County north of Mullen, Nebraska, in the early twenties, was on a mail route that was over one hundred miles long and had more than sixty gates. In order to decrease the number of gates for the mail carriers, as well as to make things easier for the ranchers and their families, the county commissioners installed a number of ladder guards. According to Robinson, these were made by taking eight-foot lengths of bridge plank and then drilling holes part way through them in order to hold the fourteen-inch lengths of one-and-one-half-inch pipe used for bars. Like the ladder guards described in chapter 3, these ladders were held in place by long rods bolted through the entire guard, and they were placed over a pit that was three feet deep. "The wooden and pipe guards were right for the Model T and A," said Robinson, "but when trucks started using them, they didn't stand up too well. It also got so the planks were of poorer wood all the time. In the Sandhills the sand blew and the auto gates as a rule were a little higher than the road. If cars and trucks didn't slow up, they would land in the middle of the gate. Even the steel auto gates got damaged that way." So, no doubt, did automobiles.

The earliest commercial manufacturers of cattle guards seem to have been Nebraskans. On 8 June 1922 the *Antioch News* published an item about a new industry for Antioch, a factory to manufacture automatic auto gates. The inventors, Walter Hoffland, William Connor, and Frank Rogers, were trying to capitalize on the inconvenience caused by having to open and close twenty-five to fifty gates that, according to the article, had to be opened and closed if one took a fifty mile drive in any direction from town. The reporter felt there would be a demand all over the West for thousands of the gates, which he then described:

> Timbers slightly raised from the ground are placed as a track for cars to run over. On each side of the gateway is erected a post from the bottom of which there is a gas pipe extending from post to post beneath the runway. Attached to the pipe are fingers the heighth *[sic]* of a gate kept in upright position by means of a spring fastened on each post horizontally and attached to the bottom bar. As a car approaches the gate, the front pushes against the fingers, lays them down between the timbers of the runway and after being released when the car passes over, the springs throw them back in position.

Hoffland and his partners were right about the demand for cattle guards, but their particular design was apparently too complicated to be commercially successful. According to Raymond R. Gentry, who ranched at Hyannis and now lives at Alliance, the fingers that were pressed down often came back up too suddenly, thus damaging the bottoms of cars as they were being driven across the gate.

More successful was the C & P Auto Gate Company of North Platte. The story about C & P comes from Everett Troyer, the long-time owner of the company and a son-in-law of one of the founders. In 1922, when Ira E. Cumpston was driving his Model T from his home in Tryon, Nebraska, to Hyannis, he had to pass through numerous gates all along the way. In one place, however, he drove across a series of poles running across the road and nailed into some timbers, which were placed in a pit and ran with the road. He was impressed by the time saved and the convenience, so he approached the commissioners of McPherson County with the idea of installing some of these auto gates on roads there. He called in his brother-in-law, Lyle Pyzer, a skilled carpenter, and the two of them agreed on a design. First, they decided that pipe would be a more uniform and permanent material for the bars than poles would be. To arrive at the optimum spacing of the bars, they made the pipes adjustable and tested them by having ten horses of various sizes walk over them. They placed the pipes as close together as possible for a smooth crossing, but far enough apart so that if a horse got in the guard, he could pull his hoof out and not be trapped or injured.

Their next step was to build by hand a few guards in Tryon and then to place them on the most heavily traveled roads in McPherson County. These guards used three-by-twelve-inch wooden planks for the sides and two-inch pipe for bars. They worked so well that within two months, officials in Arthur and Hooker counties had asked Cumpston and Pyzer to build guards there as well. At this point the two men formed the C & P Auto Gate Company. To do the drilling and cutting, they built machines which they mounted on trailers. Because Tryon was not on a railroad, lumber was shipped to either Mullen or North Platte, where the guards were assembled. In its effort to make the wooden part of the guards more durable, C & P had lumber from the West Coast shipped to Denver. A crew would go to Denver with the milling machinery, mill the lumber, then have it pressure treated before reloading it on cars and shipping it on to Nebraska. Even so, the wood did not hold up well under the progressively heavier traffic, so a decision was made to manufacture the guards entirely of metal. Because he was a carpenter, Pyzer lost some of his interest in the operation when this change was made, so he sold his share of the company to Cumpston in 1940.

At about the same time, the entire operation was being moved to North Platte, partly because there was not enough electric power in Tryon to run the welding equipment necessary for the increased demands of manufacturing. In 1954 Cumpston sold the company to his son-in-law, Everett Troyer, who ran it until he retired in 1970. Since then the company has changed managers several times, until, in 1977, the manufacturing equipment was sold at auction. Although Troyer still has a small shop in North Platte, he no longer takes on any large-scale projects. Over the years, C & P made and sold thousands of cattle guards in many states. Many of their first all-steel guards, made in 1940, are still giving good service on Nebraska roads.

During the 1920s an interesting problem with gates was developing on the Fort Berthold Indian Reservation in North Dakota. Marion Everhart of Scottsdale, Arizona, has provided copies of the correspondence between E. W. Jermark, superintendent of the reservation, and the commissioner of Indian affairs. On 19 November 1921 Jermark sent a letter to Washington in which he described the problem with fences and gates:

> There is approximately two hundred miles of boundry [sic] fence. To keep this fence in repair I am employing four lineriders.

The fence is built of native box elder and ash post and as it has been a number of years since the posts were renewed, these four lineriders have almost a hopeless task in trying to keep it repaired.

At this point I desire to call your attention to the fact that the salaries of these men is *[sic]* $48.00 per month, including the bonus, which you readily see is scarcely sufficient compensation to warrant obtaining the services of a man and saddle horses necessary to make the long rides. Another and very serious difficulty arises and that is with the white lessees on this reservation. Numerous gates have been cut in the fences. These gates provide the means for much of our trespassing stock.

The average white man as well as the Indian drives to a reservation gate in his automobile, gets out, opens the gate, draws it aside, gets back in his machine, drives through and in only rare instances stops to close the gate. As these gates occur at numerous and frequently isolated places it may be two or three days, possibly a week before a linerider passes that way and replaces the gate. In the meantime frequently several hundred head of cattle and horses get out and scatter for a radius of miles over their old range, now the homesteads of our white farmers.

Jermark goes on to ask what steps are being taken on other reservations to deal with such problems, particularly what can be done to make people shut gates. His closing sentence reveals his desperation: "I am in a position where I would greatly appreciate any advice or instruction which would serve to assist in abating this nuisance."

Jermark evidently wrote to the commissioner again on 2 March 1922 and received a reply dated 22 March 1922. In this reply Commissioner Charles H. Burke suggested that there should be a minimum number of gates, which should be kept in good repair. He also suggested various plans whereby the passage of livestock through openings in the fence could be reduced:

One method is to build a fence along both sides of the roadway for a short distance at the point where the gate is located and at right angles to the boundary fence. There are several methods of constructing such lanes at gateways, but probably the most satisfactory is the one designated as the figure-eight entrance, which would appear as in the following diagram:

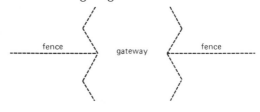

Another method is to construct an automobile runway alongside the gate so that the automobiles can pass without opening the gate. This is done by digging a trench and constructing two narrow runways across it just wide enough to accommodate each wheel of the automobile. A cattle guard is then constructed between the runways on the same principle as that used by the railroads or some other similar plan.

Later that year (23 October 1922) Assistant Commissioner E. B. Meritt wrote to Jermark, asking for a follow-up report, which was sent 30 October 1922:

In answer I have to advise that the line riders organized a corps of workers in their respective districts who spent a certain number of days repairing the fence in that district with the result that the reservation fence is in fairly good shape.

Good substantial gates were made and conspicuous notices posted, demanding that the gates be closed. This is an extremely difficult matter to control, as the whites, even more than the Indians, are prone to go through the gates and drive on without taking the trouble to close them. However, there has been very little difficulty experienced during the summer months.

In a handwritten postscript, Jermark noted: "To date we have not had finances, time, or help to install the auto gates."

This correspondence prompts a couple of observations. First, the "figure eight" fence gap described by Commissioner Burke illustrates an alternate method of avoiding gates that allows for free-moving traffic. The problem, of course, is that not all livestock will be steered away by the perpendicular fence, so it is not a very effective deterrent. Second, it is interesting to note that Andrew Johnston had built his cattle guard in 1914 on the ranch road that led to his leased pastures in the Fort Berthold Indian Reservation; therefore, Jermark had an example of an effective cattle guard much nearer than the commissioner's office.

There are dozens of other stories about cattle guards from the twenties, each interesting in its own way, but the ones given above are the most appropriate for illustrating what was happening to the cattle guard during this decade as its use spread. Sometimes this dispersal was gradual, as ranchers and farmers carried the idea from one place to another; sometimes it was rapid, as oilmen and mail carriers hastened its spread. The commercial manufacturing that began in this decade also contributed to the spread of cattle guards. The use of cattle guards has increased in each decade since this time.

5

THE

RAILROAD CATTLE GUARD

As Charles Dickens was touring America in 1842, he maintained a journal of his observations. Some Americans find these candid observations rather imperfect, and in at least one instance I am inclined to agree. When, early in his stay, Dickens rode a train from Boston to Lowell, Massachusetts, he was impressed not only with the speed of the locomotive but also by its apparent disregard for pedestrians and livestock along the wayside. "[The locomotive] rushes across the turnpike road, where there is no gate, no policeman, no signal: nothing but a rough wooden arch, on which is painted 'WHEN THE BELL RINGS, LOOK OUT FOR THE LOCOMOTIVE.'" If Dickens had not been traveling so fast and had he not been so intent on observing his fellow travelers, he might well have seen, on each side of this turnpike crossing, a slat-covered pit that extended under the tracks from shoulder to shoulder of the grade—in other words, a cattle guard.

Dickens was quite perceptive in noting details that distinguished the American character and experience from that of the British, but he missed two features of American railroading that certainly help to point up these distinctions. Both features—the cowcatcher and the cattle guard—reflect especially the openness of America, the notion of great spaces (even in the East) where livestock could roam, unrestrained by hedges, fences, or herders. In England these devices were not immediately necessary for early railroad use, because livestock did not normally have access to the tracks. The English locomotive, in fact, had a square front end, according to Clarence P. Hornung in

71

Wheels across America; thus, when the John Bull was imported into this country, it was fitted out with a cowcatcher. As soon as trains had begun to attain the exhilarating speed of twenty miles per hour, the cowcatcher did little to save the life of an animal in the path of the locomotive, but it did tend to move the carcass along and thus helped to prevent derailments, which commonly resulted from collisions between trains and livestock.

Isaac Drips is credited with inventing the cowcatcher, but we do not know who invented the railroad cattle guard. Although railroad buffs and historians, a diverse and dedicated lot, have explored many facets of American railroading, the cattle guard has attracted none of this effort. Even the Association of American Railroads and the Transportation Division of the Smithsonian Institution, with their extensive collections of documents, offer little to the researcher seeking the origins of the cattle guard. Despite these handicaps, the outlines of the development of the railroad cattle guard can be traced.

We know, for example, that the railroad cattle guard is an American invention. *The Oxford English Dictionary* lists the term "cattle guard" as of American origin, and Mitford Matthews includes it in his *Dictionary of Americanisms.* As documentation, both sources quote from legal testimony published in 1843: "The first cattle guards he saw were in one thousand eight hundred and thirty six." We do not know where this 1836 cattle guard was seen. Nor do we know who devised and built it. We do know, however, that on 11 March 1837 Thomas J. West of Whitehall, Virginia, filed for the first United States patent (number 146) on a railroad cattle guard. A reproduction of this patent application is included in the Appendix.

Although it has been exciting to try to discover biographical data about West, the results have been inconclusive. What fame he had was apparently local, for his name does not appear in any of the standard biographical reference works. Mabel Apple Talley, of the Albemarle County Historical Society Library in Charlottesville, Virginia, has provided information about a West family (or families), probably of English ancestry, including a Thomas J. West, in the Albemarle County area during the late eighteenth and early nineteenth centuries. (1) A Thomas West is listed in a 29 August 1794 record as a witness to the marriage of James H. West and Susannah Harlow. (2) At least one Thomas West figures in two guardian bonds. On 4 September 1815 a Thomas West is listed as an orphan son of James H. West, with Robert Brooks named as guardian. On 8 April 1817 James West is listed as an orphan son of James H. West, with Thomas West named as guardian. Probably the orphaned Thomas West was a young nephew or cousin of the Thomas West who witnessed the marriage of James H. West. (3) The single reference to a Thomas J. West (who logically could have been either the younger or the older West) occurs when he marries Lucy Ann Randolph on 27 May 1820. (4)

Finally, a rather complicated indenture of 16 July 1823 lists Thomas West as the seller of a large number of household items (including "a negro woman slave named Aggy") to Nathaniel Harlow, with West pledging $132.36 to Smith Massie.

The little existing evidence suggests that the West family was of English heritage. Most persons named West had their origins in Cornwall. This link to the West Country of England is important, because, as will be seen in chapter 6, the earliest forerunner of the cattle guard can be traced to the ancient flat stone stiles of that county. The flat stile and the railroad cattle guard patented by West share the concept of parallel bars spaced over a pit.

One cannot prove that there was any connection between the Cornish flat stile and the invention of the railroad cattle guard merely by establishing a link between Cornwall and Thomas J. West of Whitehall, Virginia. For one thing, there seems to be another White Hall in Frederick County, Virginia. Moreover, we do not know for certain that Thomas J. West actually invented the first railroad cattle guard (which was in use at least by 1836) or, indeed, that he invented one at all. We only know that he patented the first railroad cattle guard in 1837. Mrs. Talley reports that although some mention of a cattle guard has been passed down in the West family and another story in the area associates the invention of the cattle guard with a black man, no documentation exists for either of these local traditions. Miscegenation may be one reason for the difficulty in tracking down the history of Thomas J. West; someone in one of the West families in the area seems to have married a mulatto woman, probably in the late part of the nineteenth century. Even in today's more tolerant social atmosphere, that subject is not readily discussed.

It is possible that the railroad cattle guard was invented by a black, but it is highly unlikely that Thomas West was black, for the indenture of 1823 indicates that he himself was a slaveholder. Undoubtedly in 1837 a white man could have taken out a patent much more easily than a black man could have, so it is likely that if a black man had invented this particular cattle guard, West may have patented it, whether for selfish or altruistic reasons is not clear. More probably, however, West's patent was on a device of his own invention.

Because of the identical concepts underlying the Cornish flat stile and the first railroad (as well as the first highway) cattle guard, it is tempting to look for someone with a Cornish background when seeking the originator of the cattle guard. Whether or not Thomas J. West is that man is an apparently insoluble puzzle. Adding to the puzzle is the fact that hundreds of Cornish miners, who had walked across flat stiles on their way to work in the tin mines of Cornwall, were brought into Central City, Colorado, in the late nineteenth century to work the gold mines. As noted in chapter 3, the earliest known highway cattle guard was located at Barr Lake, Colorado, which is less than fifty miles from Central City. This is but speculation, however. Undoubtedly the inventor of the first cattle guard—railroad or highway—will remain nameless. In any case, the cattle guard was in use remarkably soon after railroading itself began.

Two of the earliest railroad cattle guards in Canada were patented in 1856 and 1861. The first one, "a moving and self-acting cattle guard for railway purposes," was patented on 6 February 1856 by D'arcy Porter of Hamilton, Ontario. The other, a "self-acting cattle guard," was patented 14 February 1861 by James T. Forrest, a machinist from Wentworth County, Ontario. Porter's mechanism was rather complicated, consisting of levers, posts, pulleys, weights, cranks, rollers, pickets, and a platform. When an animal stepped on the platform, it caused the platform to sink, in turn causing the levers to operate the cranks that turned the rollers, thereby raising the pickets to a vertical position to form a gate of sorts for stopping livestock. The posts, pulleys, and weights were used to prevent the platform from rising above the level of the tracks and thus getting hit by a train. Although Forrest's cattle guard also involved moving parts, it was much simpler in design: it had a series of revolving bars which were shaped like four-pointed stars in cross section. When an animal stepped onto the grid, the bars would roll inward, causing the animal's leg to be pinched so severely that it would at once back out.

Results of a preliminary survey made in the British Patent Office by a classification section examiner named Mrs. J. A. Sullivan suggest that no railroad cattle guards were patented in Britain until late in the nineteenth century.

In the United States, as well as in England and Europe, travel by steam locomotive began in the early 1830s. The first regularly scheduled service by steam-powered trains in this country, the forerunner of today's 190,000 miles of track, was provided in 1831 by the South Carolina Canal and Railroad Company. (This line also gave us our first derailment and our first locomotive explosion, which occurred when the engineer sat on the steam escape valve in order to stop its annoying hiss.) By 1835 over two hundred charters had been granted for railroad operation on about 1,000 miles of track in eleven states. Some fifteen years later, track mileage had increased to 7,400, of which 6,671 miles were along the seaboard. There was no track west of the Mississippi at this time.

In the 1830s, railroad builders were competing with canal promoters for superiority of transportation. Many of the latter considered the steam locomotive an impractical but dangerous toy that would succumb, if to nothing else, to the wrath of farmers who would "destroy the tracks . . . as soon as they discovered that their cows would no longer give milk nor would their hens let down eggs when the smoke-belching, ugly black monster came chugging

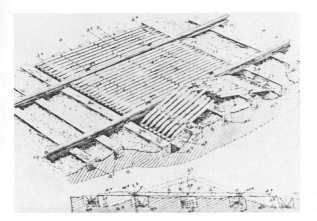

A railroad cattle guard patented in 1896 by Charles V. Compton, New Albany, Indiana. Livestock stepping on the ends of the grid would cause it to rise up. (Photo from *U.S. Patent Gazette*)

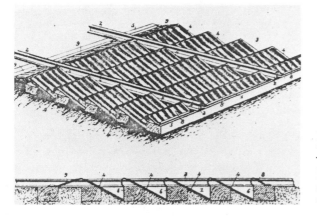

A railroad cattle guard patented in 1892 by John J. Callaghan and Albro R. Horn, Stevens' Point, Wisconsin. (Photo from *U.S. Patent Gazette*)

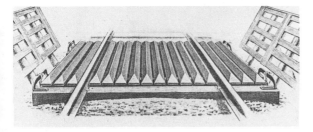

Buda Oscillating Cattle Guard, as pictured in *Railway and Engineering Review* (31 December 1904)

through," as Madeline Sadler Waggoner puts it in *The Long Haul West*.

Some cows did stop giving milk, but the cause was considerably more drastic than mere noise and smoke. Collisions between trains and livestock were a serious problem, and the cowcatcher was far from being totally effective in preventing derailments. Besides posing a threat to the physical safety of passengers, employees, and equipment, livestock on the right of way also posed an economic threat to the railroads. Farmers usually sued if trains killed their animals, and the juries, invariably made up of the farmers' peers, not those of the railroad magnate, tended to support the plaintiffs. Joseph A. Noble, who spent half of the twentieth century as an employee of the Atchison, Topeka, and Santa Fe Railroad, attests to this tendency:

> Of course, in spite of all the precautions to prevent accidents, now and then a cow got on the track and was struck by a train. The owner immediately demanded payment for this "fine animal which probably would have won a prize at the next stock show." The matter was usually settled on the basis of whether it could be shown that the cow, heedless of the cuts and scratches inflicted by the barbed wire, had ruthlessly torn down the well-maintained right-of-way fence, or whether the section foreman had neglected it to such an extent that, when the cow rubbed against a post, the fence fell down and the animal just walked over it. I believe in most cases tried before a jury, Justice prevailed and the railroad paid off.

Although materials were expensive in the 1830s, fencing the right of way was the most effective way to keep animals off the track. Grade crossings, however, could not be fenced, and, as Charles Dickens noted, many crossings did not have gates or watchmen. Thus, livestock that was either straying or grazing on the open range could rather easily mount the tracks. Actually, neither gates nor watchmen, despite their undoubted effectiveness, would have been a practical solution for warding off livestock. Posting a twenty-four-hour watch at every grade crossing would have been prohibitively expensive for a railroad company, not to mention the problems of weather and darkness. Gates have proven, in this century especially, to be a better solution, particularly the type of automatic gates found on British and European railways. These gates close across the tracks when no trains are near, then, upon the approach of a train, they swing through a 90° angle to block off the highway completely. In the 1830s such automatic gates were not available, while the existing manually operated gates suffered from two disadvantages: they were bothersome to the traveler, and consequently they were often left open.

Thus, by at least 1836, responding to safety and economic pressures, some unknown innovator—possibly a railroad employee, a farmer, or a passenger—had created the first cattle guard ever used in conjunction with mechanically powered transportation. As railroading progressed, and especially as the western cattle ranges began to be organized into fenced ranches in the late 1800s, cattle guards became more and more important. Literally hundreds of designs were patented, although not nearly that many were successfully marketed. Journals such as *Engineering News, Railway and Engineering Review,* and *Scientific American* kept their readers posted on innovations by carrying notices and descriptions of newly invented guards.

A good way to gain an understanding of the railroad cattle guard is to examine a few of the track manuals current at the turn of the century. Railroad historians have particularly recommended three of these manuals: *Notes on Track,* by W. M. Camp; volume 3 of *The Science of Railways,* by Marshall M. Kirkman; and *Railway and Track Work,* by E. E. Russell Tratman. In addition, retired railroad workers have suggested two other manuals: *The Trackman's Helper,* by J. Kindelan, used by the Kansas-Missouri-Texas line in the early 1900s; and *The Road-Master's Assistant and Section-Master's Guide,* by William S. Huntington, revised by Charles Latimer, which is the earliest of all these particular manuals. Camp and Tratman give the most attention to cattle guards; Kindelan and Huntington, the least.

Huntington seemed to know of only two types of guards, the more effective of which he considered to be the open pit, devoid even of cross sleepers. More troublesome to use was the wooden-slat guard placed over a shallow pit. Cattle often became trapped in this type of guard. Then a passing train would kill the cattle and simultaneously be derailed. Apparently, when Huntington first published his manual (1871), surface railroad cattle guards were not yet widely used or even available. His final comment on the subject suggests that the railroad cattle guards of the time were more often than not ramshackle affairs, "cobbled up on ties and fence-posts. . . . Nothing gives our railroads a more poverty stricken, slovenly appearance than a shabby and unsafe manner of building cattle-guards and culverts."

In his manual, Kindelan states that steel surface guards, which were rapidly growing in favor with railroad men, were much better than open-pit guards. His manual also explained why such a boom in the promotion of surface cattle guards occurred: "It is just what the railroads need at the present time, and . . . if the proper kind is offered railroad companies would purchase them and put them in." In other words, in the 1880s and 1890s the market in railroad cattle guards was there, waiting to be exploited. The advantages of the steel surface guard, in Kindelan's opinion, were many: it did not require a deep pit, it did not trap cattle, it was not expensive, it was easy to install, and it did not weaken the track.

Kirkman devotes only these three paragraphs to the cattle guard:

> [Cattle] guards should be placed at all farm and public road crossings where there is no protection by gates or otherwise; to prevent cattle running along the track, a fence should be built from the

right of way fence on both sides of the opening to as near the rail as practicable. There are various forms of cattle guards. One plan in particular commends itself, being effective and cheap. It is a space of not less than six feet stretching the entire width of the track parallel to the road, laid with two and one-half by four inch oak pieces laid across the ties parallel to the rails, cut to a sharp edge on the upper face, spaced with two-inch spacing blocks, and spiked down to the ties. The most effective plan, however, is to build a pit the entire width of the road about six feet wide, and of sufficient depth to enable a cow to drop entirely clear of the trains. This, however, is too expensive, requiring the building of retaining walls and bridged for the rails only. This style of a cattle guard is perfectly effective.

. . . .

Cattle guards are the means of continuing fences across railroad tracks without interfering with the passage of trains. They form a very considerable portion of the expenses of a road, and therefore it is desirable to obtain a device as simple as possible, and yet it must effectually exclude all stock from the enclosure. A framed pit sufficiently wide for the connecting fences to afford proper clearance for the cars, and with stringers for the rails to rest on, was, until recent years, the form in most general use. The danger of stringers spreading and the disastrous effect of a derailment at these pits led to the addition of ties and guard timbers; these additions permitted a much shallower pit. As cattle, sheep and goats learned to walk these ties or guard timbers, it became necessary to have them chamfered.

Many other forms of stock guards, principally surface guards intended to do away with the pit entirely, have been suggested and patented.

The first paragraph refers to the two types of cattle guard that Huntington described — a grid of wooden panels, and an open pit — and Kirkman seems to favor the latter despite its greater expense. Several important points are raised in the second paragraph. First is the notion that railroad cattle guards are considered primarily as an extension of the fence, whereas automotive cattle guards are thought of primarily as gates (although both types serve both functions). Second, Kirkman emphasizes the economic importance of the cattle guard. He then points out some of the disadvantages of the pit cattle guard, which have led to its being replaced by surface guards, but he no more than mentions these replacements, even though at least 173 railroad cattle guards had been patented by 1902, the date of Kirkman's revised edition. Obviously his sympathies lay with the pit guard.

Both Tratman and Camp, in concurrence with the editors of *Engineering News,* disagreed with Kirkman about the desirability of the pit cattle guard. Tratman devoted nearly six pages to the cattle guard; Camp, over nine; and both authors went into much greater detail concerning the construction and use of each type of cattle guard. Both pointed out that cattle guards were being used not only at grade crossings but also at approaches to bridges, tunnels, and deep cuts—any place, in other words, where it was important to keep the track clear of trespassing animals.

Tratman discusses the difficulty of making an effective cattle guard, primarily because cattle are persistent in their attempts to evade constraints:

> It is not as easy to turn cattle as might be supposed, and very generally they will become accustomed to the guards and find a way to cross them. If straying along the road they will sometimes spend considerable time in trying the guards, either from a desire to wander or to reach a tempting patch of grass or hay. Hungry cattle are especially venturesome. Some cattle are inveterate wanderers, and will cross almost any form of guard, even as others are inveterate fence breakers or jumpers. If being driven they will often either run blindly into or over the guard, and the length of the guard should be sufficient to deter them from jumping. Hogs and sheep are difficult to stop, and are very persistent in their attempts to reach forbidden ground.

He also noted that a standing cow, if struck by a train, would probably be thrown clear of the track, but if the cow were lying down when struck, the train would usually be derailed. Camp emphatically stated that the only sure way of keeping the track clear of livestock was with pits:

> It is safe to say that the open pit properly constructed will stop stock. There are, of course, those who will declare they have seen some old cow do the tight-rope act and walk the rail over the pit, but such exhibitions may properly be considered unusual and of infrequent occurrence; and no doubt room could be found for all such rare animals in menageries, where they could make their living easier than by picking it along the track.

Camp was just as emphatic, however, in condemning the use of the pit cattle guard. Both he and Tratman pointed out problems of maintenance: the track could heave or settle, resulting in an uneven riding spot on the rails; frost and rain could damage the pit; timbers could rot or burn. The most serious objection, however, was safety. A derailed wheel or truck would invariably drop into the pit and cause a wreck. Moreover, persons who walked along the tracks at night, whether trainmen or members of the public, often fell into these pits, and if the stringers holding the rails had been joined together with a switch rod, the chances of a broken neck were considerable. The *Chicago Times* for 14 May 1881, for example, carried a story about a man who had suffered a fatal accident when he fell into an open-pit cattle guard at night. According to railroad law, the railroads were not liable for damages if a trespassing pedestrian accidentally fell into a pit cattle guard. Charles A. Dana once recalled that during the Civil War, trains were sabotaged by placing ties in cattle guards so that the engine would strike them and then run down an embankment.

Camp further pointed out that a shallow pit was even worse than a deep one (he recommended that a pit be ten feet long, ten feet wide, and three to six feet deep). A shallow pit posed the same maintenance problems as a deep one, yet it would not turn stock as effectively. If the pit were too shallow, animals could walk across it, and if they slipped on a deeper one, they would become stranded and cause a derailment. Both Tratman and Camp discouraged the use of the open-pit cattle guard, although Camp was the more vehement: "Thus it seems almost criminal to place open pits in the track and their use ought to be illegal."

Camp mentioned only one railroad that was still using a form of the pit cattle guard in 1904, the Florida East Coast Railway. The design of these guards on that railroad featured eight-by-eight-inch ties laid on corner (presenting a diamond shape when viewed from the side) so that they offered no footing to livestock. These ties were strong enough to hold up any derailed trucks. In Florida there was no danger that a track would heave due to freezing ground, but because of the damp climate, maintaining good pit drainage could be troublesome.

Pits were used on a railroad that ran through Parker and Palo Pinto counties in Texas, according to Tracy King of Roby, Texas, who saw them on his grandfather's farm around 1900. Pit cattle guards were also used around 1891 by the Baltimore & Ohio Railroad near Rittman, Ohio, according to Marcus Lind of Salem, Oregon: "My late father, 1881–1968, used to tell how, as a boy, he would crawl down into the cattle guard, which evidently was in the form of a pit, when the train went over. He spoke of the terrific noise it made, which I can very well believe. And Father was hard of hearing all the time I knew him."

Pit cattle guards were no doubt used at one time or another by many other railroads, but by 1900 pits were rapidly being supplanted by surface cattle guards. There was an overwhelming variety of surface guards from which a roadmaster could select a design he deemed appropriate for his railroad. Over the years, some 409 railroad cattle guards have been patented, at least 290 of them by 1910. There are two major reasons for this onslaught of cattle-guard designs. First, cattle guards had a significant, if sometimes indirect, economic impact on railroads. If an inventor built a better cattle guard, the railroad companies beat a path to his door, bringing with them fistfuls of dollars. Second, the problem with all these inventions was that none, with the exception of the pit, was totally effective. As Camp put it, "The two essential conditions of a perfect cattle guard—a structure which will safely carry the wheels of a derailed truck and which will form an impassable barrier to stock without entrapping the animals to the peril of trains—are incompatible with each other." Tratman was more prosaic, but no less demanding in his specifications:

> Besides being effective in turning cattle, the guard should meet the following requirements: 1, Reasonable in first cost and maintenance expense; 2, Permit of proper maintenance of track; 3, Not liable to cause derailment or wreck a derailed train; 4, Not liable to become loose or to be caught by low-hung brake rigging, etc.; 5, Easily and safely passed by employees; 6, Not liable to trap or throw cattle attempting to pass; 7, Not noisy or rattling under the trains.

Both authors agreed that it was more difficult to turn livestock than many persons might suppose, and they both agreed that surface cattle guards were ineffective because they were not made long enough. Camp notes:

> Horses will clear an 8-ft. guard at a single jump, and by stepping as far as possible with their front feet cattle will leap the rest of the way over a guard 10 ft. long. If cattle guards were made 15 or 20 ft. long, measured with the track, and well flanked by side fence, there would be but very few animals better domesticated than the Texas steer or the southern "razorback" hog that would attempt to clamber over them.

He added that the Chesapeake & Ohio Railroad preferred twelve-foot guards to eight-foot ones, while the Nashville, Chattanooga, & St. Louis line got good results from a sixteen-foot guard made by placing two eight-foot sections end to end.

With few exceptions, railroad cattle guards relied either on insecure footing or on the potential to cause pain as the deterring factor in their various designs. Those few exceptions were guards constructed on a principle of novelty. Of over 400 guards, probably fewer than two dozen ever achieved much commercial success. Here are descriptions of some of the more widely used, and some of the more novel, railroad cattle guards.

The simplest cattle guard, and one of the most widely used, was made of wooden slats. It was cheap to build, easy to repair, and uncomplicated in design—a series of wooden arris bars, roughly four to six inches wide at the base and eight feet long, running parallel to the track and spaced so that hooves could not slip between them. The bars could be spiked directly to the ties, or they could be bolted, with spacing blocks, into sections that could be placed onto the ties and could more easily be removed for repairs. The slats were usually made of oak or hard pine. They were also usually kept freshly whitewashed on the theory that paint would be more effective in deterring livestock than would natural wood; paint also helped to preserve the wood. Some guards were painted black; others had black slats and white slats alternating. The Wabash Railroad coated its cattle guards with hot tar, and the Chicago Terminal Transfer Railroad used white glue and whitewash for a coating that would last up to a full year between repaintings. Among other railroads, the Canadian Pacific, the Missouri Pacific, the Union Pacific, the Northern Pacific, and the Wabash all used the wooden-slat cattle guard at one time or another.

Insecure footing was the principle behind most wooden-slat cattle guards, but the potential for pain was incorporated in the guards used by some railroads. The Louisville & Nashville, for example, used twists of thickset buckthorn ribbon wire between and parallel to each slat. This variation was particularly effective against range cattle, as was the Kennedy Cattle Guard, made of slats and strips of barbed wire, which was used by the Oregon Railway & Navigation Line. The Western Pacific Railway used the same guard with eight-inch spacing, so that a horse could get its foot out without damage. Camp described a barbed-wire guard designed by a Rock Island Roadmaster, J. D. Sullivan:

> The strands of barbed wire in each section of the guard are stretched over a frame made of two strips running parallel with the rails, with four cross pieces of wood of triangular section, covered with sheet metal. The ends of the section are held together by bolts and the barbed wires are woven back and forth from end to end of the section, on lines parallel with the track. This guard is used on parts of the road in Indian Territory and northern Texas, where the cattle are hard to hold and where other forms of surface guard have failed.

Camp also noted that when a dragging brake beam had caught in one of these interlaces of barbed wire, it created an appearance that would frighten anything, man or beast.

The National Surface Guard Company made two types of cattle guard. The first used flat metal slats, which were serrated and barbed, set on edge, and fitted into slotted cross pieces of triangular sections at the ends and in the middle. Alternate slats were two and one-half and three and one-half inches deep and were spaced from two and three-quarters to three and three-quarters inches apart. Each section (it took four to make a complete unit— two between the rails and one on each side) weighed 140 pounds. In an attempt to deter smaller animals, such as the practically unstoppable razorback hog of the southern states, the serrated slats were furnished with barbs punched out on the sides. The other type of guard made by National had slats of angle iron, with the angle on top, like an inverted V. A complete unit was nine feet long and ten feet wide, and it weighed about four hundred pounds.

National Surface Guards were used quite extensively, thanks in part to the endorsement they received from the New England Road Masters' Association.

In the original Kalamazoo Guard, triangular slats alternated with rows of triangular teeth that were punched up out of the flat strips of plate between the ridges. An animal's hoof would slip down off the ridges onto the teeth, but a person who fell across the guard would be held off the teeth by the slats. This guard was nine feet long and weighed 375 pounds. It was approved by the Western Railroad Association. What is today known as the Kalamazoo Guard was originally manufactured under the name of Perfect Steel Surface Cattle Guard. It was made of sheet metal and looked somewhat like a series of low shed roofs with peaks about ten inches apart and eaves about five inches lower than the peaks. The peaks reached just below the level of the rails. The advertising copy of the 1907 edition of *Railway, Mining, Municipal and Contractor's Supplier Catalogue* describes this guard:

> An effective stock turner for any section of country. Renders crossing physically impossible and does not punish the animals. At initial step they slide toe first against slot at base and cannot advance, but are free to withdraw without slightest injury. Made in three sections only, ready-to-place. Offers no catching points for dragging chains. Is readily removable during track overhauling. Chokes weed growth. Has a solid anchorage in track; can not rattle to pieces. After assembling, guards are dipped in an asphaltum bath to fill all crevices and cover all surfaces with a thick tenacious coat. Is proof against corrosion. Is self-cleansing of snow and rubbish by draught. Prevents personal injury from accidental falling. Length 9 ft. Weight 475 lbs. Prices on application.

This guard does indeed sound perfect, but, like all the others, it was not. The Union Pacific Railroad is currently having some trouble with this type of guard in Wyoming, a problem that will be discussed later.

The Bush Surface Cattle Guard, promoted as the "common sense steel guard," had seven slats of inverted T-irons, two inches apart and held in slotted triangular pressed-steel cross pieces. The slats were held at different heights. This guard was made in four interchangeable nine-foot-long sections and weighed about 475 pounds. Each slat could support a center load of 1,800 pounds. The complete guard sold for $20 plus the cost of delivery.

The Bartlett Cattle Guard was used on the Great Northern Railroad during the 1920s. This guard consisted of thirty-two separate pieces of heavy sheet metal, spiked in four rows onto eight adjacent ties. These triangular metal sheets sloped forward like the prow of a a ship. An animal could put its foot down between the rows formed by the sections but could not step forward; it could only pull up its hoof and draw it backward.

The Merrill-Stevens Guard had T-iron slats, one and one-fourth by one

83

and one-fourth inches, set aslant of and parallel to the rails. The slats were set diagonally in the end cross pieces and were level with the top of the rail. Thus it relied on insecure footing to turn cattle.

The Standard Company made two cattle guards. One used slats of Z-bar, set at an angle in order to offer an upturned corner for insecure footing. The other had slats of angle bar, one leg of which was much longer than the other. Both guards were spaced by supporting rods that passed through holes in the slats, and both were nailed onto the ties. The ends of the slats were beveled in order to prevent dragging brake lines from catching on the guard.

The Cook Cattle Guard was made of four interchangeable sections, each of which had nine serrated slats fastened to metal channel section cross pieces which were nailed to the ties. The serrated teeth were staggered, thereby presenting an uneven appearance and unstable footing for cattle. Each section was spiked to the end ties only; thus the guard vibrated under the weight of an animal, an added deterrent. This guard operated on the principle of pain, but the teeth did not cause serious injury. The guard was available with an auxiliary hog slat which went between the regular slats. This slat was shorter, and its teeth were like saw teeth. It could also be fitted with rows of link-belt chain stretched parallel with the rail over suitable cross pieces, placed at appropriate intervals. By 1904 some thirty-five thousand Cook Guards were being used.

The Sheffield Car Company of Three Rivers, Michigan, a subsidiary of Fairbanks-Morse, produced a cattle guard that was made by punching out rows of triangular teeth, each tooth with a three-inch base and spaced three inches apart, in a flat steel plate twenty-six inches wide and eight feet long, or slightly longer. This guard had several advantages besides its forbidding appearance. It could be fastened to ties without any special preparation. No pit was needed, and no dragging brake gear could catch on it and tear it out. The soft steel teeth, if bent accidentally, could easily be straightened with a spike hammer. This guard was widely used throughout the country; the Santa Fe was one of its chief customers.

The Walhaupter and the Positive cattle guards were similar to each other. Both were made of buckled plate, with folds that ran crosswise of the track and reached to the bottom of the ties, the pitch of the folds or corrugations corresponding in length to the spacing between the ties. The folds were shaped like ratchet teeth, and when in place on the track, they presented an inclined surface that ran from an upper corner of one tie to a lower corner of the next tie. When an animal stepped on one of these guards, its hoof would slide into the fold and strike the ridge or upper corner of the next fold; thus its leg would be obstructed just above the ankle and the animal would not be able to move forward. It could, however, back out unharmed.

The Trackman's Cattle Guard worked similarly, but the folded metal was made in separate pieces, each of which was spiked to a different tie. The advantage of this design was that ties could be easily removed for replacement, the track could be lined or surfaced without dismantling the guard, and the entire guard did not have to be replaced if part of it got damaged.

The Columbian Guard consisted of steel angle irons, one and one-half by one and one-half inches, laid parallel in order to form inverted-V slats. An eight-foot section of this guard weighed about 320 pounds.

The Wallace Surface Cattle Guard Manufacturing Company of Monroe, Arkansas, made a guard composed of a longitudinal triangular-shaped wooden strip spiked to the tie, over which was placed a covering of galvanized steel which sloped on each side to the tie into a deep V-shaped box. One of these boxes was laid between each two ties, with the top an inch or two higher than the level of the bottom face of the ties. An animal attempting to walk over the guard would have its feet pinched into the tight, converging sides of the box.

The Climax Stock Guard Company of Chicago made a metal guard without slats. An inverted V-shaped strip of expanded metal was placed on each tie, its edges projecting beyond the tie so as to hit the leg of any animal that tried to step between the ties. This guard had the advantage of not having to be removed in order for section hands to go about their normal work of lining, surfacing, and ballasting.

Climax also produced an unusual railroad cattle guard made of blocks of vitrified shale clay. These blocks were twenty-four inches long, eight and one-half inches wide, and four and one-half inches high. Each block was formed of two longitudinal triangular ridges molded into shells one and one-fourth inches thick and joined at the base. A complete cattle guard was composed of forty blocks weighing thirty-three pounds each and arranged on five ties in two-foot rows. It was held in place by a two-inch wooden cleat fastened around the guard, and end blocks were slotted and beveled to accommodate spikes.

Another unusual railroad cattle guard used clay sewer-pipe tiles. A series of ten pipes, eighteen inches in length, was buried vertically between each of four successive ties. The tiles were set on a bed of gravel in order to ensure proper drainage, and they reached just to the top of the rails. The ties were capped with a triangular wooden piece so that they afforded no footing. One of the major attractions of this guard was its cost: forty tiles at fifteen cents each, and almost no maintenance. According to its promoters, only in snow did this guard require attention, and then it could be dipped out with a light scoop. The idea for this guard was patented by Kellogg, Baker, and Stearnes of Garden Grove, Iowa, in 1889. They could not manufacture and ship this kind of cattle guard, but they did sell to railroads the right to install it.

Within two years the Rock Island, the Keokuk & Western, and the Chicago, Burlington, & Quincy were among the railroads using this guard.

Still another unusual cattle guard was made by the Buda Foundry and Manufacturing Company of Chicago. It was called the Oscillating Cattle Guard, and it did just that when stepped on, for its panels of triangular-shaped wooden slats were suspended by chains from each of its four corners. The chains were attached to arched brackets that spanned the space between two ties. The guard was nine feet long and eight feet wide. Its slats were spaced three-quarters of an inch apart and were spiked to wooden bolsters in three sections. The section between the rails had ten slats, and the two outer sections had three slats each. Two cross bars hung below the track rail between two adjacent ties near the end of the guards, and the chains from the brackets were attached to the crossbars at that point. In addition to its cattle-turning advantages, this guard did not have to be removed for snow plows, and all or part of it could be easily removed for track work by simply removing the cotter pins that held the guard sections to the cross bars.

The Conical-Roller Cattle Guard was another movable guard. It was made of four sections, each twenty-four inches long and each composed of about twenty wooden cylinders that were three inches in diameter at one end and four inches at the other. The cylinders were held in a frame of steel side and end pieces. The rollers rotated on metal rods and were installed with the large and small ends alternating. If an animal attempted to cross the guard, the rolling bars discouraged it from doing so.

In 1903 William H. McLaren of Highgate, Canada, patented what could best be termed a liquid cattle guard. His invention consisted of four shallow metal pans, two of which were to be placed between the rails and one on the outside of each rail. These pans were supposed to contain water and a second (unspecified) liquid of a lower specific gravity that would float on the water. This second liquid was also to possess a highly reflective surface and have a bad taste so that cattle would not drink it.

Finally, there were some mechanical cattle guards on the market — which may or may not have actually been used by railroads — that could be termed "trip and flip" cattle guards. These guards usually had loose trip boards (connected by transverse rods to several prongs) which would, when stepped on, spring the prongs into the air and form a sort of fence, much like the workings of the Canadian cattle guard discussed above. Others would, when tripped, hammer an animal's leg, as a piano hammer strikes a string. None of these devices seems to have been very practical, but that did not stop inventors from trying. Camp put it best: "Cattle guards are as numerous as Yankee ingenuity has been able to devise, but only a comparatively small number of the inventions in this line have succeeded in being put to use."

Today Yankee ingenuity has created a world of miniature railroads, cor-

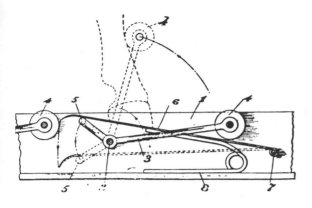

A "trip and flip" railroad cattle guard patented in 1909 by Robert B. Walker, Strathcona, Alberta, Canada. (Photo from *U.S. Patent Gazette*)

A Kalamazoo-type cattle guard near Craig, Colorado

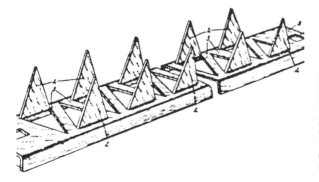

A railroad cattle guard patented in 1914 by Eugene Cook, Niles, Michigan. This cattle guard is the type described by A. F. Young and Jesse Jordan. (Photo from *U.S. Patent Gazette*)

rect in every detail, including cattle guards. The 1980 edition of *Walthers HO Railroad Catalog and Craft Train Reference Manual* is 425 pages long, and it carries the product lines of some two hundred and fifty manufacturers. On page 390, among a number of accessories (such as an oil can, a fire-alarm box, and a set of track tools) produced by the Sequoia Company, is a miniature railroad cattle guard, one which appears to be patterned after the National Surface Guard Company's metal cattle guard. Six pages later, a model of the widely used wooden arris-board railroad cattle guard is offered for sale by the Kadee Company.

Kalamazoo, Michigan, seems to have been a hotbed of railroad-cattle-guard activity around the turn of the century. Many of the cattle guards listed above were manufactured there by the Kalamazoo Steel Cattle Guard Company, the Bush Surface Cattle Guard Company, and the Merrill-Stevens Manufacturing Company (which also made the Cook Cattle Guard). In addition, the Kalamazoo Railroad Velocipede and Car Company manufactured a cattle guard made of woven steel wire.

A result of the invention of barbed wire was increased pressure to fence railroad right of ways, and a result of this pressure was the formation of fencing companies, one of the largest of which was the Western Fence Company. Between May and October of 1880, its first year in business, Western Fence had built literally hundreds of miles of railroad fences, along with numerous gates and cattle guards. This Chicago-based company furnished all materials for fences, wings, gates, and cattle guards. They built pit cattle guards with wooden slats spaced over the pit, according to an advertisement in Poor's *Manual of Railroads* (1890). During the first ten years of its existence, the Western Fence Company built an average of one thousand miles of fence per year and, presumably, hundreds of cattle guards as well.

A decision handed down by the Iowa Supreme Court in 1885 typifies the economic pressure that was being put on railroads to continue their search for an effective, durable cattle guard. The Rock Island passed through land owned by a farmer named Miller. The railroad had constructed a crossing for Miller and had properly installed fences, gates, wings, and cattle guards. When a gate was left open, however, some cattle got through the lane fence (which was in poor repair) and were killed by a train. The Rock Island used as its defense the claim that Miller had not requested that the fence and the cattle guard be repaired. The court decided in favor of Miller anyway, and the railroad had to pay him double the value of his cattle.

In fact, by the late 1800s the legal requirements and ramifications of railroad fencing had become so complex and pervasive that a book of more than 550 pages was devoted exclusively to the subject. A look into this book, *The Law of Railroad Fences,* by W. W. Thornton (1892), and into some other pertinent legal records, reveals much about the use of railroad cattle guards at a time just prior to the introduction of the automobile, and thus just prior to the time when the railroad cattle guard would have served as either the conscious or the subconscious model for the automotive cattle guard.

From a legal standpoint, the term "cattle guard" is used interchangeably with "cattle pit." Both terms refer to some sort of structure that, according to Thornton, "will prevent animals from going over the right of way upon . . . inclosed land; and [a cattle guard] must extend quite across the right of way, or wing fences must be built from it to the fences along the outer edge of the right of way." Most states in 1892 had laws governing a railroad's obligation to fence its right of way, but the legal requirements concerning cattle guards varied from state to state. Some state laws explicitly required cattle guards; in other states the obligation to build them was implicitly contained in the laws requiring the construction of fences. Also, under certain circumstances, a railroad was allowed to forego the building of fences and cattle guards.

For the most part, railroad companies were required to fence both in rural and in urban areas, except where fences would interfere with the rights of the public or with the ability of the railroad to conduct its normal business. Thus, towns with numerous street crossings, alleyways, and railroad service areas tended to have less fencing (and fewer cattle guards) than did the countryside. Railroads were not forced to fence depot areas, sidings and switch areas, coal yards, or freight yards. Part of this exception to the normal fencing requirement resulted from court decisions that allowed the company a reasonable freedom in conducting its business, and part came from considerations of safety. Decisions from Indiana courts express these concepts quite clearly:

> To have securely fenced [the right of way] at that place . . . would have required a cattle-guard near the south end of the bridge and another at or near the switch. The evidence . . . shows without conflict that a cattle-guard near the switch would have greatly endangered the lives of . . . employees in operating . . . trains. It is well settled law that a railroad company is not required to fence its road where such fence interferes with its own rights in operating its road or transacting its business, nor where the rights of the public in travelling or doing business with the company are interfered with.

An 1891 Montana statute concerning fences and cattle guards can also be considered typical:

> Railroad corporations must make and maintain a good and legal fence on both sides of their track and property, and maintain, at all crossings, cattle guards over which cattle or other domestic animals cannot pass. In case they do not make and maintain such fence and guards, if their engines or cars shall kill or maim any cattle or other domestic animals upon their line of road, they must pay

to the owner of such cattle or other domestic animals, in all cases, a fair market price for the same, unless it occurs through the neglect or fault of the owner of the animal so killed or maimed; provided, that nothing herein shall be construed so as to prevent any person or persons from recovering damages from any railroad corporation for its negligent killing or injury to any cattle, or other domestic animals, at spurs, sidings, Y's, crossings, and turntables.

This statement of law is supplemented by three pages of commentary, cross references, and applications. Two years later, Montana passed legislation mandating, in grazing country only, the construction of crossings through railroad fences at intervals of at most four miles. These openings had to be no less than sixty feet wide and had to have a cattle guard on each side. Other states in range country had similar laws.

Where a company was required to fence, the laws could be quite strict. Not only did cattle guards have to be installed; they also had to have been installed by railroad personnel (not the farmer whose land was crossed by the railroad), and they had to have been installed in appropriate places. A Texas decision, for instance, declared that the farmer was not responsible for building cattle guards to protect his crops because "it is a work requiring skill and experience, beyond ordinary labor, such as a farmer is not supposed to have, nor is it supposed that he has such knowledge of the business to choose a competent and skillful person to prepare them for him." Although some farmers might not have liked the implication, contained in the foregoing decision, that they were incompetent, all of them were undoubtedly happy that the responsibility for cattle guards was placed upon the railroads. Concerning installation at proper places, decisions from many courts required that cattle guards be placed precisely on the margin of the highway at a grade crossing. Even an unintentional error of five feet in constructing the cattle guard could be cause for holding the railroad liable for livestock that might be struck at that crossing.

In addition to paying costs for livestock killed or injured by passing trains, railroads sometimes were also liable to pay for damage done to crops by livestock that had strayed through right-of-way fences. Only if cattle were unlawfully on the highway or if they were in an area where the railroad was not legally bound to fence was the company not liable for crop damages.

Not all decisions went against the railroads, however. Companies were not required to go beyond what was reasonable in constructing and installing cattle guards. In New York in 1860, for example, the railroad was held liable for damages only until fences, gates, and cattle guards had been constructed. Farmers could not legally allow their stock onto the right of way, unless they had permission to do so, nor could anyone except railroad employees legally walk along the tracks other than at public crossings.

Moreover, unusual circumstances, such as a heavy snow, could alter the liability status of a railroad. Snow was a problem for railroads particularly in Canada and the northern United States, and many of the cattle guards used in those areas were removable. They would be put in place in the spring, when livestock was turned out to pasture, then taken up in winter, when most animals had been moved to winter quarters and when snow plows were needed on the tracks. Only fairly recently did the Canadian Pacific reach an agreement with some of the cities along its route in Alberta whereby it was allowed to cease altogether the installation and maintenance of cattle guards.

Finally, railroads were not held accountable for animals that were especially difficult to keep behind fences: "The company is bound to put in guards that will turn ordinary stock; and if it does, and stock leap over them, the company is not liable." In a New York decision, the owner of a cow that had crossed a cattle guard during a snow storm could not collect damages because the animal was illegally running loose already.

Present-day fence laws are not in all cases identical to those of ninety years ago, and livestock owners are now more likely to be responsible for keeping their animals fenced in than are grain farmers (or railroads) to keep that same stock fenced out. This generalization, however, does not hold true in all states, particularly those, such as Wyoming, that have large areas of open range. Although most western railroads had their right of ways fenced by 1900, the Northern Pacific in Montana had, in the early decades of this century, fenced only those portions of its line where concentrations of cattle were especially heavy. A fifteen-mile stretch of fence (with cattle guards) might be followed, for example, by a fifty-mile stretch of unfenced track.

As Joseph Noble noted in his book, rarely if ever did a train seem to strike a scrub animal, or even an ordinary one. Several correspondents have mentioned that only purebreds seem to have been drawn, seemingly irresistibly, into the paths of trains. Joel F. Overholser, publisher of the *Fort Benton* (Montana) *River Press* suggested a survey "on whether any railroad ever hit any but pedigreed stock. The quality slaughtered by the Great Northern trains from 1887 until Jim Hill fenced his line was substantial — the few items on claims I've run across indicate that the quality was excellent!" Other people have also alluded to James Hill as someone who had to pay for the carcasses of many purebred animals. Thus it is somewhat ironic that Hill did indeed believe in upgrading the quality of livestock, as this quotation from the 15 June 1916 *Breeder's Gazette* indicates: "One of the chief factors in the success of the late James J. Hill as the builder of a great railway system was his active, personal interest in promoting improved methods of farming and the breeding of better livestock in the territory depending upon and supporting his lines." Perhaps Hill decided that as long as he had to pay for top-quality livestock when his trains hit any, he might as well do what he could to see that what was hit was indeed of top quality.

Most of the material referred to thus far comes from around the turn of the century. Although railroads continued to use cattle guards extensively for the first few decades of the twentieth century, during the past thirty years or so the use of cattle guards on railroads has greatly decreased, a circumstance noted in the 1978 edition of *Track Cyclopedia:* "Cattle guards are rapidly disappearing in this country, even though their use is required by law in some states. The guards are very costly to maintain and claims paid for livestock may be less than the maintenance cost."

The American Railway Engineering Association developed four criteria for stock guards. These have not been changed since before 1962, and they are essentially the same as the criteria developed as early as 1915:

1. A stock guard should be so constructed as to avoid projecting surfaces liable to be caught by loose or dragging portions of equipment.
2. It should be effective against all livestock, have no parts which would catch or hold animals or unnecessarily endanger employees who pass over it in the discharge of their duties.
3. It should be reasonable in first cost, durable and easily applied and removed, so as to permit repairs to track at minimum expense.
4. It should not rattle during passage of trains.

Many correspondents have provided copies of the cattle-guard standards used by various railroads, almost none of which have been updated since the 1920s. The most recent patent for a railroad cattle guard I have been able to locate was issued in 1934. Likewise, during the 1930s, such journals as *Railway Age* ceased to publish articles about cattle guards. One man who worked thirty-four years for the Delaware & Hudson cannot remember ever having seen a cattle guard in place on that line, according to D. E. Hoadley; and Bill Armstrong of the Chicago & North Western Railway said that cattle guards were removed when new track was installed and were simply not put back, as was the case with the Katy in 1943 on its Kansas City Division. On the Central Vermont Railroad, natural forces were responsible for the removal of cattle guards; in the late 1930s a hurricane washed out most of them, and they were never replaced. In short, the use of railroad cattle guards appears to have been on the decline for several decades.

Interesting things have happened to some of the old cattle guards after they have been removed. The Santa Fe branch that runs through the Kansas Flint Hills near my hometown of Cassoday tore out all its old Sheffield Guards during the early 1970s, at the same time that it was tearing down many of the stockyards along that route. (Cattle shipping on the railroad in this particular area effectively ended in the 1960s, when trucks took over.) Some of these old guards are still to be found in the gravel along the right of way on the north edge of town, where they were discarded after having been ripped out. I salvaged one in 1978 for my personal collection of cattle guards. Another donation to this collection came from Jesse Jordan, curator of the Western Trails Museum in Clinton, Oklahoma, who sent me a piece of a Rock Island cattle guard installed there in 1901. He had gone out to take photographs for me of some of these old guards, which are now being used as braces for fence posts, and on his way he stumbled over a broken piece in the grass, which he tagged and mailed to me. Other correspondents have told about placing sections of old railroad cattle guards in their local historical museums.

Sometimes, old cattle guards are put to further service. On the F. B. McCann ranch at Culbertson, Montana, for instance, the windbreaks around the stock watering tanks are nothing more than sections of old wooden Northern Pacific cattle guards. These guards are ten feet long, and the slats have been cut into a triangular shape.

The cattle guard sent to me by Jesse Jordan was one patented in 1915 by Eugene Cook of Niles, Michigan. It came in eight-foot strips of U-shaped iron bar approximately three inches by three inches. The open sides were notched to form a saw-toothed edge. When in use as cattle guards, five of these strips were nailed outside each rail, and ten strips were fastened between the rails. A. F. Young of Riley, Kansas, a long-time employee (now retired) of the Rock Island, used these metal strips for right-of-way posts soon after the Rock Island discontinued using them as cattle guards around 1930: "It was the first metal post I ever saw used. Sure different than the posts used now." Young thought that the Rock Island cattle guards worked well and were attractive; the biggest problem encountered was when a dragging brake beam would hook the end of a guard and tear it loose. It was usually easy, however, to nail down the loose end and get the guard back into working order. In the late 1970s Larry Greer discovered some of these Cook Cattle Guards, discarded from the old St. Louis and San Francisco Railroad, being used as fence posts along Kansas Highway 254 between El Dorado and Wichita. Because of the toothlike appearance of the punched-out serrations, Greer says, these posts are often called "'gator posts."

As of 1981 apparently only one supply company, the Tamper Division of the Canron Railgroup of West Columbia, South Carolina, was offering railroad cattle guards for sale. In 1969 Tamper bought the Kalamazoo Railway Products Division, thus adding the Kalamazoo Perfect Steel Cattle Guard to its line of products. This guard was being built at least as early as the turn of the century. According to the specification sheet from Tamper, the design has not been changed since 1929. Each unit of the Kalamazoo Perfect Guard is eight feet eight inches long, and it is available in widths of seventeen, twenty-two, thirty-four, thirty-six, and forty-six inches. In 1978 Tamper sold fifty-five units; in 1979 that figure dropped to seventeen; in 1980 it rose to twenty-seven. Although sale of the guards is obviously not a major factor in Tamper's balance sheet, the company does intend to continue to manufacture and sell them as long as there is any demand at all, according to Richard Teeter, public information director for Tamper.

Overall the use of railroad cattle guards may be declining, but some railroads are actually having to increase their installations of cattle guards, particularly in the northern plains, where new branch lines are being laid into coal-producing areas. The Burlington Northern, for example, recently built a 116-mile line into the Powder River Basin of Wyoming, a line requiring new cattle guards all along the right of way. Rather than buying commercially produced guards, Burlington Northern has developed standard plans (revised and updated in 1975) for a single-track and a double-track railroad cattle guard, as well as for an automotive cattle guard to be used at grade crossings. These guards are then constructed locally as needed. Some are made by large manufacturing companies, others by small-town welders. As far as Burlington Northern is concerned, according to W. A. McKenzie, director of information services, the future of cattle guards will remain vital as long as open-range conditions exist in the West.

A cattle-guard controversy of sorts between southern Wyoming ranchers and the Union Pacific developed early in 1980, according to a story by Ron Franck in the *Laramie Boomerang* (24 February 1980). Trains on the Coalmont Route between Laramie, Wyoming, and Walden, Colorado, had run on an unfenced track through open-range country for years without doing much damage to stock, but recently, because of the boom in Wyoming coal, more and faster trains have been traveling the route, and more animals have been hit and killed. According to one rancher, "Up until just a couple years ago we never lost any livestock to the trains. What few trains did go through here went pretty slow. Now, though, since they started hauling coal from Walden, there are about four trains a day going through, and they go a lot faster. With a heavy load of coal, they can't stop when they want to. And I think the engineers have come to feel that, what if they do hit a horse or cow? The railroad will pay for it. One of those fellows told me it costs the railroad about $10,000 every time they have to stop a train. Maybe they just think it's cheaper to go ahead and hit the animals." Fence law in Wyoming places responsibility for fencing, not on the owners of the livestock, but on landowners who want to keep livestock off their property. Thus, in the 1980s, just as in the 1880s, the Union Pacific must either fence its Wyoming right of way or continue to pay claims for damage to livestock.

Along with fencing goes the cattle guard, but even that is causing trouble for the Union Pacific, which, according to railroad spokesman Barry Combs, uses the new model Kalamazoo Cattle Guard. This guard is made of thin strips of sheet metal bent into the shape of a rooftop and laid over the cross ties. Between the crossties no support is provided for the edges of these sheet-metal strips, and the weight of a horse or cow can cause the animal's hoof to slip down between the metal strips. When this happens, especially with horses, the Kalamazoo Guard becomes, according to Wyoming rancher Richard Smith, "a trap; the animal gets its foot down in it and it can't get out without badly injuring itself and often breaking its leg." Smith lost a horse when it caught a hind foot, broke an ankle, severed some arteries, and stripped the leg to the bone. Not all ranchers have lodged complaints against the Kalamazoo Guards, according to Combs; but where discontent exists, the Kalamazoos are being replaced with the old-style guards made of wooden slats. In other instances, the railroad guards are apparently being augmented by putting automotive guards on the approach roads that cross the railroad tracks. Warren Godfrey of Madison, Kansas, received a contract from the Union Pacific in the summer of 1980 to make nearly one hundred guards to be placed on roads crossing Union Pacific tracks in Wyoming and Colorado.

Godfrey figures in another contemporary story about railroad cattle guards. The need for railroad cattle guards in the present day can arise not only in the open range of Wyoming but also in the small-farm region of eastern Kansas. Around 1978 a spur was run from the Missouri Pacific near Westphalia to the construction site of the Wolf Creek Nuclear Power Plant near Burlington. This seven-mile spur, built by Kansas Gas and Electric Company (K G & E), angles through more than three dozen fence lines. Although the Missouri Pacific had used wooden-slat cattle guards in its Kansas operations during the teens, apparently no one who was connected with the Wolf Creek spur was aware that railroad cattle guards could still be purchased, for K G & E commissioned an original design. The utility company purportedly spent around forty thousand dollars building and installing these sheet-metal guards, and all for naught.

The guard itself offered no footing for livestock, and it was formidable in appearance, but animals could (and did) step between the sections of the guard at will. Proper installation required that the crossties be placed more closely together than usual and that no ballast be put between them, thus creating at least the semblance of a pit. Unfortunately these instructions did not reach Kansas, and the guard sections were simply placed on ties in their normal positions. The problem was solved only by scrapping the sheet-metal guards and replacing them with ones made of pipe, which Godfrey designed and built.

Paul Longrigg has developed an unusual way for railroads to use cattle guards. Longrigg, an electrical engineer, applied some of his expertise in radar and laser technology to the invention of an effective warning device to

Warren Godfrey standing beside one of his railroad cattle guards on the Wolf Creek spur of the Missouri Pacific Railroad

A wooden arris-bar cattle guard used on British railroads, Summercourt, Cornwall, England

be used at highway-railroad grade crossings. The result was a system that included, among many complicated and sophisticated mechanical devices, bar-grid cattle guards forty feet long embedded in the highway about 850 feet from the railroad tracks. The grid of the cattle guard serves as a tactile warning to drivers, much as a series of asphalt ridges is sometimes used to warn drivers that they are approaching a detour. Moreover, alternate bars of the grid are capable of automatic vertical displacement if a train is on the tracks or approaching the crossing when the car first hits the cattle guard. The result is an even rougher tactile warning to the driver. The cattle-guard part of the system is intended to be used on those crossings where auditory and visual warning devices would not be effective. Potential problems with the cattle guard include freezing weather or dirt and dust that could clog the actuating mechanisms.

J. G. Côté, a retired official of Canadian National Railways, provided an interesting account of what can happen when cattle evade a cattle guard and get onto the right of way. Usually an animal, when struck by a train, is killed at once and causes only limited damage to the engine (except in the case of derailment), but Côté was not in a regular train when this incident occurred.

The once that cattle did get away from a farmer's field, through a cattle guard, and onto the track happened on the Edmonton, Dunvegan & British Columbia Railway (now the Northern Alberta Railway) on which my father, in 1921, as Member of the (provincial) Legislature for Athabaska/Grouard, had rented or chartered a Packard inspection automobile on steel wheels (flanged) for use on that railway. He was to tour his constituency, and decided to take my mother and myself, a mere lad of 12 years. A derailment of the switch engine at Smith, Alberta, delayed us (the west switch was blocked) until 10 P.M. or so, and past midnight we hit a herd of cows on the track on a curve, as our headlights didn't show them up in time! We spent the next several hours until dawn trying (the conductor and driver and my father) to raise the wheels off the mooing cow under it. I had the trainman's lantern and with my mother went back to flag the following freight. When it came, the engine pulled the Packard off the cow with a chain; and we proceeded Westward.

More often than not, such accidents were fatal for livestock, but sometimes the cattle guards themselves could be equally dangerous. One of the most unusual cattle-guard fatalities I have learned of occurred in the 1930s on Wayne Rogler's ranch just north of Matfield Green, Kansas. The Santa Fe used the Sheffield Guard (a piece of sheet metal with three-inch triangular teeth punched out and pointing nearly straight up) on both sides of the private crossing between Rogler's ranch pens and a pasture on the west side of the tracks. While some cattle were being driven across, one especially wild cow ignored the jagged teeth of the guards and ran across a double section of them. A couple of the ranch hands opened a gate alongside the tracks and went in after her, but when she came out, she ignored the gate and again ran across the guard. Because the cow was hot and excited, Rogler cut her off into a side pen while sorting the rest of the herd. He said that she immediately went to a corner and lay down, and when he noticed her a few minutes later, she was lying on her side. When the hands had finished with the other cattle about twenty minutes later, they went to get the troublesome cow and found her on her back with her feet in the air, dead. Rogler thinks that the guard hurt her feet so much that she was trying to take all the pressure off them she could and that while she was on her back, her lungs must have collapsed. The heat and her nervous state may also have contributed to her death. Whatever the exact cause, it is the only instance that I am aware of where just running over a cattle guard caused an animal to die.

As noted earlier, many cattle guards are based on the principle that cattle are frightened by the prospect of insecure footing. Occasionally, however, a cow comes along that proves to be an exception to the rule. Dallas Perry of Kimball, Nebraska, tells the following story about a man named Shirl, a clever cow, and the triangular-shaped wooden cattle guards used in Kimball near the turn of the century:

> Shirl was town raised and remembered only the cattle guards at railroad crossings. Said his family had a cow that solved the problem of walking over them. Shirl thinks she went straight across, instead of at an angle, which might have helped a little. She would spread her feet out, and turn them enough to keep the clove of each hoof from slipping down on the upper edges of the triangular shaped timbers. It might have been fairly easy to so maneuver the front feet, but must have needed a heap of practice with the rear ones. Perhaps she watched humans sidle or "toes-out" their way across the three-sided planking. In any event that must have been one smart bovine; which may be the reason no iron horse ever caught up with her. I have to believe Shirl. He isn't the malarkey type of person.

A cow in eastern Kansas was equally adept at evading cattle guards, but once she had some trouble with a bridge trestle, James Kiser recalls. Kiser, who now lives in Chanute, Kansas, worked for the Katy for over fifty years before his retirement in 1960. One night in the 1920s he and a section crew were on a handcar heading north of Burlington when they hit a cow, and the handcar ran right up her back. The cow had gotten past a cattle guard and was crossing a bridge when she had slipped through the timbers and got stuck, her feet dangling through the ties of the trestle. Kiser and his men got the car off the cow, then took some poles and ties and pried her up a little at a time, blocking and getting a new hold, until she was raised up high enough to be able to get her feet on the ties. Kiser said she then hurried on across the bridge, never missing a tie: obviously it was not her first time to cross that bridge. A few weeks later, Kiser happened to be in town talking with the farmer who owned the cow. The farmer was mystified by what had seemed to be (and in fact were) cogwheel marks on the cow's back, but when Kiser told him about the bridge incident, the farmer refused to believe him.

Most of the material in this chapter has dealt with the use of cattle guards by railroads in the United States, with some reference to Canadian and British guards. I do not know to what extent railroad cattle guards are found in other parts of the world, although I have learned that they are found in countries as far apart and diverse as Argentina and India. In addition, I was fortunate enough to receive from B. Gallagher of the British Railways Board a survey history of the use of cattle guards on British railroads, with which this chapter will end.

According to terms of the 1845 Railways Clauses Consolidation Act, British Rails is required to keep all "cattle" (a term that includes all domestic farm animals) off the railway. In practical terms this means that nearly ten million dollars must be spent annually for fencing, crossing keepers (i.e., men

A ground-level view of a Sheffield Cattle Guard, the type that caused the death of Wayne Rogler's cow

hired to open and close gates), automatic antitrespass gates (gates that raise and lower or swing open and shut automatically), and cattle guards. The typical cattle guard used on British railway lines is made of wooden arris bars (i.e., triangular-shaped slats, with the pointed side angled up at a slant) spaced about two inches or so apart. These slats are fixed on timbers and are spiked to the ties on either side of a crossing.

Since 1910, when many of the railways, particularly in southeastern England, were electrified on the conductor rail system, antitrespass guards have been used in conjunction with cattle guards, especially at busy crossings. Even in the middle of cities such as Canterbury, one finds such a system of dual protection, although cattle guards used within a city are aimed primarily at discouraging trespass by humans, not by animals.

Beginning in 1955, many crossing barriers that had formerly been controlled by hand were converted to lightweight automatic barriers. Ten years later the railroads were allowed to install automatic half-barriers (i.e., single arms that raise and lower, covering, as do most American barriers, only one lane of traffic). In 1979 further measures were taken to replace many of the antitrespass guards with automatic single-lane barrier arms. As a consequence, many of the British crossings that are not now equipped with cattle guards soon will be.

The British are currently experimenting with potential replacements for the wooden-slat railroad cattle guards. One alternative is a "Bomac concrete slab panel," which wedges against the rails and can be lifted out more easily than wooden guards can be removed, thus enabling normal maintenance operations to be carried out more smoothly than is currently possible. Wooden guards are often damaged while being removed and then must be repaired or replaced, at not insignificant cost. Another alternative is a concrete guard made in a honeycomb pattern, which can also be relatively easily lifted out and replaced.

In drawing conclusions from this survey of British use, it would seem that the railroad cattle guard, despite the late start it got in Britain, is now probably being used more widely there than in this country. Even here, however, the cattle guard will not disappear from railroad crossings for many years, if indeed it ever does.

6

CORNISH STILES, LICH GATES, & CATTLE GUARDS

Folk wisdom says that there is nothing new under the sun. As far as cattle guards are concerned, this axiom contains more than a grain of truth, for the ancestors of the cattle guard can be traced back hundreds of years. Even though Jacob's pits and poles in Genesis 30 were not really cattle guards, still one can find many examples, ranging from contemporaneous to ancient, of progenitors for both railroad and automotive cattle guards.

Probably the concept of the cattle guard developed almost simultaneously with that of the gate, which in turn must have developed with the invention of fencing. A fence is of limited value, after all, if there is not a gate to allow one to get through it. Anthropologists now hypothesize that the earliest prototypes of fencing were developed to protect early man from his natural predators. In fact, a Dutch researcher, Adriaan Kortlandt of the University of Amsterdam, has demonstrated how effective thorn-tree branches are for turning lions away from fresh meat, even live sheep. He therefore concludes that prehistoric man could well have protected himself with barriers of thorns. Following this logic, one can easily imagine how our Neanderthal or Australopithecine ancestors might have built a bridge of logs, with thorn branches buttressing any weak spots (a prehistoric guard against predators), around a mesa or cave that could not be reached otherwise. (An analogy can be seen in the protective devices used by residents of Churchill, Manitoba, who happen to live on the migration path of Hudson Bay polar bears. In order to keep the bears from breaking in, home owners drive large nails through heavy sheets of plywood, then place these bristling sheets—a sort of unwelcome mat—on their doorsteps.)

By the eighteenth century, just this sort of protected entryway had been developed into a livestock barrier in the most recent progenitor of cattle guards, the dry moat. A dry moat (undoubtedly developed from its defensive counterpart in the medieval castle) was a steep-sided ditch dug around a garden or a house and yard (much as the Dutch today use water ditches as fences), with a footbridge where people could cross. This footbridge, often made of logs spaced in parallel fashion over the ditch, looked almost like, and worked exactly like, a modern-day cattle guard. Dry moats were used in New England as early as the middle of the eighteenth century, and they continued to be used into this century, according to Eric Sloane. Sloane has included a sketch of a dry moat from Ohio in *Our Vanishing Landscape*, and he notes that dry moats moved west as New England settlers followed the frontier.

The ditch part of a dry moat, without the footbridge, bears more than a passing resemblance to the ha-ha. A ha-ha, which may be of either Continental or English origin, is a sunken fence set in a ditch with a gradual slope on one side and a perpendicular wall made of stone or brick on the other. In England this kind of fence was first used at Stowe in Buckinghamshire in the early eighteenth century by Charles Bridgeman (d. 1738) and was thereafter often used in conjunction with landscape gardens or parks. The ha-ha had two advantages: it kept large animals out, and it did not obstruct the view. One of England's most famous landscape designers, Capability Brown, used the ha-ha in many of his projects, most notably at Blenheim Palace. Ha-has were once found on large estates all over England, and even today not all of them have fallen into disuse. In the summer of 1980, I saw a ha-ha at Trelissick Gardens in Cornwall. Along part of the wall, steel posts had been attached in order to keep stock from grazing along the top edge. Along the rest of the wall, however, the stones and the ditch kept cattle out of the main garden as well now as they had for centuries.

The link between the dry moat and the cattle guard may well have been an explicit one in western Kansas in the mid teens of this century. Near Quinter, Ray Purinton built a cattle guard with ash poles in 1916. The idea for this cattle guard, the first that Purinton had built or even heard of, was given to him by his grandfather, a native of Vermont who had moved to Kansas after the Civil War. Ray Purinton has no way of knowing, but perhaps his grandfather had seen a dry moat in Vermont, where they were quite likely to have been in common use.

The oldest extant manifestations of the concept of the cattle guard—spaced bars over a pit in the roadway—are in Cornwall. There, and nowhere else according to all available evidence, the inhabitants invented and installed a flat fence stile of stone, which they placed in gateways in their many stone

A ha-ha at Trelissick Gardens, Cornwall, England. The posts and wire have been added in modern times.

A flat stile in use on a footpath near Treslothan, Cornwall

walls and hedges. The exact age of these stiles, which still deter livestock today, is not known, but they are centuries old. Because little is known, and nothing has been written, about their history, an extended examination of them is in order.

Stone monuments abound in Cornwall: the Dancing Maidens (a circle of nineteen standing stones), the Tristan Stone (a commemoration to this legendary Arthurian hero), the Lanyon Quoit (one of many prehistoric burial chambers), the Men-an-tol (a doughnut-shaped stone that is big enough to crawl through), and Chysauster (the remains of an Iron Age village) are only a few of the silent granite memorials to Cornwall's past. A more prosaic, and even more pervasive, reminder of Cornwall's ancient heritage is contained in the rock walls that divide the peninsula into countless fields. Many of these walls, which are often overgrown with grass, flowers, and hedges, are quite old: Bronze Age artifacts have been discovered amidst the stones.

Incorporated in Cornwall's stone fences — as in hedges and stone walls almost everywhere — are stiles of many sorts: stiles that go completely over a fence like a set of steps; stiles, again like steps, that are placed within the fence line itself; stiles that have a high center slab or ridge of thin stone that must be crawled over; stiles that have a narrow perpendicular slot that must be slipped through. One kind of stile, however, is unique to Cornwall — the flat stone stile. This stile looks like, and works like, a cattle guard, even though it is intended strictly for foot traffic. Its bars, usually from three to six in number, are made of rectangular granite slabs spaced over a shallow pit. These granite bars vary in size, but a typical one measures about six by eight inches (narrow side up) by three feet long.

Except for three such stiles on St. Mary's in the Isles of Scilly (these islands lie twenty-eight miles west of Land's End and may at one time have been almost connected to the mainland; they are completely Cornish in culture), flat stiles seem to be found nowhere else. One might think that because of a common Celtic (or even pre-Celtic) heritage, Cornish flat stiles might be found in such countries or regions as Brittany, Ireland, Wales, and Scotland, but this does not seem to be the case. Through my own observations, a search of relevant scholarship, and correspondence with English, Irish, Scottish, French, and other European folklorists, I have not been able to turn up any evidence of flat stiles except in Cornwall. Apparently the geology of the region, the abundance of easily worked granite, and the ancient farming and settlement practices combined to make the use of flat stiles practical only there. Even so, these reasons do not fully explain why the design for this particular type of stile, one so easily crossed over yet so effective against livestock, occurred only to Cornishmen and not to others living in regions with similar raw materials and agricultural practices.

However that may be, the flat stone stile is definitely a hallmark of Cornish stone walls wherever they are crossed by footpaths. Closely related to this fence stile is the distinctive lich gate found in many old Cornish churchyards. Especially in southwestern Cornwall, there are three components of almost every churchyard entrance: (1) a flat stile (with stone bars that are narrower and invariably cut much more smoothly than are those found in the stiles of ordinary footpaths), (2) stone benches built into the gateway on either side of the stile, and (3) a lich stone (also termed a coffin rock or coffin slab) in the middle of, and running at right angles to, the bars of the stile. In addition, many of these entrances have a roof. The coffin rock, which is long, narrow, and usually rectangular in shape, was used as a rest for the coffin after the pallbearers had carried it to the churchyard. After placing the coffin on the lich stone, the pallbearers would rest, sitting on the stone benches of the lich gate while waiting for the priest to come forth for the service.

Like the flat stile, this type of lich gate is found only in Cornwall. Roofed lich gates are not uncommon in Britain; I have seen some as far north as the Scottish Highlands. I have also seen a coffin rock in a cemetery entrance at Escrick in Yorkshire. But so far as I have been able to learn, nowhere except in Cornwall can all these elements (roof, benches, and coffin rock) be found in conjunction with the spaced stone bars of a flat stile.

Many flat stiles and lich gates are still to be found in Cornwall. On my re-

A roofed lich gate at St. Minver, Cornwall, with benches and flat stile

A lich gate with coffin rock at Tintagel, Cornwall

search trip there during the summer of 1980, I found literally scores of them in use. Unfortunately, according to many sources, far fewer stiles are extant today than was the case a few decades ago. Some, on the footpaths especially, have been overgrown and forgotten, as was one only recently discovered on John C. Lyall's Bonallack Barton Farm near Helston. Others have been bull-dozed in or taken apart, victims of the merging of small farms into larger units as agriculture has become more mechanized over the years. In the churchyards, most of the lich-gate stiles have been filled in or paved over in recent years in order to provide safer footing, particularly for women wearing high-heeled shoes. For example, I examined twenty-one Cornish churches that had a total of twenty-six flat-stiled lich gates. Of these twenty-six gates, only seven still had operative stiles; all the others had been filled in.

Probably the most famous — certainly the most photographed — of all Cornish lich gates are to be found in the beautiful churchyard of St. Just-in-Roseland, where, amid luxuriant subtropical vegetation, stand two roofed gates. The walkway of the upper one has been paved over, but the lower one still houses a flat stile. The coffin slabs that were in place there in 1620 are now gone, presumably removed when the two stiles were rebuilt in 1632 and a roof was added to each. Here is the relevant passage from the churchwarden's accounts for that year: "Pd two days work riddinge the old stile 2/5. Item bestowed in beere upon the men which carried up the moore stones for the church stile and for helping them in their places 2/-. Pd the sexton for 7 days work in July about the style 8/6. Pd Alice Grub for 8 days carrying belling-stone and other work about the stile 4/-. Pd for timber for the stile 2/- and nayles 8^s. Pd for 4 bords for the seats in the style 8^d." Old records such as these often contain fascinating details — for instance, the men who carried the moor stones (i.e., the granite slabs for the stile) received their pay in beer. Interesting too is that the bellingstone (a rough slate used for roofing the gate) was hauled by a woman, Alice Grub. This name seems most appropriate for someone employed in manual labor, particularly a woman at that time. Most intriguing is the relative cost of lumber and nails; today nails would be cheap and the wood dear.

The spaces between the bars of the main lich gate were filled in a few years ago after a visitor had sprained her ankle, but the bars are still visible. The upper gate is seven feet wide and ten feet long and contains five granite bars with twelve-inch spaces between bars. The lower gate is narrower by two feet and longer by two feet. It has six granite bars with twelve-inch spaces and is placed over a pit that is twelve inches deep. The arcade roof of each gate is seven feet high, and each gate has wooden benches. These two stiles date from at least as early as 1620, when they appear on a terrier map, and they are probably at least several decades older. Lawrence Powell of St. Just-in-Roseland, one of the first people to send me information about Cornish stiles, thinks that these and other stiles can reasonably be dated to the sixteenth century. His reasoning is partly on the evidence of manor court records, such as the Menheniot manorial accounts, now kept at the Records Office in Truro, which insist that pigs be ringed because they are going into churchyards and rooting up bodies. These stiles are probably one of several responses to the damage caused by grave-robbing pigs.

A lich gate that is less picturesque than those at St. Just, but perhaps more typical, is located at the churchyard near Mabe. This church was built more than a mile from town, at the site of a menhir (an upright monumental stone), still standing, that marks a spot where people have gathered to worship for more than a thousand years, perhaps even since pre-Christian times. Because the church was built at this traditional site of worship rather than in the town, the public footpaths, many of which originally contained flat stiles, radiate in toward the church from the surrounding countryside like spokes to the hub of a wheel. A long, tree-canopied lane leads east from the road down to the unroofed lich gate, which is constructed entirely of stone with two good-sized benches built into either side. A coffin rock sits in the middle of the stile, which is composed of six bars, each eight inches wide. The bars are spaced very evenly, four and one-half inches apart, and the pit depth between the bars is eight inches.

The church at St. Levan has two lich gates, neither of which is roofed and one of which has been filled in. This church, like the one at Mabe, is colorful but is not readily accessible to tourists. It is noteworthy for two reasons. The first concerns the folk tales that are associated with it. One of these, told by the man who gave me directions to the church, recounts how the church was originally slated to be built on a hill some distance from where it now stands. Each night after the masons had spent a day laying stone, however, the "little people" would take the stones down and carry them to the site of the present church. After some time spent in trying to build the church in the spot originally planned, the builders gave up and built it where the "little people" wanted it. The other aspect worth noting is more germane to this study. The stile in the lower lich gate at St. Levan has been filled and has a narrow rectangular coffin rock, but the upper, and larger, gate retains an operative flat stile. The most intriguing aspect of this lich gate is a coffin rock that is actually shaped like an old-fashioned coffin — the only coffin rock with this shape that I have seen. In fact, I have seen only one other coffin rock that was anything other than rectangular. The stone at Perranarworthal has rounded ends; it is shaped like a long oval with straight, parallel sides.

The relationship between lich gates and fence stiles is seen most clearly at Zennor, a small village in the harsh but compelling southwestern region of Cornwall between St. Ives and Land's End. Originally most, if not all, Cornish churches were at the ends of footpaths that contained many flat stiles. Today, however, only Zennor — which has public footpaths going off in two directions, southwestward towards Gurnard's Head and northward to St. Ives, some four miles away — has flat stone stiles within a few hundred feet of its lich gates, which, unfortunately, have been filled in.

Most people have heard the nursery rhyme riddle about going to St. Ives and meeting a man with seven wives. In the early fifteenth century, there were no wagon roads between Zennor and St. Ives, only footpaths. With my family, I walked a single mile of one of these footpaths, and on this stretch of what was for hundreds of years a, if not the, major thoroughfare between these two towns, we crossed twenty flat stone stiles. All but one of these stiles was still performing its original duty of keeping livestock out of fields.

The most fascinating thing about this path and about the flat stiles along it concerns its use during the Middle Ages. St. Ives had no church of its own until 1428, although its residents had petitioned for one as early as 1409. Before then, citizens of St. Ives had had to travel from two to four miles in order to attend either the Zennor or the Lelant church. Even after a chapel had been built at St. Ives, its clergy was not granted a license to conduct burials. Instead, the privilege of performing this lucrative rite was retained by the clergy of the churches at Lelant and Zennor. Only in 1542 did St. Ives get its own cemetery. How burials from St. Ives were accomplished before then was related to me by Canon J. B. D. Cotter, vicar of Zennor. (Canon Cotter, by the way, is Irish, and he told me that he had never seen anything like the flat stone stiles of Cornish fences or lich gates in his native country.) Along the old church route from Zennor to St. Ives, in addition to the scores of stiles, there used to be twelve Celtic crosses. As bodies were carried to Zennor for last rites, the cortège would stop at each cross to say a prayer. About midway between the two villages there was a large boulder with a hole hollowed into it. Holy water was kept in this depression, and there the accompanying priest would sprinkle the coffin before the party continued on its way. Some of these processions were as much as one-quarter of a mile long, and relief bearers helped the pallbearers in transporting the deceased. In addition to stops for prayer, there reportedly were also frequent stops for refreshments of ale. Whether or not the flat stiles were developed for these funeral processions cannot be known for sure, but certainly such stiles lend themselves much more readily to the carrying of a bier than do step-up or step-over stiles. In fact, most flat stiles in Cornwall are to be found on public footpaths, while stiles that are intended strictly for use on private farms tend to be step-up-and-over stiles. In more recent times, Cornish landowners in some localities have been required by law to keep stiles in good repair for use by funeral processions, and undertakers have been heard to warn pallbearers about cracked bars or especially treacherous footing on certain stiles.

The age of these stiles on the road between St. Ives and Zennor is not known for sure, but some of the stone walls, particularly in this area of Cornwall, are pre-Christian. The small-field patterns in this part of the peninsula, a result of the superabundance of stone that had to be cleared before the land could be tilled, have been estimated by scholars to date from as early as 2,000 B.C. In contrast, many of the hedges in the rest of England date from the Enclosure Acts of the late Renaissance and afterwards. There were Cornish crosses at Zennor before the eleventh century, and Christianity was being practiced in the area by the sixth century. The Zennor church itself shows evidence of architecture from many periods. The south side of the nave is thirteenth century, and the southeastern portion of the chancel, the oldest part of the building, dates from the Norman period. The stiles conceivably could have been built at any of these times.

The Cornish have generally taken their unique flat stiles for granted, but at least one person has consciously attempted to adapt them to contemporary use. Just south of Praze-an-Beeble, I saw that builders of a new house had installed a brand-new flat stile (cut much more neatly than an ordinary fence stile, almost as trimly as a lich-gate stile) as a foot passage into the yard next to the wooden gate that closed across the driveway. Unfortunately, no one was at home, so I could not ask the owners what had inspired them to incorporate this particular aspect of Cornwall's past into their new home.

Travelers to Cornwall have not been so indifferent to the stiles as the natives have been. On the day that I was inspecting the lich gates at St. Just-in-Roseland, for instance, I overheard two Englishmen who were a bit perplexed by the stile in the lower gate. When I explained to them the uniqueness of the Cornish flat stile and its relationship to the cattle guard, the two men, who were from Devon, the neighboring county, told me that they had never seen anything like the flat stile in their own region. Letters published in such journals as *Field* and *Country Life* confirm the observations of the two men from Devonshire — other areas of England have nothing like the flat stile. Some other writers have noted its similarity to the cattle guard, and one even posited a causal link between them. These letters are welcome support to my thesis that the Cornish flat stile is the ancestor of the cattle guard.

The first traveler to comment in print about the peculiar stiles found in Cornwall seems to have been Celia Fiennes, who kept a written log of her travels throughout the English countryside during the period 1695 to 1697. These journals, published posthumously, have been lauded as an important source for the study of English social and architectural history. Here are her comments on Cornish stiles:

> From Redruth I went to Truro 8 mile, which is a pretty Little town and seaport and formerly was Esteemed the best town in Cornwall, now is the second next Lanstone. . . . I could hear but one Sermon at Church, but by it saw the fashion of the Country being obliged to go a mile to the parish Church over some Grounds which are divided by such stiles and bridges uncommon, and I never saw any such before; they are severall stones fixed across and so are like a Grate or Large Steps over a Ditch that is full of mudd or water, and over this just in the middle is a Great stone fixed side wayes which is the style to be Clambered over. There I find are the ffences and Guards of their Grounds one from another, and Indeed they are very troublesome and dangerous for strangers and Children.

I am especially struck by the similarity between her term "Guards of their Grounds" and the modern term "cattle guard." The stile that she is describing in this passage seems to be a flat stile ("a Grate or Large Steps over a Ditch that is full of mudd or water") with a center slab several inches (perhaps more than one foot) higher than the grid ("and over this just in the middle is a Great stone . . . to be Clambered over"). I have seen several of these combination flat and step-over stiles in Cornwall; they seem to be most common today in the St. Buryan area.

Fiennes's recollections prove that Cornish stiles, different from any others she had ever seen in any of her extensive travels, were commonly used at the end of the seventeenth century. Church records at St. Just-in-Roseland document that they were being used nearly a century earlier. Although no definite dates can be proven earlier than about 1600, circumstantial evidence strongly suggests that flat stiles in the lich gates and footpaths were used during the Middle Ages, and many British folk-life specialists and antiquarians think that these stiles could be as old as the Iron Age and Bronze Age stone fences that they cross.

Not only is the flat stile old, but as I have emphasized earlier, it is not found anywhere but in Cornwall. As the forerunner of the cattle guard it is indeed without comparison. Although there is no way to prove that the inventor of the cattle guard, either of the railroad or of the automotive variety, drew his inspiration directly from the Cornish stile, still the similarity between them is so striking as to strongly suggest at least some sort of indirect influence. Certainly the concept of the cattle guard, through the flat stile, had been in the realm of Cornish, and thus British, folk life for centuries. The sudden emergence of the first railroad cattle guards (which bore a strong resemblance to the flat stile), followed seventy-five years later by the simultaneous development of automotive cattle guards all over the Great Plains, is a remarkable example of folk transmission and re-creation.

7
LORE
ABOUT CATTLE GUARDS

At first, my reason for studying cattle guards was to explore their role in the folk life of the Great Plains. Although the scope of this study has expanded greatly since then, its original thesis has proven to be accurate: the cattle guard has played and still plays a significant role in the folklore of range country. Its major folk characteristics include anonymity of invention, traditional transmission of form and concept, variation within a formularized construct, lore regarding its use and efficacy, aesthetic considerations, and humor. Also within the context of lore about cattle guards is their role in popular culture—such things as social attitudes toward cattle guards and their appearance in literature and the visual arts.

The cattle guard is a prime example of folk technology—that is, of a mechanism or device (or the concept for that mechanism or device) that is generally built according to directions transmitted orally (although sometimes the concept is carried in the popular press) and that is built by its users from materials at hand (as opposed to commercial production from printed plans and standardized materials). Log-cabin construction techniques are a prime example of folk technology. So are stone walls, rail fences, and sod houses. In short, almost any noncommercial technology used by any subculture (i.e., a folk group) within the population would qualify as folk technology.

Folk technology is sometimes adapted to games and the construction of playthings, but often it is used to help folk groups adapt to certain conditions within their environments. The extensive use of sod-house technology on the high plains, for instance, was the direct result of dry, treeless conditions there. So, too, the cattle guard can be seen as a response by fence-dominated agrarians in a motorized society (as opposed to agrarians living under true open-range conditions) to the problem of gates. As seen in chapters 2 and 6, the origins of the cattle guard are traceable to cemetery gates and stone stiles in Cornwall, to ingenious treatments of gaps in rail fences, and to the moat in either its dry or its wet form; but the actual inventors of these devices are lost in the mists of history. One correspondent, T. Elwess of Chadron, Nebraska, has even suggested that Jacob invented the cattle guard. As related in Genesis 30:31–43, Jacob and his father-in-law, Laban, reached an agreement whereby Jacob would have all spotted livestock, and Laban all the solid-colored ones. In order to increase the size of his herd, Jacob erected some sort of structure of rods and gutters: "And Jacob took him rods of green poplar, and of the hazel and chestnut tree; and pilled white strakes in them, and made the white appear which *was* in the rods. And he set the rods which he had pilled before the flocks in the gutters in the watering troughs when the flocks came to drink, that they should conceive when they came to drink." Jacob probably intended the white-streaked rods to function as some sort of sympathetic magic that would make the livestock varicolored, not as fencelike structures that would allow some animals to pass through but hold back others. Still, Jacob was attempting to practice some kind of selective breeding and was employing, in the process, what at least Elwess thinks could be called the first cattle guards.

The concept of using an open pit to deter animals was readily implemented, again anonymously, by the people involved in the development of American railroads during the 1830s. We do know the names of some people who invented cattle guards, but the spontaneity and anonymity that are characteristic of folk transmission are evident in the way the automotive cattle guard appeared all over the Great Plains and beyond at roughly the same time and without apparent causal links. In other words, the concept of using spaced bars over a pit as a deterrent to livestock was conveyed in a traditional manner. Even today, despite its modern, mass-produced manifestations, the cattle guard is in a very real sense an item of rural folk life.

Not only has the concept of cattle guards been transmitted by tradition; use of them has also been a matter of custom. Traditionally, cattle guards consist of four parts: (1) a rectangular grid of bars (usually of pipe or rail), (2) a pit dug in the fence line (ranging in depth from a few inches to several feet), (3) a base or foundation upon which the grid rests, and (4) wings on either end of the grid which connect the guard to the fence. The *sine qua non* of a cattle guard is the grid. Sometimes a grid is placed directly on the ground, without any pit at all. Sometimes a grid is placed directly over a pit that has

A western-Kansas cattle guard showing the four-part structure: grid, wings, base, and pit

A cattle guard made of sucker rod, intended exclusively for car traffic, on the David Miller farm, Albert, Kansas

A rectangular wing, Ellis County, Kansas

no foundation other than dirt. Sometimes during the early years the grid took the form of troughs or ladders. And some cattle guards have no wings, the fence coming directly up to (sometimes into) the grid. But there is no cattle guard that does not have a grid of some sort.

Other types of variation also exist within this traditional design. Variations may take several forms, some of which result from the idiosyncracies of individual builders but others from local conditions or local opinions of efficacy that in turn help to create true distinctions, sometimes subtle, in cattle guards. These distinctions are to a degree regional, to a degree occupational (i.e., depending upon the major intended users—oilmen, loggers, miners, or cattlemen), and to a degree dependent upon the kind of stock to be held behind the cattle guard.

Some of my observations suggest that regional variations in the construction of cattle guards do indeed exist, even though I cannot yet offer enough documentation to confirm this belief. Thus it is not possible to specify, for instance, the elements that make a California cattle guard different, say, from one in Oklahoma; or on an intrastate basis, one in the Oklahoma Panhandle from one in the Osage Hills of that state. At this point, in other words, a field guide to cattle guards is not feasible. I can, however, point out the regional variations that I have noticed. Cattle guards in the gas fields of the Texas Panhandle, for example, tend to be short, and their wings are almost straight up and down, slanting out only slightly. In north-central Texas, many cattle guards are framed by elaborate entryways, often complete archways of brick or native stone, while in the hill country north of San Antonio, concrete wings are common. Many cattle guards in southwestern Missouri lack true wings, that function being taken over by rectangular panels of board fence. New Mexico cattle guards on the frontage and access roads along Interstate 40 have heavy pipe wings, sometimes triangular, sometimes rectangular, that are painted in alternate stripes of aluminum and black, apparently to increase visibility for night drivers. One of the most clear-cut regional distinctions in cattle guards exists in Wyoming, where many guards, particularly in the north-central area, are placed upon extremely solid bases, with as many as a dozen heavy I-beam stringers supporting the grid. Moreover, the grid itself has bars that are spaced exceptionally far apart—as much as eight inches. Guards that I have seen in other states generally have spaces ranging from two to five inches; in these areas the eight-inch gap is the exception, not the rule, as it is in the Wyoming guard.

Perhaps the fact that logging and mining trucks use these Wyoming guards helps to explain the heavy-duty underpinning of the grid. Guards on oil leases are usually less heavily built than those used on mine property but are more substantial than those used strictly at entrances to farms or ranches. One also often finds wider gaps on cattle guards intended for use with horses; those used exclusively with cattle tend to have a narrower space between bars.

TABLE 7.1

A COMPARISON OF CATTLE GUARDS
USED IN THE FLINT HILLS AND IN THE GYPSUM HILLS OF KANSAS

	FLINT HILLS	GYPSUM HILLS
Material used in bars	*Percentage*	*Percentage*
Pipe	80.00	67.00
Railroad rails	11.00	25.00
I-beams	1.50	8.00
Bridge planking	5.00	
Other	2.50	
Size of bars	*Inches*	*Inches*
Average	3.11	3.00
Smallest	1.50	1.75
Largest	6.50	5.00
Median	2.50 and 3.00*	3.00
Spacing of bars	*Inches*	*Inches*
Average	4.08	4.36
Narrowest	1.75	2.50
Widest	8.00	7.00
Median	3.50	3.00
Number of bars per grid		
Average	12.32	11.50
Least	4.00	6.00
Greatest	22.00	17.00
Median	11.00	13.00
Length of grid	*Inches*	*Inches*
Average	181.71	221.25
Least	93.00	168.00
Greatest	360.00	360.00
Median	168.00	180.00
Width of grid	*Inches*	*Inches*
Average	80.67	78.71
Least	40.00	60.00
Greatest	120.00	96.00
Median	84.00	60.00 and 84.00*
Depth of pit	*Inches*	*Inches*
Average	18.39	15.71
Least	0.00	3.00
Greatest	98.00	32.00
Median	16.00	15.00

* Equal number of each.

Thus far I have made a thorough survey (measuring, describing, and photographing) of nearly three hundred cattle guards in the Flint Hills big-pasture region just southwest of Emporia, and I have made an initial survey of two dozen guards in the Gypsum Hills around Medicine Lodge, Lake City, and Sun City. A comparison of the results does not reveal any spectacular differences, but some subtle ones do emerge, as can be seen in table 7.1. Consider, for instance, bar material. In the Flint Hills, four out of every five cattle guards have grids made of pipe, compared to only two out of three in the Gypsum Hills. On the other hand, one out of three cattle guards in the Gypsum Hills is made out of heavy-duty bar material — railroad rails or I-beams — compared to only one out of eight in the Flint Hills. Finally, Flint Hills cattle guards show greater diversity in bar material — bridge planking, railroad ties, T-bars, sucker rods, and concrete. These differences can be explained, at least in part, by the ways the cattle guards are used. Cattle guards on oil leases, for instance, are almost invariably made of pipe, a material that is readily available to builders of cattle guards in oil-producing areas. Such areas are found both in the Gypsum Hills and in the Flint Hills, although the most pervasive oil activity and the most pervasive use of the pipe grids are in Butler and Greenwood counties in the Flint Hills. Moreover, the Gypsum Hills, as the name suggests, contain gypsum mines, and the trucks that carry the raw gypsum demand extra-heavy-duty cattle guards; thus most of the railroad rails and I-beams are found there. As for the diversity of bar material found in the Flint Hills, I can only note that, except for bridge planking, every example of unusual bar material was found on the guards of private ranch and farm roads. Perhaps the stockmen of the Flint Hills are more inclined to use materials at hand or are apt to have more diverse materials at hand than are their counterparts to the southwest. Another area that warrants comment is the length of the grids. Grids in the Gypsum Hills are over four feet longer, on the average, than are those in the Flint Hills. This difference can be explained in part by the greater number of Flint Hills cattle guards found on private ranch or farm roads, roads that are nearly always only one lane wide.

The cattle-guard wings in both regions are similar — most are triangular, made of pipe and rod; a few are rectangular or trapezoidal; a few have single posts; and some are wingless. Guards in the Gypsum Hills occasionally have wooden triangular wings, whereas the only wooden wings found in the Flint Hills survey had a single post. Two wings had individualized touches that deserve special mention. Wings are often used as posts to which the fence wires are attached, but barbed wire can easily slide up or down on the perpendicular endpiece of a wing. One welder in the Flint Hills, however, has countered this problem by sticking half-rings every few inches along the inside of this pipe. The barbed wire is passed through the rings and thus held in place. In the Gypsum Hills, one guard leading into an oil lease had wings with a reverse slant. In other words, instead of slanting from the top of the end post down *toward* the grid, these wings slanted down *away* from the grid, just opposite from the norm. Because wings are slanted so that automotive traffic will have a slightly wider surface upon which to cross, this particular innovation would seem to serve no practical function.

None of the above observations can prove without doubt that cattle guards, like log cabins, are constructed differently in different parts of the country. But these observations do show that regional variations in the design and construction of cattle guards do exist. Another type of variation in cattle guards is quite important from a folklore perspective — naming. In all, I have collected over fifty terms by which the cattle guard is known in various places, and the list continues to grow. The most widely used term is "cattle guard"; it occurs all over the United States and Canada. In parts of Canada, however, particularly in the prairie provinces, the term "cattle guard" is applied almost exclusively to railroad cattle guards, while automotive guards are called "pit gates," "vehicle passes," or, most often, "Texas gates," apparently because it was thought that, like longhorns, everything connected with the cattle industry must have originated in Texas. Other Canadians have told me that the term came into being after Texas oilmen had introduced cattle guards into the Alberta oil fields. Outside of Canada, I have collected the term "Texas gate" in Texas, Maryland, and Kansas. Steven A. Bealby recalls that the early guards on the ranch where he was reared in Osborne County, Kansas, were made of hedge poles and were called Texas gates, but when his father replaced the poles with pipe grids in the 1960s, the Texas gates became, without any fanfare or conscious thought, cattle guards.

The cattle guard is called a "cattle grid" in England and South Africa, a *"guarda ganado"* in Argentina, a *"mato burro"* in Venezuela and Brazil. In the United States the second most popular type of name usually has the word "auto" or "car" in the title: "auto gate" (particularly common in the Nebraska Sandhills, but also used in other areas of the Great Plains), "car gate" (Sandhills, Gypsum Hills, eastern Colorado), "car crossing" (Kansas), and "car pass" (western North Dakota). There are also descriptive or humorous names: "razorback gate" (Ozarks), "corduroy gate" (Flint Hills, because of the rippling vibrations that occur when a car is driven over the grid), "spook" (Wyoming, used especially for the cowhide often thrown on a grid), and "cow filter" (Cornwall, England, because it filters out cows while letting cars pass). Other humorous terms include "Model T trap" (Kansas), "lazy man's gate" (Idaho and Wyoming), "wife saver" (Kansas), and "gee whiz gate" (Kansas, from "Gee whiz, that sure beats opening a gate!").

Some of the other names for the cattle guard, listed alphabetically and, when possible, where they are used, are: "auto chute" (Nebraska); "barrier

117

gate"; "buffalo gate" (Custer State Park, South Dakota, home of a sizable herd of bison); "cattle crossing guard" (California); "cattle gap" (Mississippi); "cattle gate" (Colorado, Kansas, Nebraska, New Jersey); "cattle grate" (Kansas); "cattle grill" (Kansas); "cattle guard gate" (Idaho); "cattle pass" (North Dakota); "cattle stop" (California, Kansas, Nebraska); "cattle stopper" (Montana); "cow catcher" (Kansas); "cow pit"; "cow trap" (Kansas); "crossover" (Nebraska); "drive-over gate" (Wisconsin); "fence stile" (Nebraska); "gap" (Tennessee); "Kalamazoo" (Wyoming, from the manufactured guard used on railroads); "livestock barrier" (Texas); "Mexican gate" (Wyoming-Nebraska border); "pit guard" (Santa Fe Railroad); "run-over" (Nebraska); "stock bridge" (Texas); "stock gap" (Tennessee, Texas); "stock guard" (Kansas, Wyoming); "stock pit"; and "Wyoming guard" (Nevada).

The term "fence gap," from eastern Colorado in the early 1900s, suggests a possible borrowing from the common fencing term "water gap." In Montana in the early 1920s the device was called an "automobile runway cattle guard." The first half of this term refers to wheel troughs for the automobile, while the latter half describes the pit with poles, similar to those used on the railroad. From this composite usage one can surmise that such terms as "run-over," "crossover," and "auto gate" originally referred to the trough or arched-crossover guard and that the term "cattle guard" came to be applied to the pit-and-pole guard. One old-time cowboy, who obviously preferred riding horses to driving pickups, gave me this answer when I asked him if he knew the cattle guard by any other names: "I call it a rough son of a bitch."

At least one cattle guard has, like a teen-ager's hot rod, been given a proper name. Fred B. Curry of New Braunfels, Texas, told me about a particularly noisy cattle guard, one designed with loose bars that would rattle when driven over, that was known locally as "Thunder Bridge."

Another type of variation in cattle guards concerns the use of folk substitutes for the grid, the pit, or both. For instance, a substitute found in many areas of the West might be called the rubber-band cattle guard. People have learned that by stretching (and usually twisting) strips of inner tube (usually from tractor or truck tires) between two wooden end pieces at about four or five inches above the ground, they can effect a light, inexpensive, and adequate replacement for the regular kind of cattle guard. The rubber strips can be driven over without causing bumps, and the driver does not even have to slow down. Because there is no pit, cattle could escape by stepping between the strips, but they do not seem inclined to do so, at least not on the Tom Wyse Ranch near Lindsay, Montana. According to Mrs. Wyse, no animal has ever gotten out of their pasture where this kind of guard was being used. Their guard is made of only six strips, but the vibrating and shimmering that occurs in the slightest breeze helps to frighten the cattle away. Mrs. Wyse also commented on the ease with which a broken strip can be replaced. Other

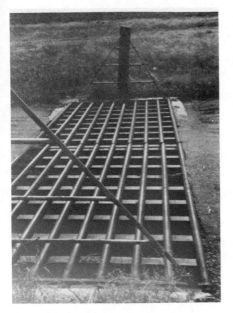 

A cattle guard in north-central Wyoming. Note the extra-wide spacing of the bars and the extra-heavy base supports.

A railroad-tie cattle guard made by Dale Remsberg, Cassoday, Kansas

rubber-strip guards have been built in Wyoming, California, Texas, and New Mexico, among other places. One near Magdalena, New Mexico, was built in a potentially high-water area where a regular pit guard could have had its dirt approach ramps washed out. This guard was built specifically for use by heavy cattle-hauling trucks.

A related cattle guard, but one that is much less convenient for driving over, can be made by bolting worn-out tires together. One such guard was built by Julius Trescony of San Lucas, California, who fastened together five rows of tires, five tires each in the middle and outside rows, four tires each in the other two rows. These rows fitted snugly into each other, and then four tires were bolted vertically in a row on each end in order to form the wings. Art Dorsett of Olpe, Kansas, saw similar guards on a ranch where he had worked in South Dakota. "You couldn't cross it going very fast," he said, "and we used them only in pastures where we mostly drove pickups. They kept the sight-seers out and the cattle in."

Cattle guards used in the late 1970s in southern Texas were made by placing cinder blocks with the hole side up. A quarter of a century earlier in Exmoor National Park in England, a guard was made by vertically embedding round drainage tiles into a concrete base. I have also seen other con-crete-block cattle guards in southern England. These guards turn cattle rea-sonably well, but their practicality is limited because of the ease with which dirt and debris will fill up the holes. A road running through Crazy Woman Canyon in the Bighorn Mountains of Wyoming has a cattle guard that was made by forming rows containing three concrete parking abutments, then making eight such rows into a grid. This guard had no pit, and it was ex-tremely rough to cross.

In Colorado in the early 1920s, some ranchers merely laid cedar posts (usually split so that they would not roll) directly onto the ground and drove over them. Lack of a pit and the roughness of crossing were two major disad-vantages of this guard. Other Coloradans have put old bedsprings on the ground to drive over, while an Arizona rancher put his bedsprings into a shallow pit. Around 1954 a Utah rancher made a guard by hanging some bedsprings about four inches off the ground. In Wyoming and Montana, old harrow sections, minus teeth, have been placed on the ground or in a shallow pit and used as cattle guards. One rancher in Texas put an old World War II landing mat over a pit and used it as a grid for a cattle guard. In the northern plains a winter cattle guard was sometimes made by digging a shallow pit in the gateway and then filling it with water. The water would remain frozen all winter long, and the slick ice would effectively turn cattle.

In the summer of 1978, while driving north of Watford City, North Da-kota, to the ranch where the late Andrew Johnston invented his cattle guard in 1914 (see chapter 3), on one road I crossed a sheet of flat steel, the kind of metal siding used for the walls of grain bins or heavy storage tanks. This flat metal covered the road from fence line to fence line and was some eight to ten feet wide. It was not only completely smooth to drive over but apparently was also effective in turning stock. In Wyoming a similar sheet-metal cattle guard, painted bright orange to increase its effectiveness, is reportedly being used near the Big Horn National Forest. Colorado farmers have claimed that a series of corrugated roofing tin, laid two strips wide on a road, will stop livestock. The crackling noise, along with the slippery footing, serves as a deterrent.

In Alberta, cowmen have substituted a cowskin for tin, stretching it across a gateway to keep cattle from crossing. In some areas of northern Mex-ico no gates are used. Rather, each of the two posts that frame the gateway is draped with a cowhide. Cattle will not voluntarily pass through them, and sometimes the hides must be removed before the cattle can even be driven through the openings. Because animals inevitably shy away from the dead of their own species, cowhides are often used in conjunction with regular cattle guards in order to improve efficacy, an instance, perhaps, of what Sir James Frazer might have termed a sort of sympathetic magic in reverse.

A cattle guard incorporated into a bridge over the White River near Meeker, Colorado. The board panels can be lowered if cattle are to be driven over the bridge.

A wingless cattle guard, Ellis County, Kansas

Unusual cattle-guard wings made by bending grid bars, near Lovewell Reservoir, Kansas

Of all the makeshift cattle guards I have encountered, none was as intriguing or as sensational as the dog cattle guard. This was the only instance of a living cattle guard (not counting cowboys) that I have heard of; the story was related by Lon J. Godley of Hardesty, Oklahoma. As a boy, Godley lived with his family on the J. K. Hitch Ranch in the northern panhandle of Texas. A neighboring ranch had a county road passing through its pastures, so the owner was not allowed to erect a gate to keep his stock in. Although cattle guards were widely used by the period 1918 to 1925 (the dates Godley remembers seeing the dog guard in operation), for some reason this rancher chose to chain a shepherd watch dog to the post on either side of the gateway. Each dog was provided with a house and was fed and watered daily. Their chains were short enough that they could only come within eight or ten feet of each other. Thus, they could not get their chains tangled, nor could they get run over if a car passed between them. Their barking and snarling, however, was enough to keep cattle from trying to escape from the pasture. Being kept on chains made the dogs irritable, and their barking not only kept cattle away, it also caused most mule- or horse-drawn wagons to take a detour through a wire gate some distance to the side. Teams might have been afraid to pass between the dogs (I wonder if they were named Charybdis and Scylla?), but horseback riders, like Godley and the ranch cowboy who worked with his father, could ride through; nevertheless, the experience was exciting and daring, just the sort of exploit to fix itself in a young boy's memory: "I was just a boy eight or ten years old at that time, but the dogs made me remember them because they were so mean."

Although cattle guards work reasonably well, they are not foolproof, and folk opinion about their efficacy and its improvement forms a major part of cattle-guard lore. People agree, for instance, that wild cattle are more likely to jump a guard, if pushed, and that tame cattle, particularly milk cows and roping steers, are more likely to learn to walk across guards. Shallow pits and wide spacing of bars allow animals to cross by stepping between bars; wide, flat support stringers can be walked over; even a two-inch ledge on the sides of the grid where it joins the wings can be negotiated by a determined cow. Some people say that a cattle guard that is to be used in a pasture with brahma cattle should be half again as wide as a regular guard. In short, popular opinion holds that cattle guards will not be totally effective against a determined bovine; but that same opinion also holds that such an animal will usually get through almost any other kind of barrier as well. One Colorado rancher, for instance, told me that while his cattle and horses would jump an eight-foot cattle guard to get out of the pasture, he always had to open a gate in order to get them back in.

That a horse's hoof can sometimes span the bars of a cattle guard perhaps accounts for the folk belief that a cloven-hoofed animal is more likely to

A cattle-guard wing with rings to hold barbed wire, Greenwood County, Kansas

A noise-making cattle guard constructed with loose bars, Greenwood County, Kansas

be turned away by a cattle guard than is a horse. This belief is reasonably accurate with regard to cows and sheep (although sheep have been known to jump cattle guards six feet across and wider), but very few cattle guards are able to turn the cloven-hoofed goat. Some cattle guards have been specifically designed for goats. These have straight sides (goats often cross at the junction of the wing and the grid) or angle irons, pointed side up, along the stringers and pit edges; nevertheless, according to one Texan, "the goats cross in flocks."

Like almost every other aspect of the cattle guard, its operating principle has received little study. Very few persons, even among ranchers and oil pumpers, were able to give a clear and quick response when asked what made a cattle guard work. Those who did respond quickly usually answered, only half facetiously, to ask a cow. There is more than a little truth in this answer, yet some observation and deduction can suggest plausible theories concerning the effectiveness of cattle guards. In fact, when given time to ponder, most persons I talked with agreed that livestock probably have an instinctive fear of injury, particularly to their legs. Thus a surface offering obviously poor footing, coupled with an open pit underneath, would be a formidable obstacle to the average head of livestock — goats excepted.

This idea is well expressed by two correspondents from Texas. C. W. Wimberley of San Angelo observed that cattle, when crossing rocky and rough terrain, will often lower their heads and become very careful and selective of their footing. If given a choice, they will avoid rocky areas scarred by wide cracks and crevices, thus indicating that they will instinctively avoid any opening in the earth where the bottom is not clearly visible — which is the basic principle behind cattle guards. Tracy King of Roby suggested that cows and horses have an innate danger signal. For example, in heavy fog or on a dark night, cattle will not allow themselves to be driven over a bluff. Moreover, a horse that is familiar with the terrain will, if given his head, pick his way home despite any darkness or fog. If he comes to a gate or fence, he will stop rather than walk into it. Thus, says King, when a cow or horse comes to a cattle guard, its innate sense of danger tells it to stay off.

Other persons agree that this fear is general, that livestock will shy away from shadows, holes, and insecure footing, much as a green colt will balk at being ridden through a mudhole. A telling example of this intuitive desire for firm footing is found in *cavalletti*, obstacle courses used at some horse shows as a test of a horse's training. These structures, which are made by laying a series of poles on the ground or just above ground level, bear a general resemblance to a cattle guard. Persons who know about such things have told me that an untrained horse tends to be spooked by these obstacles; sometimes great efforts are necessary in order to train a horse to go through *cavalletti* smoothly and confidently.

Fear of cattle guards may be innate in most animals, but many of my informants agreed that livestock will occasionally try to cross a cattle guard, especially if the animals are heavily concentrated in a small area. Once a cow or horse has been caught in a guard, however, and escapes without having to be destroyed, that animal will be especially wary of getting caught again. In other respects people disagree about what makes a good cattle guard, particularly concerning the pit and the spacing of the bars. Some have told me that the pit should be boxed in, because a dark hole is more frightening to an animal than is a lighted hole. Others have insisted that the most effective pit should be open at one or both ends so that daylight can show through. Most agree that the pit should be relatively deep, free from grass and weeds, and cleaned of dirt and gravel. Yet I have seen cattle guards that were placed directly on the ground with no pit whatever, guards that must have worked reasonably well because they opened onto a well-traveled highway. In fact, some highway departments in western states have substituted stripes of paint for regular cattle guards and apparently have no major problems with livestock crossing the highways.

Concerning bars and spacing, some persons think not only that pipes offer more slippery footing than do wooden slats but also that the sound and feel of hoof on metal is what turns the animal. Others say that wooden bars are just as effective and are much smoother to drive across. Some ranchers want to have the bars close enough together so that if an animal happens to get pushed onto a guard, it will not slip through and break a leg. Others want the bars eight inches or more apart so that there will not be any footing at all on the grid itself. Wide spacing only works well (although it is rougher to

Julius Trescony and a cattle guard he made by bolting tires together. (Courtesy of Reuben Albaugh)

A cattle grid made of drainage tiles in Exmoor National Park, Devonshire, England. (Photo taken in 1941, courtesy of Richard Jemmett)

A cattle guard supplemented with an innertube strip, Blanco County, Texas

125

drive across) if a deep pit is maintained. When a pit begins to fill up, animals can simply step between the bars and walk right across. Therefore, many grids are built so that they can be easily removed in order to clean the pit. Some persons consider railroad rail to be the best material for bars because of its great resistance to bending. Others dislike it for the same reason; the slightly rounded top of the rail tends to make an animal slip off, and once its leg is caught, the bars cannot be pried apart to release it. Rail is also more difficult to cut than is pipe. Some persons prefer the trapezoidal-shaped formed-steel bars found in many commercially produced cattle guards because of their strength and the smoothness of the ride when one crosses in a car. But others have found that the shape of the bars, with the base of the trapezoid on the bottom, forms a trap that holds an animal's hoof more effectively than does any other type of bar. Horsemen have told me that the space between the bars should either be close enough together to be spanned by a horse's hoof or far enough apart so that a horse could step between the bars and pull his hoof out easily. Because a horse's hoof is solid, it neither spreads out when he places weight on it nor contracts when he draws it up. By contrast, cows have more flexible hooves and are therefore much less likely to be caught or seriously injured in cattle guards than are horses. The ideal space between bars is wide enough to let an animal's foot go through and to let the foot be pulled back out of the pit without serious injury but narrow enough to hinder forward motion.

Many welders believe that the bars should be far enough apart to scare cattle and close enough together to allow a smooth crossing for vehicles. Ralph L. Ricketts, professor emeritus of agricultural engineering at the University of Missouri-Columbia, is the only person I know of who has attempted to study the problem from anything approaching a scientific point of view. He has spent many years in the field as an extension specialist. In his attempts to design an economical but effective cattle guard, he determined that the pit, along with proper bar size and spacing, was crucial. One incident proved to him that a totally effective cattle guard required both bars and a pit:

> I spent a lot of time trying to design a cattle guard that could be easily built and yet one that would keep livestock from crossing it. Some co-workers and I built an experimental guard out of concrete. It was just a slab poured on the ground with six-inch-high ribs sticking up—no pit. We poured one on a farm as an experiment in the Ozark area. It sure was pretty. This farmer and his neighbor were driving cattle up the lane and approaching the cattle guard. The neighbor had been bragging about this guard and said he surely would build one of his own. The gate was open at the side of the guard and the cattle were supposed to approach the guard, smell it, and then go through the open gate. They approached it, smelled it,

A cattle guard made of concrete parking abutments, Bighorn Mountains, Wyoming

A sheet-metal cattle guard north of Watford City, North Dakota

and then every one of the cattle in the herd walked or stumbled over the guard. Apparently they thought this was no more rough than some of the stony land adjacent to the cattle guard.

This answers the question as to why cattle guards work. It is not because they are rough; it is because cattle fear the space under the rails. They can't keep their feet on top of the rails and they know this. With the guard that failed, their feet simply slipped off the top of the concrete rails into the shallow space between the rails with no damage. With a grid and a pit, their feet slip off the rails and go down in the space below the guards. The cattle know this will happen and don't try to cross a good guard. If they do happen to get into a guard, they always lose hide and hair from the leg or legs and they respect the guard much more in the future than before they got mixed up in it.

In a good plan the rails will be narrow, two inches maximum, and preferably rounded at the top. They will be spaced six inches apart (farther would be good, only a little rougher to cross with a car), and there should be 18 inches of space under the rails.

Another crucial element for the effectiveness of a cattle guard is the manner in which the guard is connected with the fence; it is also important to make sure that cattle cannot cross along the lip between the grid and the wings.

For whatever reasons, most cattle guards, properly installed, do work. Many ranchers find that cattle, in trying to escape, are more likely to rub down a gate or crawl through the fence rather than to escape through or over a cattle guard. Cattle guards have even been used to keep recently captured mustangs in a pasture. On the other hand, there seem to be more gates and fewer cattle guards on ranches that handle registered stock, because breeders cannot take the chance of getting livestock from one pasture mixed with those of another.

The controversy over the effectiveness of cattle guards remains active, and one stockraiser's experiences with cattle guards will differ from those of another. One of the most convincing (and entertaining) testimonies to the effectiveness of cattle guards was related by Larry Whitmer, who operates a ranch near Zenda, Kansas. A few years back, near his house, Whitmer had a pasture full of heifers that adjoined a lot where he was keeping some bulls. Besides a good barbed-wire fence, the two enclosures shared a cattle guard and a pond. The line fence had been stretched across the pond, the bottom wire just a few inches above the water. Whitmer did not particularly want the bulls in with the heifers, but bovine nature being what it is, he was not surprised one day to find that a couple of bulls had gotten into the heifers' pasture. The gate was still up, and no wire had been torn loose from the fence, so he assumed that they had somehow crossed the cattle guard. He ran the bulls back into their pasture and then went back to the barn to get some material for a wire gate to string across the cattle guard. He got back to the pasture just in time to see one of the bulls swim across the pond, duck its head under the barbed wire, and come out into the heifers' pasture. The mating urge was strong, but apparently, in this instance at least, the instinct to avoid cattle guards was even stronger.

Cattle guards have proven to be effective against bison at, among other places, the Maxwell Game Preserve in Kansas, Custer State Park in South Dakota, and the Wichita Mountains Wildlife Refuge in Oklahoma (which also uses cattle guards to control elk, deer, and longhorn cattle). Many national forests and parks, such as Yellowstone, use cattle guards to control bison. Yet some correspondents have reported that bison will run over cattle guards at will: "Buffalo are crazy, anyway," one experienced handler said. The assertion is probably correct at times, especially when bison are riled. Yet gentled, undisturbed bison will stay behind not only cattle guards but also fences that tame cows will crawl through.

Cattle guards have even been known to be effective with dogs and coyotes. Several persons have told me that they have had to carry their dogs across a guard, and others have said that a good woven wire fence with a cattle guard could keep sheep safe from coyotes — if anything could. Still others, however, have found that both dogs and coyotes were quite willing to jump or run across cattle guards.

A folk observation, made especially in desert states and in the Nebraska Sandhills, is that rattlesnakes often live in the pit area of cattle guards. In the northern states they will sun themselves near their homes; in hotter climes they will stay in the shade of the pit walls and grid. In either case, an unwary

A cattle guard near Virgil, Kansas, built by Mick Sage. Tires were added to help deter livestock.

A cattle guard with pipe-bar gate to keep out unwanted automobile traffic, Greenwood County, Kansas

rider, coming up to open the gate beside a cattle guard, may find himself either on a horse that has been bitten by a snake or on one that has been spooked by stepping on or near a snake.

Many persons have told me stories about livestock that had been trapped in cattle guards, and most agree that the consequences are usually more serious for a horse than for a cow. One story, however, about a young goat that got stuck in a Texas cattle guard has all the trappings of an incipient folk anecdote. C. W. Wimberley tells this story:

> During the 1930s my wife mothered two angora pet kids and one evening while we were away from home, the antics of these kids on the nearby cattle guard turned traffic on that country road into a comedy of errors. One of the kids managed to fall through the center opening into the pit of the cattle guard. While it spent its day imprisoned, its partner wandered about the immediate vicinity, frequently returning to check on his buddy.
>
> On hearing a car approach, the prisoner would stick its head up through the railings to see what was going on and, in the last split-second, would jerk its head back as the car passed overhead. From that point the behavior patterns of each kid varied from car to car.

Afterwards, the way Wimberley heard the story while sitting around the general store, it ran something like this:

> "Yeah, when I sees this goat's head sticking up between the bars, I jams the brakes—too late. And when I do stop and look back there that goat's head is looking at me—nary a scratch. I go back

and get in the cattle guard to get it out, but after the scramble I figure a goat that's that hard to catch can take care of itself without any help from me."

"I done nearly the same thing. Only when I looked back that danged kid was standing in the middle of the road. Of course I was glad it wasn't hurt, but I'll never figure out how it got out of that cattle guard so quick."

"That's nothing. When I hit my brakes, old John was right behind me and his truck rams mine right on top of the cattle guard and he comes out mad as blazes. I tried to get him to look under my truck to see if there was a goat down there in that cattle guard, but he points his finger at a goat standing beside the fence and says, 'There's your blamed old goat.'"

Wimberley concluded his story by saying: "And that's the way it went on all day. Those two goats had everybody all stirred up with their cattle guard game."

Because cattle guards are not always totally effective, folk methods have arisen to improve them. The simplest way to ensure that a cattle guard will stop stock is to supplement it with a gate. I have seen scores of cattle guards that have had a barbed-wire gate, an aluminum gate, or a single pipe stretching from wing to wing. Sometimes these extra gates have been placed there specifically to keep unwanted motorists from purposelessly (or purposefully, for that matter) driving into a pasture; more often, however, these added deterrents have been placed on little-used cattle guards. Thus the wire gate, for instance, can be left open for a day or a week of heavy use, but kept closed at other times.

Using a gate with a cattle guard, however, is self-defeating, because cattle guards were designed so as to eliminate the necessity of opening and closing gates. Thus, when a cattle guard fails to work adequately, other methods are often put into play in order to make it more effective. Sometimes common-sense additions are made to the original guard. In Wyoming, for example, I have seen a too-wide concrete lip between wing and grid that was made effective by fastening a piece of angle iron, pointed side up, in the middle of the lip. Near Ellis, Kansas, a piece of seven-inch pipe, cut in half lengthwise, was laid between wing and grid in order to deny footing to errant livestock.

Other means have been used in attempting to frighten away animals that might want to walk across cattle guards. Ray Purinton of WaKeeney, Kansas, found that a piece of loose roofing tin laid on the grid stopped a troublesome horse from getting out. The bars were close enough together so that the horse's hoof could span the space between two of them, but the sound and feel of the loose tin on the grid stopped him from walking out. People have also tied rags to the wings and grid, placed newspapers and white paper in the pit,

An old harrow section used as a cattle-guard wing near Lake City, Kansas

Truck and tractor tires used as wings on the Pioneer Ranch, Nebraska Sandhills. (Courtesy of Mary Ann Koch)

and even put chunks of broken mirror into the pit in order to make their cattle guards more effective.

Besides the main part of the guard, the wing is another part that has yielded to the folk impulse to improve its effectiveness. In addition to, or sometimes instead of, the usual wooden or metal wings, people have placed wheels from old wagons or implements and old tires from trucks or tractors between the grid and the fence in order to discourage animals from trying to crawl through. Sometimes mere sticks, boards, or broken fence posts have been slanted down from the fence to the grid. Sections from old harrows and the headboards from old-fashioned metal beds have been used as wings. In desert regions, ranchers will often buttress the wings with chunks of cactus or branches of tree cactus.

A spectacular use of tree cactus was reported from New Mexico, where a rancher had constructed a pitless variation of a trough cattle guard. He had leveled off and hollowed out two logs for the troughs. The logs were about fourteen inches above the ground, and dirt had been mounded up to each for an approach ramp. The rancher had kept the tracks clear; but in between, on both sides, and all around for several yards, he had filled every available space with pieces of tree cactus. Instead of using wings, he had tied big chunks of tree cactus to the fence posts in order to steer cattle away from the crossing. According to George W. McKinney, who saw this cattle guard in the 1930s, it was an awesome sight: "I bet it would have made an old Model T stand on its toes as it crossed."

The attempt to keep animals away from the grid, particularly those that might be inclined to try to jump or walk over it, is a commonly practiced folk method of improving the effectiveness of cattle guards. E. A. Stephenson of

Bucklin, Kansas, had a problem with cattle walking along the fence near the guard. He devised a method for heading them back into the middle of the pasture. He built a wire wishbone by setting a post behind each end of the wing at the point where it joined the outside edge of the grid; he then angled the wire back ten feet or so to a post in the fence line. Another method of trying to frighten the animals away is by setting a tall post on each side of the guard, stringing a wire on the poles, then hanging gunny sacks down from the wire. The wire can be strung high enough to give clearance to trucks, and the gunny sacks will not damage them. In Montana a more ingenious—but more complicated—system has been devised by Tom McCrea of Plains. He placed a hot wire, charged by an electric fencer, about four or five inches above the ground and directly in front of the first bar of the grid. He first tried using inner tubes for insulators (which also act as springs, allowing vehicles to pass over the wire by pressing it down), but later he found that the rubber straps used in tying down truck cargo work best. He says, however, that this device works well only if livestock will stop to sniff it. Then, once shocked, a cow will not try to cross. In order to draw the animal's attention to the wire, McCrea has placed such things as old tires or a cowhide under it.

Although opinion is divided on whether cows are less likely to cross metal bars than wooden ones, many persons from both sides believe that the deterring powers of either type of bar material will be enhanced by paint. The majority of cattle guards are plain, but many have been painted. Paint also protects metal bars against rust. Colors commonly used are silver, black, and white; but some guards are painted with bright colors such as yellow, orange, red, blue, and green. The most effective method, according to conventional range-country wisdom, is to paint every other bar black, and the others white. Thus, since the spaces between the bars will appear farther apart to a cow, she will not attempt to cross the guard. I have seen many guards painted this way—or in some other variation, such as painting two bars white, then two black, and so forth. One new cattle guard on the eastern edge of the Flint Hills was not keeping cattle in. Painting the bars did not solve the problem either until two additional pipe bars were installed and painted.

Next to painting the grid, probably the most widely used means of improving the effectiveness of a cattle guard is with a cowhide. I have already mentioned the use of a cowhide by itself as a deterrent, but more often it is used in conjunction with a cattle guard. Sometimes a dried cowhide is thrown onto a grid where it will rattle; sometimes a fresher hide is fastened to the grid; sometimes a hide is tied onto each wing of the cattle guard or to the fence just beyond the wing.

One Flint Hills rancher, Raymond Prewitt of Cassoday, Kansas, told me about a problem he had with some roping steers that had gone sour and ornery over the course of the summer roping season. Among other bad habits,

Cowhide on a cattle
guard in central New
Mexico. (Courtesy of Jay
Taylor)

A cattle guard and
arched entryway near
San Angelo, Texas

A symmetrical grid cat-
tle guard in the Teter-
ville Oil Field, Green-
wood County, Kansas

these steers had learned to walk the narrow concrete ledge of the cattle-guard pit just west of his house. He tried painting every other bar with aluminum paint, but this did not work. He tried painting each bar in alternate twelve-inch sections of black and aluminum, again with no effect. He tried pouring the paint in concentric semicircles on the gravel road in front of the guard, but traffic soon erased these efforts. Finally, he draped a fresh cowhide over the bars of the grid. The steers, completely oblivious to the hide, continued to cross; but his daughter's horse, a family pet that was used to jumping the guard at will, would not come within fifty feet of the cattle guard until the hide had been removed. Conversely, Montana rancher James Murphy of Livingston found that a cowhide over a cattle guard kept his cattle in but had no effect whatever on his horses, which continued to jump the guard. Ranchers from the Ruby Mountains of Nevada and from the Sandhills of Nebraska, however, have told me that hides work with any kind of animal.

Earlier in the history of the development of the cattle guard, when the ladder guard with an open pit in the middle was used, a hide was often placed in the pit to help scare cattle away. In the sheep country of Nevada a sheepskin is sometimes substituted for a cowhide. In Kansas I have seen dead snakes laid across a grid, ostensibly to frighten livestock.

The cowhide technique is employed all over North American range country, and possibly elsewhere. It seems to work because animals tend to jump and snort and bellow and shy away from signs of death and blood, as anyone can attest who has ever driven cattle past an animal that has recently been struck by lightning. In general, the operating principle seems to be similar to that used in a Navajo scarecrow, which consists of a dead crow hung from a string on a post in the cornfield.

The innate desire to beautify one's surroundings often finds expression in functional, workaday objects. Folklorists have often noted the results of this aesthetic urge in such things as rural mailboxes, quilts, and embroidered blue jeans. Like these items, cattle guards are primarily utilitarian; but unlike these items, cattle guards are not normally the objects of beautification. Occasionally, however, someone has attempted to make a guard aesthetically pleasing, above and beyond the clean, hard geometric lines inherent in cattle guards. Often the aesthetic effect of a cattle guard is enhanced, not by the guard itself, but by a fancy entryway of which the guard is only a part. High poles, for instance, with the name of the ranch in wrought metal suspended between them, are commonly used to frame cattle guards in the Kansas Flint Hills and elsewhere. There is an especially fancy entryway of this sort in east-central Wyoming, where old wagon wheels have been welded into the structure of the cattle guard's wings on both sides of the gateway. In north-central Texas, prosperous-looking ranches often have elaborate gateposts of native stone or brick. Sometimes these masonry entryways arch completely over the driveway, with the cattle guard directly underneath. In some instances these arched frames are intentionally constructed so that only cars and pickups will have the necessary clearance to drive under them; large trucks (which might damage the grid) must go through the gate at the side.

The guard itself can be beautified (as well as having its effectiveness improved) by painting the grid, although if the paint is not maintained, the resulting chipped and scraped cattle guard soon turns into an eyesore. Usually, if the guard itself is decorated, one also finds the artistic impulse displayed in the wings. For instance, wings lend themselves to such things as having the owner's name or brand spelled out in metal rod and worked into the design of the wing. The most unusual wing design I have seen was on an oil lease near Lovell, Wyoming. There the wings of the cattle guards that led into the lease were made of rod that had been formed into the shape of an oil derrick. I have also seen the tops of the center posts of wings adorned with metal rings, drilling bits, and other such decorative items.

One of the nicest — and most subtle — aesthetic touches I have seen in cattle guards is found in several guards east of the Teterville oil field in Greenwood County, Kansas. Here the pipe bars are arranged symmetrically so as to form a point at each end where the grid and the wing join. The middle bar of an eleven-bar grid, in other words, might be fourteen feet long, while the two bars on either side would each be six inches shorter (three inches on each end), and so forth, so that the two outside bars would each be eleven and one-half feet in length. The ends of the wings are then attached to the ends of these outside bars, and the wings slope back and up towards the center bar of the grid. Thus, all lines, both of the grid and of the wings, come to an arrow-like point. Because this design does not afford any pit edge or any space between the grid and the wings on which cattle may cross (usually the weak link in a cattle guard), it provides a prime example of that happy instance in folk expression where function and aesthetics meet in perfect form.

Because cattle guards are so much a part of range country and are taken for granted by most of the people who live among them, there has developed around cattle guards a set of customs, actions, and beliefs. Some of this lore is related to custom, some is utilitarian, and some concerns values. Cattle guards became necessary because of cars; therefore, it is not surprising that much of this lore concerns automobiles. In open-range country, for instance, where crossroads are few and signposts even fewer, cattle guards are used in giving directions, much as one uses traffic lights in a city: "Take the fork to the right after you cross the fifth cattle guard."

Some travelers in range country use the cattle guard as a game, much as passengers would pass time by "collecting" license tags from as many different states as possible when going through more heavily traveled regions. Patricia Diness of Middletown, New York, for example, was raised in Dartmoor National Park in Devonshire, England, an open-range area containing many cattle guards. She remembers, as a child, playing a game of guessing the number of cattle guards to be crossed before reaching home. Once she had grown old enough to remember where each cattle guard was, the game lost its challenge, but she reports that her young daughter has enjoyed the same game on visits to her grandparents in Devon. Similarly, Kaye Y. Turner of Pocatello, Idaho, remembers that as a girl she used to ride at sixty-five miles per hour along the Medicine Bow cutoff in Wyoming, a stretch of road that had many cattle guards. "With nothing else to do (other than count antelope), we would take turns hollering 'cattle guard—lazy man's gate' for each one. Drove my mother crazy!"

Many persons have told me about this stretch of Wyoming highway, which is rather renowned as far as cattle guards are concerned. One of the most intriguing customs concerning the Medicine Bow cutoff was reported by some instructors at Casper College. Apparently, some students, when they leave for holidays, take along a supply of beer in the car. The object is to finish a beer before the car crosses each of the cattle guards. The mounds of empty cans tossed out at each guard are treasure troves for gatherers of aluminum cans.

Changing social attitudes are revealed in a story about cattle guards told by Margaret Hailey of Phoenix. In 1922 her husband, Rob L. Hailey of Willcox, Arizona, attended a high-school dance with some fellow students in Bowie. On the way home to Willcox, they found that the sheriff had strung a chain across a cattle guard as a roadblock. He was checking for illegal booze, and the cattle guard made a perfect spot to stop traffic. Because the sheriff knew the students and knew that they were not bootleggers, he let them pass, then he refastened the chain for the next car. Mrs. Hailey went on to say: "We like this story because it is a contrast to what goes on now. Needless to say, the amount of traffic through that area is very heavy in 1980 and stopping cars would be a big operation. Also, our son, who is a policeman (just one generation later) wouldn't think of trying to operate in this manner."

Because it is more expensive to construct a cattle guard than a barbed-wire gate, cattle guards on private roads tend to be associated with rich ranchers. Roy Alleman, in a 1957 article in *American Cattle Producer,* indicated that this was the case in the Sandhills of Nebraska: "If one passes through a range which [has] a lot of fancy auto gates, he lifts his eyebrows and remarks to himself, 'Hm-m, wonder which vice-president of what corporation owns this place?'" Other persons have told me that in the early days, a cattle guard on a public road was considered a sign that the rancher whose ranch was crossed by that road was on especially friendly terms with his county commissioner.

Scholars and laymen alike recognize the effect that barbed wire has had on the development of the West. The automobile made range country even more accessible. The cattle guard has also played its part in helping to urbanize rural America. The long search for a practical automatic gate (see chapter 2) proves how strong was the pressure for a time- and labor-saving device such as the cattle guard. With improved roads, faster cars, and cattle guards, ranch country that was scores of miles from a city could become a rural suburbia for erstwhile city dwellers who did not mind commuting to their jobs. C. W. Wimberley has mused upon this subject: "The cattle guard was the bane of the old time country people and did more than any other contraption to urbanize the rural areas of Texas with city dudes too lazy to open a gate. It destroyed the family unit productive farm by making them playgrounds of country living." While the cattle guard does not deserve the entire blame for the demise of the family farm (which resulted from many forces), it undoubtedly did have some influence.

The line between folklore and popular culture is sometimes vague. Probably, however, the few depictions of cattle guards in the visual arts or in literature belong to the realm of popular culture. I have seen very few western paintings of cattle guards. In 1948 Ross Stefan did a pastel entitled *A New Experience*. This painting, set in the desert Southwest, shows a skinny, leggy weanling Hereford calf encountering its first cattle guard — eight wooden bars set between a nearly vertical set of wooden wings. One of the tall end fence posts carries a sign: "No Trezpasing." I have also seen a few cattle guards in paintings by regional artists and a few photographs using a cattle guard to frame the main subject of the picture, such as an old windmill or a snow-topped mountain.

A cattle guard can occasionally be seen fleetingly in the background of a movie or television show, usually one set in the contemporary American West. A few years ago, however, a cattle guard appeared in the opening frames of a Robert Mitchum movie that was set in England, a film version of Raymond Chandler's detective story *The Big Sleep*. The few appearances of cattle guards on film seem to have been totally accidental, but this was not so in an animated "Peanuts" television program, "Run for Your Life, Charlie Brown." In an early scene, Snoopy is shown on his way to camp riding on a low-slung motorcycle. En route he bounces and vibrates across a cattle guard, thus providing a small laugh to those who are familiar with cattle guards and also giving his persona a needed shaking up.

Cattle guards in fiction are rare. Mary O'Hara is representative of those authors who include a few cattle guards in their work in order to add realistic detail (although the fifteen-foot-wide cattle guard in *My Friend Flicka* lacks verisimilitude; it is nearly twice the width of a typical cattle guard and three feet wider than any cattle guard I have surveyed). In my reading of novels set in the twentieth-century West, cattle guards have figured importantly in only three. One of these was Edward Abbey's *The Monkey Wrench Gang,* in which two of the protagonists, Smith and Hayduke, are in a jeep, trying to elude a posse of pickups and Chevy Blazers. Abbey has the two men cross an old wooden cattle guard, which they then set fire to in an attempt to slow the pursuit:

> The fence appeared, stretching right-angled across the line of their advance, from cliff to canyon. An opening for the road was formed by a rack or grill of two-by-fours set on edge, resting on a pair of railway ties. Cattle guard. Wheels could cross; hoofed animals like sheep, cows, and horses could not. There was a closed gate beside the cattle guard, through which livestock might be driven, but this, like most of the fenceline, was banked thick and solid with years' accumulation of windblown tumbleweeds. From a distance the fence resembled a hedgerow, brown and tangled.   [Pp. 119-20]

I am not sure why Abbey included this cattle guard in his story, for, although Smith and Hayduke successfully set it ablaze, their pursuers are able to jump their vehicles across it anyway. I also found it interesting that Abbey, who normally has a good eye for detail, had the cattle guard made of two-by-fours; very few wooden guards, especially on public roads, are made with such small lumber.

In John Nichols' novel *The Milagro Beanfield War,* Bernabe Montoya, the sheriff, braces himself and shudders in a conditioned response every time he drives over a painted-stripe cattle guard just outside the town. This painted-stripe guard is used as a major image in the novel, a metaphor for the way in which the natural things in life are being cheated by artificial substitutes.

> [Bernabe] flinched and, shaking his head, muttered to himself: "It sure beats me how a handful of white stripes can fool cows like that."   [P. 30]
>
> . . . .
>
> Bernabe likened the painted cattleguard to the sort of stickers — "Protected by Acme Burglar Alarm System" — store owners who could not afford burglar alarm systems put on prominent display in their business windows.
>
> Or to those signs — "Beware of the Dog" — that surburban folks too cheap to invest in a ferocious mutt, but nevertheless terrified of burglars, displayed on their lawns.
>
> Or then again, Bernabe figured a painted cattleguard might be said to share a common soul with a shapely woman who wore falsies.
>
> And Bernabe wondered: Did the painted cattleguard concept have some relationship to artificial insemination, also? . . .
>
> Bernabe never truly understood the deep down discomfort caused in himself by that painted cattleguard.   [P. 164]

In *Horseman, Pass By,* Larry McMurtry's novel that was made into the movie *Hud,* the cattle guard on the prosperous Bannon Ranch is solidly built of pipe. The poverty of a young neighbor who helps Bannon work cattle, on the other hand, is subtly symbolized by a rickety, cheap cattle guard made of two-by-four lumber.

The brevity of the foregoing comments shows that the cattle guard has not had the same sort of symbolic or general appeal as the windmill, the locomotive, or barbed wire in the popular mind and in the popular arts. Still, a few artists have recognized, and utilized, its symbolism.

Jokes about cattle guards will never replace situation comedy or knock-knock jokes as a major form of American humor, but there have been some successful cattle-guard jokes and humor, in addition to the humorous names cited earlier — "corduroy gate," "cow filter," "wife saver."

Some of the cattle-guard humor I have encountered has been of a personal nature. A cowboy friend from my home town, for example, sent me a note that closed with the admonition, "Keep your cattle guard up." Then, in response to one of my newspaper queries, I received this letter: "Enclosed is a photograph of the cattle guards we are using during the 1980s in Chanute, Kansas. The older one was made in 1927, the other two in 1963 and 1967. The two newer ones are efficient, but it seems the older they get the more it costs to maintain them." I had not yet looked at the accompanying photograph, but when I saw the signature on the letter, Britton Thompson (my wife's cousin), I realized that my leg had been pulled. Britton is not considered to be the most serious-minded member of the family, a reputation that was not altered by the enclosed photograph — a picture of himself (the 1927 model) and his two sons, Dan and Ted, guarding their Holstein milking herd by brandishing clubs and shotguns.

Less personal but equally amusing is the humor found in the memoirs of a Wyoming schoolteacher, Paul Swaffar. This passage on the cattle guard is from his book *Look What I Stepped In,* published in 1972:

> I have no notion why they should be called cattle-guards instead of horse-guards, sheep-guards, pig-guards or billy-goat guards. I can only say — and I am widely quoted in this statement — "Cattle-guards are sure nice." You make them by leaving a hole in the fence, much as if you were going to put a gate there. The length of the hole will depend some on whether your wife drives the car — in case she does you make it real long. Then you dig a square hole right there in the gap. I don't know how deep this hole ought to be, but be sure to make it deep enough. You make the hole, say six feet across, depending some on whether you have mules or goats — if you do, I'd suggest around twenty feet. Then you take some heavy logs and lay them crosswise of the hole. Leave them stick over the edges quite

aways so's you don't fall in with a load of hay. Then lengthwise and on top of the logs you put 2 x 6s on edge, or poles, or old railroad irons, or pipe about say six or eight inches apart. You nail, bolt, or haywire these down good and you have the slickest gate you ever saw — without having a gate. Some people get real fancy and box the hole with concrete which is all right, but it costs quite a bit more — and this is pretty important in this day of high taxes.

Advantages of a cattle-guard are:
(1) Kids love them — so do older people.
Disadvantages of the cattle-guard:
(1) They are useless on a chicken farm.   [Pp. 48–49]

Swaffar's view of the cattle guard, while humorous, is also accurate. Like much humor, it contains more than a grain of truth.

One joke about cattle guards made use of the practice of placing a cowhide over the grid. An "Out Our Way" cartoon by the late J. R. Williams shows a vacationing city family of four who have just driven over a cattle guard covered by a hide, with hoofs, head, and tail still attached. Quite apparently this was the father's first encounter with a cattle guard. While the kids were bickering in the back seat, he was probably trying simultaneously to drive and to read a road map. He has hit something that felt like it was shaking his car apart, and when he looked into the rearview mirror, all he could see was a cow flattened out on the road. His trepidation will not be eased by either his son's keen interest in the disaster (a typical reaction of small boys) or by the devious comments the two cowboys are planning at his expense. "I put old dry hides in all the cattle guards to spook our cattle from jumpin' 'em — those people think they run over a cow," says one. To which his companion replies with typical cowboy deadpan humor: "We'll tell him this dry air and hot sun dries 'em up awful fast out here."

"Ace" Reid, creator of the cartoon "Cowpokes," includes cattle guards in his work, sometimes as realistic background detail and sometimes as part of the joke. One that illustrates perfectly the reason for the invention of cattle guards shows a cowboy driving a battered pickup through the last (or at least the latest) in a long series of barbed-wire gates as his wife struggles to close the gate. This long-suffering woman has evidently made a suggestion that completely fails to penetrate his consciousness: "What do we need cattle guards for?" he asks.

Mary Weberg wrote a humorous article "Honey, You Get the Gate" for *Farm Journal* (September 1959), in which she noted that ranch dwellers will often feign indifference about who will drive, but actually getting to drive is a very competitive game in which the loser "gets the gates." She had a neighbor who lived seven fences away — fourteen gates for the wife to open and shut when she came visiting. The suggestion was made to this long-suffering

140

Build cattle guards! What we need with them?

woman that she ask her husband for a cattle guard for their wedding anniversary each year for seven years, but we are not told the result. Perhaps her husband served as the model for Ace Reid's cartoon.

By far the most prevalent motif in cattle-guard humor concerns the mistaking of metal or wooden cattle guards for humans who guard cattle (one of the term's original dictionary meanings, by the way). The version I have heard and read most often is similar to this one printed in the September 1979 issue of *California Mining Journal:*

> Nick Franklin, New Mexico's secretary for energy and minerals, received an inquiry from Washington. The bureaucracy wanted to know how many cattle guards there were in New Mexico.
>
> The state official scratched his head and made a guesstimate. He advised Washington that there were approximately 50,000 cattle guards in his state.
>
> A reply from Washington informed him that there were too many cattle guards on the state payroll and there would be no more federal money for state highway programs until New Mexico fired at least half of them.
>
> It's reassuring to know there are people in Washington with that kind of mentality looking after you and me.

This story gained wide currency when Paul Harvey used it on his broadcast (as fact, not as joke, needless to say) on 8 September 1978. Later, Tracy King of Roby, Texas, sent me a letter containing a summary of Harvey's item. Doug McDonough, farm editor of the *Plainview* (Texas) *Herald* sent me a copy of his column, which told the story at three removes — the *American Agriculture News* account of Harvey's broadcast. A number of persons from several states have told me the story, often citing Harvey as the source. I had first heard the story, however, a good two months before Harvey's broadcast. A roughneck on an oil lease near Virgil, Kansas, stopped to check me out as I was measuring a cattle guard, and after he had learned that I was doing research on cattle guards, he told me the story as a joke, minus Franklin's name and a specific setting. I have tried several times, unsuccessfully, to communicate with both Harvey and Franklin in order to trace the story to its origins.

Recently, the joke seems to be spreading independently of the media coverage it received in 1978. I heard two versions in October 1981, both told as humorous but supposedly true stories. Donald Thompson of Arlington, Texas, for example, heard the story from a New Mexico hunting guide, who had state rather than federal officials as the objects of humor. As early as June 1981, the Reagan administration had attained the major role in the story, apparently a result of its much-publicized intent to reduce the presence of the federal bureaucracy in local affairs. According to Yvonne J. Milspaw, her father, who is from Utah, heard that a newly appointed official of the Interior Department had asked workers in the Salt Lake City office of the Bureau of Land Management for an inventory. When the resulting list showed, among other items, four hundred cattle guards, the naïve political appointee ordered that one hundred of them be fired.

Variations of this joke include one from Nebraska: "A cattle guard is someone who guards cattle from a thief and is hired by the government. More expense to the city dude to pay for in taxes." There is also this one from Montana: "We're kind of hoping, here in Montana, that not too much attention gets centered on cattle guards or else the bureaucrats will want to reorganize them and put them in uniforms." A Texas variation has a city slicker say, "I thought that a cattle guard was a deodorant for cows."

Many folk tales are based on facts, and jokes about cattle guards are probably originally related to experiences similar to the one that happened to Merle Walker, a former professor at Fort Hays State University in Kansas. When he was a young man, Walker had worked as a park ranger. One day a woman stopped to ask him how she and her party could view the major sights of the park in the least amount of time. Walker gave them directions, beginning with the phrase, "Go down to the first cattle guard and take a left turn." The woman repeated his instructions down to "the first cattle guard," at which point she asked, "Will he be wearing the same kind of uniform as you are?"

Tracing this story to the single incident that gave rise to the subsequent jokes is probably impossible, but certainly the experience that Alice Bullock had during World War II is a likely candidate for the point of origin. She was working for the New Mexico Department of Education in Santa Fe at the time this incident occurred. There were many shortages during wartime, and when her office applied for money for six cattle guards for school bus routes, Washington gave an unexpected answer: it could have two guards, but not six; manpower was just too limited.

The cattle guard, despite its previously unrecognized role, is obviously a significant factor in the folk life and the popular culture of range country.

By the end of World War I the cattle guard had become, except for such variants as the arched crossover, essentially what it is today—a series of bars over a pit in the roadway. While this design works well, it is not without draw-backs: bars will bend; cars tend to vibrate on grids; pits fill up with dirt and debris; guards are heavy, permanent, and expensive; and they are not totally effective in turning livestock. In their attempts over the years to counter one or more of these problems, inventors of cattle guards have produced many unusual (and sometimes unusual looking) cattle guards. Sometimes, for ex-ample, cattle guards have been constructed in an unusual fashion or with un-common material; some guards have relied on mechanisms, simple or com-plex; some have made noises to frighten cattle; some have been electrified; some have been portable; and some have not even actually been there—they have been replaced by stripes of paint on the pavement.

Most cattle guards have metal bars, but during at least the past forty years, some cattle guards have been made entirely or primarily of concrete. Sometimes these guards have been poured on the site by using portable forms, such as those based on plans developed by Ralph Ricketts in the late 1940s. Hundreds of guards have been built from these plans, which are still available from the University of Missouri Extension Service.

In 1960 David Smith started the Smith Cattleguard Company in Mid-land, Virginia, a company that makes and sells franchises for the making of precast concrete cattle guards. Smith sold more than fifteen thousand guards between 1960 and 1980. He may have been influenced in his innovation by an architect in his region, Randolf Carter, who built an all-concrete cattle guard about 1940. Carter's cattle guard, however, was not too successful. It measured roughly five by twelve feet and had bars six inches wide with four-inch spacing between them. The problem was that Carter ran his bars with the road, rather than across it, and car wheels could get caught in the grid.

An unusual concrete cattle guard was patented in 1948 (U.S. patent number 2,533,168) by William S. Letson and John G. Sheldon of Kansas City, Missouri. This guard was designed for use by tractors and trucks in a cattle pen, not for highway travel. It consisted of a sharply sloping ramp and a platform two or three feet high, both of concrete. The edges of the ramp sloped slightly inward, and the center portion of the guard was open and had a series of eight pipe bars over the resulting pit. Two of the bars extended all the way across the concrete, which was given a smooth (and thus slippery) surface in order further to deter livestock from crossing.

On a road in Crazy Woman Canyon in the Big Horn Mountains of Wyoming, I saw a cattle guard that had been made from twenty-four portable concrete parking abutments. These abutments were arranged in eight rows, three to a row, and placed directly on the ground (no pit). It was extremely rough to cross but apparently worked satisfactorily (see chapter 7).

Another unusual grid surface was made of sheet metal formed into a shape like ribbon candy, with a dozen channels in the grid. This guard was patented in 1946 (#2,471,551) by James A. Slaughter of Kermit, Texas. A. J. Bruner of Fort Myers, Florida, received a patent in 1975 (#3,971,546) for a grid that features three dozen parallel bars running diagonally across a rectangular pit frame. A metal grid of small, square intersecting partitions, somewhat like the cover of a floor furnace except that each square was larger than an animal's hoof, was patented in 1956 by Robert E. Hundahl of Tekamah, Nebraska (#2,876,997).

An early variation in design was patented in 1923 (#1,529,460) by Ellis H. Bremer of Garden Grove, Iowa, who ran the twelve evenly spaced parallel I-beam bars of his grid with the road instead of across it. This type of guard, by the way, is still being used in parts of Mexico and Brazil. Bremer's bars were close enough together to keep car tires from slipping through; nevertheless, a grid built in this fashion is not as effective in stopping livestock as is the grid with bars placed crosswise to the road.

Perhaps the most original of all grid designs was patented in 1962 by James Sawyers and Otis Jeff Dorsey of Tuscarora, Nevada (#2,211,299). In what seems to be an offshoot of the rubber-strip cattle guard described in chapter 7, Sawyers and Dorsey designed a framework to which were attached some seven inflatable rubber bars. Apparently, this guard was designed to be used without a pit. Just how well it worked I have not been able to discover,

A cattle grid made of concrete blocks, Cornwall, England

A painted-stripe cattle guard near Rockville, Utah. (Courtesy of John M. White)

No-passing stripes on a cattle guard in Gillespie County, Texas. (Courtesy of Robert Clarke)

but I would think that, unless placed over smooth, soft dirt, traffic would soon wear holes in the rubber tubes where they were pressed down onto rocks or weeds.

Some cattle guards have been mechanized. I have been told about—but have not seen—a cattle guard than can best be described as working on the principle of a weighted drawbridge. Weights hanging from a rope and pulley lift the middle section of this guard, which sits directly on the ground rather than over a pit. When a car crosses, the weight of the automobile presses down the center section, and the car passes smoothly over the flat-strap bars. The weights hanging from the pulley then pull the center of the guard back into the air after the car has passed.

Another guard that I have not yet been able to see is a manufactured one that, according to one correspondent, "was on a sort of coil spring on one end and you drove onto it and as you passed the coil straightened it across the gap. I only saw one so it must not have been much of a success." Paul Kottman of Ellsworth, Kansas, would quarrel with that opinion, if the guard he installed on his ranch some fifteen years ago is of the same type, and his description suggests that it is. Kottman bought one after seeing a demonstration model at the Kansas State Fair. The grid was made of two-and-one-eighth-inch flat steel straps spaced about ten inches apart on one side, about four inches apart on the other. Support straps, running with the road, were spaced every two feet. According to Kottman, the wider spacing was for cattle, and the guard could be turned over if it were to be used for sheep. These straps were fastened onto a rectangular frame, on each side of which a heavy coil spring ran parallel to the ground. No pit was necessary, for by adjusting the springs, the height at the center of the guard could be kept anywhere from one to two feet above ground level, while both approaches to the guard remained on the surface of the ground. The weight of the vehicle being driven across the guard caused the springs to stretch and caused the entire guard to flatten out along the ground. Then the springs would pull the guard back into an arch after the vehicle had passed. Gravity held the guard in place, and if it ever "walked" a little out of line, said Kottman, it could easily be pulled back. Not only did the springs raise the slats so that a pit-like effect was created, but, should an animal attempt to cross, the entire structure would start to wiggle and shake as soon as it was touched, thus presenting a double deterrent. Kottman's guard was ten feet in length (if flattened out to about twelve feet) and he paid $160 for it. The guard also came in fourteen- and sixteen-foot sizes, according to Fred Vahshotz, the implement dealer who sold it to Kottman. The chief disadvantage occurred when there was snow on the ground, for unless the guard was cleared of snow before being driven over, the bars could be bent out of shape on the packed snow.

Neither Vahshotz nor Kottman can remember the name or the manufacturer of this cattle guard; however, it fits the description of the Portable Cattle Guard (U.S. patent #3,390,484) currently being made and marketed by the Cross Machinery and Manufacturing Company of Mindenmines, Missouri. In 1981 Duane Cross purchased the manufacturing rights to this cattle guard from Bill von Demfange of Kansas City, who had developed the device some twenty-five years earlier. Like von Demfange before him, Cross builds and markets cattle guards as a side venture. Hundreds of Portable Cattle Guards have been sold throughout the United States as well as in Saskatchewan and Alberta. Cross has even had an inquiry about his cattle guards from a rancher in Brazil.

The Portable Cattle Guard sounds very much like one invented in the 1920s by Pat McGraw of Ekalaka, Montana, though I have not been able to trace a connection between them. In the spring of 1929 McGraw asked his neighbor, Otis Wheat (who gave me the story), to go to Camp Crook, South Dakota, with him in order to sign some papers for a Canadian patent. The original model of the guard used two-by-six wooden slats for bars and had a coil spring under each end for raising the grid up in the middle. Tracks along the sides guided the slats as they flattened out when being driven over. Subsequently McGraw built a model out of strap steel (at a cost of $67), and a local banker offered to finance the manufacturing of the guards in exchange for a half interest. McGraw refused, saying that he, if anyone, should be the one to make money from the idea. Wheat did not know if McGraw had ever sold any of his cattle guards or if, indeed, McGraw had even received a patent. Wheat did, however, witness a thorough and severe testing of the original wooden-slatted demonstration model, which McGraw had set up at the Ekalaka fairgrounds for people to drive over. According to Wheat, one cowboy, who had been sipping too much bootleg whisky, came tearing down the road in a small truck, headed right toward the guard. McGraw frantically waved his arms, trying to slow the cowboy down. The truck hit the cattle guard at full speed, and McGraw was sure that his invention would be broken to bits and scattered over the fairgrounds; however, "it flattened out just as pretty as could be and raised right back up."

In the summer of 1980 I saw a variation of this type of cattle guard in a small town in eastern Wales. This guard, made of light metal bars, was sitting on a concrete driveway. Springs, housed on each side of the guard, allowed the grid to flatten out when a vehicle was driven over, then pulled the guard back up after the vehicle had passed. Apparently it did not work with complete effectiveness, for the farmer had placed a small pipe across the gateway to supplement the guard.

Some persons have built guards with loose bars so that the grid would make noise when driven over or stepped on. Inventors have adopted this idea and constructed noise-producing cattle guards. In 1958 Earl Luff of Lincoln,

Nebraska, for instance, patented a guard (#2,938,711) in which two bars of angle iron, pointed side up, were placed between the regular formed-steel bars. The under bar of angle iron was welded to the channel-iron frame, while the upper bar of angle iron was left free to slide along the channel iron and would thus make noise when hit either by tires or by hoofs.

In 1953 George Harford of Redmond, Oregon, had patented (#2,790,626) a rather elaborate cattle guard, apparently designed to be used without a pit, that had nine pairs of bars fastened by tension springs to the sides of the frame and to a middle support. Alarm bells, attached to the ends of the guard, were activated when a bar was pressed down, whether by a car or a cow.

The most elaborate noise-making cattle guard was patented in 1949 (#2,576,188) by Edward S. McPherson of Upton, Wyoming. In addition to having a standard bar grid, there was an approach ramp on each side of the grid, which was made of a wooden treadle attached by levers and rods to a wheel on the side of the guard. When an auto (or a cow) depressed the treadle, the levers would revolve the wheel and activate the noisemakers. McPherson added a decorative touch by attaching a mounted cowboy, cut out of flat metal, to a rod atop the wheel. Thus when the treadle went down, the rods would move, the wheel would rotate, and the cowboy would turn on his horse to the accompaniment of the noise made by the guard.

Several guards that required no pit have already been described. Another such guard, using seven flat metal straps attached by springs to the sides of a frame, was patented by Ted B. Manuel and John B. Rauch of Lewiston, Montana, in 1954 (#2,710,173). Six years earlier, John Warner of Tucson, Arizona, used nine depressible flat straps as bars. *Successful Farming* (October 1952, pp. 34–35, and March 1956, pp. 41–48) gives plans for building pitless (and portable) cattle guards, one of wooden slats and the other of pipe bars. Another portable, pitless cattle guard was patented in 1953 by Jerold Alsburg of Santa Fe, New Mexico (#2,800,304). This guard used ten metal slats, held to the sides of the frame with tension springs several inches above the ground.

In 1946 Orville Winkler of Fort Worth, Texas, received the only patent (#2,592,225) ever granted for a portable cattle guard that was meant to be used with a pit. (The grids of many standard cattle guards can easily be transferred from pit to pit. In that sense they are portable, although they are not specifically designed to be moved readily from one location to another.) This guard was built somewhat like a painter's scaffold set on eight tubular legs with a pipe grid for a platform.

Many cattle guards are built with folding metal wings that can be laid down to let stock through the ends, or with solid wooden wings that can be laid down over the grid so that stock can cross. In 1953, however, two resi-

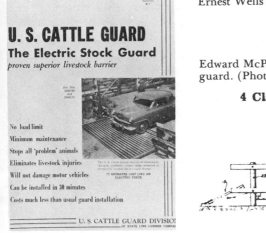

U. S. CATTLE GUARD
The Electric Stock Guard
proven superior livestock barrier

No load limit

Minimum maintenance

Stops all 'problem' animals

Eliminates livestock injuries

Will not damage motor vehicles

Can be installed in 30 minutes

Costs much less than usual guard installation

IT OPERATES JUST LIKE AN ELECTRIC FENCE

U. S. CATTLE GUARD DIVISION
OF STATE LINE LUMBER COMPAN

Ernest Wells's electric cattle guard

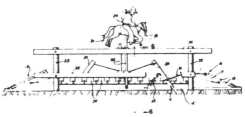

Edward McPherson's noise-making cattle guard. (Photo from *U.S. Patent Gazette*)

4 Claims.   (Cl. 256—14)

dents of Wyoming—Frank Melchert of Torrington and Edward MacClean of Cheyenne—patented (#2,774,728) a cattle guard that folded in half. It was designed to be used without a pit, and the nine flat, depressible straps were of light material. The frame was hinged at the middle, so that it could be raised to allow cattle to pass freely through the gateway thus formed. I do not know how commercially successful this guard was, but I would think that opening a gate at the side of the guard (and almost every cattle guard does have a gate in the fence line next to it) would be more convenient than lifting half of a guard, despite its lightweight construction.

Many cattle guards have been designed to double as bridges, with the grid serving as the bridge floor and the stream serving as the pit. A striking example of this type of guard can be seen on the Z Diamond Ranch road that crosses the White River near Meeker, Colorado. The bridge itself is one lane wide, approximately seventy-five feet long, and about fifteen feet above the water. About six feet of the flooring on the north edge has been removed, and a ten-bar cattle guard has been built onto the bridge stringers. Two sections of heavy wooden planking stand upright at the ends of the cattle guard; the bottom edge of each of these sections is hinged onto the side of the bridge. Although the flooring can be lowered so that livestock can be driven across, most of the time it is secured by chain in an open position. The sight and sound of the river rushing by below serves as an added disincentive for any cow that might be thinking about crossing the bridge to get to the highway beyond.

Our century has sometimes been called the Age of Electricity, so why not an electric cattle guard? In fact, at least four have been invented. In 1955 Floyd Hutchinson of Somonauk, Illinois, patented one (#2,769,617), and in

1979 Dick Pilbrow of Oxford, New Zealand, independently invented one that was remarkably similar to Hutchinson's. These guards look something like the framework of an old-fashioned metal bed. Hutchinson stretched nine wires across the frame of his guard; Pilbrow, eleven. Both guards can easily be driven across (they are pitless) with no vibration, and both can be connected to either a battery or a highline-powered fence charger. Livestock will always avoid this type of guard, if they are first familiarized with it. One danger is to children or to an animal that might get caught in the guard and not be able to escape. Although I do not know how well such a guard would work as a deterrent to varmints, it seems similar to the low-slung electric fences that some gardeners place around their sweet corn in order to keep raccoons at bay and to the rattlesnake killer that some ranchers use in the Southwest.

A safer and more elaborate electric cattle guard was built by Ernest R. Wells of Joseph, Oregon, who received two patents, in 1956 and 1957 (#2,846,194 and #2,899,174). This guard consisted of twenty current-carrying synthetic rubber strips mounted on a wooden frame. Wells invented the guard because some of his ore trucks had broken down the pipe guards on the road that led into his mining claim. After some experimentation, he was able to mass-produce the low-elasticity strips that he needed (to resist whipping when driven over), and he began to market his product as the U.S. Cattle Guard through fourteen dealers in the United States and Canada. The advantages of the guard — no pit, no maintenance, no safety problems for either cars or cows, no damage to automobiles, no need to slow down for crossing, one-third the cost of a regular guard, thirty-minute installation by one person, and effective on all animals (including dogs) — made it immediately popular. Unfortunately, Wells leased the manufacturing rights to a company that was interested in the device primarily as a tax write-off. Thus, when the electric cattle guard started making money, production was shut down, according to Wells, and none have been made since 1960.

The simplest electric cattle guard I know about is described in a promotional bulletin of the Smith Fencer Corporation of Pompano Beach, Florida. This company sells electric fence chargers, and one use for their product is a homemade cattle guard. If two separate sections of woven wire (or any other form of steel plate) are laid apart from each other on a concrete slab, one on either side of the fence line and extending nearly to the ends of the slab, and if they are then connected either to the electric fence or directly to the charger, they will form an effective cattle guard. A completely solar-powered electric cattle guard could be constructed by using this principle with the Solar-Pak Electric Fencer developed by the Parker-McCrory Manufacturing Company of Kansas City.

Many persons who might otherwise not have given cattle guards a second thought nevertheless have noticed the painted-stripe cattle guard. Dozens of respondents to my newspaper queries and questionnaires have mentioned them. Some were merely reporting that they had seen them; some were puzzled about how the guards work; some were resentful of what they perceived as a further encroachment of the artificial in our culture; but all were intrigued by them.

Although a few individuals have painted cattle-guard stripes on private roads, most painted-stripe guards are found on state or federal highways in the eleven states west of the central plains. A typical painted guard has around ten yellow or white stripes, each about four inches in width and spaced about six inches apart. A major advantage of this type of guard is economy of initial cost—perhaps one-twentieth of the expense of a pit-and-pole guard with a concrete foundation. Painted stripes do not turn stock quite as well as regular cattle guards; moreover, they must be repainted periodically. Thus a painted-stripe guard may eventually cost more than a well-constructed metal guard. Unlike the metal cattle guard, however, painted-stripe guards are completely smooth to drive over.

The following summary of the use of painted-stripe guards is based on information supplied by state highway officials in the western states. New Mexico has about three hundred, even though state officials concede that these guards do not work as well as metal ones. Although Arizona has only a few, its officials are satisfied with their effectiveness. Painted stripes were first used in Arizona around 1960. California uses the painted-stripe guard fairly extensively, and sometimes attempts to augment its effectiveness by adding an arrow-shaped triangular series of ten stripes in front of the stripes of the guard itself. These arrows point toward the open-range pasture into which the road runs, thus steering cattle away from the opening in the fence line. Washington uses some painted guards, primarily on county roads and private approach roads. Oregon painted its first guards in 1943. In the early 1970s, some forty guards were painted on highways in eastern Oregon. These guards consisted of eight bars that were six inches wide and spaced six inches apart. Oregon officials consider the painted guards to be quite effective, much less expensive than regular guards, and much more convenient for traffic. Idaho uses twelve stripes of four-inch width, which are repainted at least once every two years, one time with white paint and the next time with yellow paint. Officials believe that this change in color helps to make the guards more effective for range stock; otherwise cattle get used to them and cross them at will. Utah has used a ten-stripe guard for many years. Nevada has used painted stripes since the 1940s, with each grid having from twelve to twenty stripes four inches wide. In 1977, however, Nevada officials began to replace the fifty painted guards on their highways with regular ones because of dissatisfaction with the effectiveness of paint alone. Although Colorado has several striped guards in use, each made of eight painted bars of three-inch width, officials there do not consider them to be especially effective. Wyoming, like Washington, tends to use painted-stripe guards on county or Forest Service roads. Montana first used painted guards with the interstate highway system beginning in 1957, but did not find them satisfactory. Ten years later they were replaced by metal guards. Highway officials in Texas, Oklahoma, Kansas, Nebraska, South Dakota, and North Dakota told me that they had no painted-stripe guards on state or federal highways. I do not know how extensively painted stripes are used abroad (I have not heard of any in Canada or Mexico), though I did learn from a highway official in South Africa that his country painted its first highway cattle guard in the late 1970s.

Nor am I sure just when the painted-stripe cattle guard was first used, although both Oregon and Nevada were using them in the 1940s. Highway Department officials from New Mexico told me that the idea developed in Wyoming; however, no Wyoming official has been able to confirm that assertion. John A. Kennedy, who became New Mexico's traffic services engineer in 1931, does not remember having seen any painted guards there before the late 1940s, but he told me that the old Highway Department records that might have disclosed such information had been destroyed by his successor. Oregon's 1943 date has been challenged as the earliest only by Virgil Johnson of Crowell, Texas. Johnson took a trip with some friends in 1929, driving from Muleshoe, Texas, into New Mexico. He noticed (although whether in western Texas or eastern New Mexico he is not certain) that fences had been built right up to the road and that painted stripes were serving as cattle guards.

Painted stripes have the advantages of cheapness and smoothness, and those advantages are sometimes important enough to outweigh the major disadvantage: paint does not stop livestock as effectively as pipe does. That stripes work at all is probably attributable, not to the cow's stupidity, but to its visual system. Experts on animal behavior say that a cow's depth perception is such that it makes little or no distinction between painted stripes on a dark background and bars over a pit. I know from personal experience that cattle do not particularly like to walk on pavement, and many times when crossing a highway an especially skittish animal might have to be taken down the road past a yellow no-passing line before it can be forced across. Frank Smyth, public information officer for the Nevada Department of Highways, phrased the theory well: "No one seems to know *why* painted guards work, but we do know that range cattle are extremely suspicious of white stripes on a black background. There are cases on record of herded half-wild animals balking at the white center line on asphalt highways. The solution? Cover the stripe with sand, rope one steer and drag it across the highway. Then the others are prone to follow."

Painted-stripe cattle guards work less well with tamer stock than with wilder animals. (But then, what can keep roping steers or milk cows in?) Also,

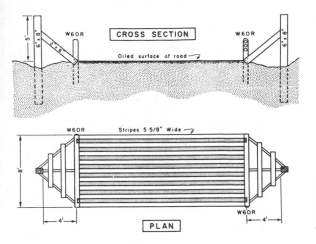

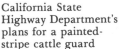

California State
Highway Department's
plans for a painted-
stripe cattle guard

according to highway engineers, painted guards do not work well in snow, rain, darkness, or when covered with gravel or sand. One respondent asked whether it was necessary to sweep gravel off a painted guard, and another wanted to know how a painted-stripe guard could work with cattle that had never been exposed to a real guard. The animal's lack of depth perception and its natural fear of poor footing are the answers. Another wanted to know how cattle that had learned to cross a painted guard would react to a real one. As far as I can tell, that is not a problem. One step onto a real guard, and the cow will pull back. I have also been told that some open-range roads in states like Wyoming have bright stripes (of orange or white) painted along both shoulders of the pavement in order to discourage animals from getting onto the highway where they would interfere with traffic.

C. G. Wood had some interesting experiences with painted-stripe cattle guards. Wood, who had a lengthy career with the Texas Highway Department, noted that sheep would seldom cross a regular pipe guard, but goats regularly do. In order to deter goats from passing from one pasture to another, Wood decided to try painting the pavement immediately in front of the cattle guard with three twenty-inch stripes—one yellow, one white, one yellow. These stripes worked excellently: "The goats would stop some thirty or more feet from the guard, then sometimes they detoured in a run. After clearing the structure by several yards, they would go back to the fence and continue walking along it."

Wood used a variation of this technique to save the lives of deer in Kerr County. Many ranchers had built high deer-proof fences along their property, so that when a deer got into the road between two of these fences, it was trapped. Especially at night, the deer would often run in front of a car, get killed, and cause extensive damage to the car. Wood got ranchers to cooperate in building a deer-proof wing fence from the existing border fence to a point about four feet from the edge of the pavement. The highway department would then pave the few feet from the highway's verge to the corner post, so that four stripes of yellow and three of white paint could be brushed on the asphalt. This ploy worked as well with deer as it had with the goats. During a two-year period only one deer got into the tunnel between the fences.

Wood related another anecdote that graphically illustrates just why and how the painted-stripe cattle guard works. Just as one deer guard was being finished, a rancher arrived, riding a saddle horse. He intended to go down the highway, but the horse refused to cross the freshly painted stripes. When the rider spurred him, the horse reared and shied away from the entire area. When the rancher applied both quirt and spurs, the horse leaped across the entire set of stripes, some seven feet of them, and ran away down the highway, with the rider frantically working to bring it under control.

Undoubtedly, future years will see as many unusual variations in the design and construction of cattle guards as past years have, if only because both human and bovine nature will continue to work at cross purposes where gates and fences are concerned.

9
MAKERS
OF CATTLE GUARDS

Although not so varied as the users of cattle guards, makers of cattle guards constitute a diverse lot. Traditionally, many farmers and ranchers have built their own cattle guards out of whatever materials were available to them — wooden poles, dimension lumber, boiler flues, old pipe — and that tradition is still operative. Nowadays, however, even homemade guards have a more uniform appearance than formerly, partly because many of them are built according to plans issued by the United States Department of Agriculture, by state extension services, or by farm magazines and partly because most of the rest have been modeled on cattle guards that the builder has seen. Some cattle guards installed in farm and ranch driveways have resulted from a project in a 4-H Club, the Future Farmers of America, or a vocational-technical school. Many cattle guards, however, are products either of local blacksmith shops and welders or of commercial production. Some typical and some unusual examples from each of these two major areas of production will be examined.

This is not a complete list of companies that manufacture cattle guards commercially, but three organizations — the Farm Equipment Manufacturers Association, the Farm and Industrial Equipment Institute, and Implement and Tractor — have helped me come up with the names of over fifteen companies that either make or have made cattle guards. I have communicated with ten of these manufacturers: Christianson Pipe Ltd., Calgary, Alberta; Clark Materials Company, Lexington, Kentucky; Goshute Enterprises, Salt Lake

City, Utah; Lincoln Steel, Lincoln, Nebraska; Northland Steel, Billings, Montana; Powder River Enterprises, Provo, Utah; Smith Cattleguard Company, Midland, Virginia; J & W Manufacturing Company, Virgil, Kansas; Wedco Manufacturing Company, Jackson, Wyoming; and Wikco Industries, Inc., Broken Bow, Nebraska. Undoubtedly many other companies manufacture cattle guards commercially.

Most manufactured cattle guards use form-welded steel, rather than pipe, as bar material, mainly for economic reasons but also because it is smoother to drive over. A typical example of this type of guard is manufactured by Goshute Enterprises of Salt Lake City. In 1969 this firm began to produce cattle guards for two reasons: to meet a rising demand for cattle guards, and to help elevate the living standards of the Goshute Nation. The entire operation is managed by Goshute Indians, and all employees are tribesmen. In addition to many other products, this firm makes twenty models of cattle guards, some of which are currently in place at the LBJ National Historic Site, Johnson City, Texas. These guards are divided into five categories, depending on their load-bearing capabilities. Grid sizes range from six feet three inches by eight feet to eight feet by fourteen feet. The lightest guard weighs 685 pounds, and the heaviest weighs 2,455 pounds. The number of bars per grid in Goshute Guards ranges from nine to twelve. As of spring 1980, Goshute's best-selling model was of medium weight, with twelve bars, measuring eight by twelve feet, and weighing 1,868 pounds, and it cost $1,178 plus freight (from $100 to $700 per load) and an extra charge of $50 for delivery on a dirt road. When Goshute first started making cattle guards in 1969, its least expensive model sold for $440. Eleven years later, inflation had boosted prices to $534 for the lightest model to $1,650 for the heaviest. Add delivery and installation expenses, and it is easy to see that a cattle guard placed on a concrete foundation over a wide road (where several units would have to be bolted together) could soon run into a five-figure item.

Northland Steel's Flying L Autogates, made in Billings, Montana, all have eleven-bar grids that are seven feet nine inches wide. They come in a choice of eight-, ten-, twelve-, and fourteen-foot lengths. Weights range from 760 to 2,140 pounds per unit. These cattle guards are made in four classes, designed to handle single-axle weights ranging from four to sixteen tons. The grid unit of these guards includes I-beam stringers and plate-steel walls, but wings cost extra.

Powder River Enterprises of Provo, Utah, is one of the country's largest manufacturers of livestock-related equipment: squeeze chutes, portable pens, loading ramps, creep feeders, livestock oilers — and cattle guards. The first Powder River Cattle Guard was built in 1949 and sold for $37. As of 1980, Powder River's smallest guard sold for $430. This jump in price is a bit misleading, however, because today's buyer gets quite a bit more for his money than did Baker County, Oregon, Powder River's first customer. The 1949 guards were nothing more than a grid of angle-iron bars welded to a few straps of flat iron. The customer had to furnish the pit and base, stringers, and wings. Powder River's formed-steel bar cattle guards now come in several different sizes (from six feet three inches by eight feet to eight feet by fourteen feet) and several different weights (from 636 to 2,796 pounds). Wings and end posts are sold separately, and the guard unit itself is composed of a grid of from eleven to fourteen bars electrically welded onto an understructure of heavy channel-iron stringers. These cattle guards are made on an assembly line that requires four workers. The most unusual custom order for a Powder River Guard came from Asotin County, Washington, where road engineers needed a cattle guard that would double as a bridge. So the entire surface of the bridge was nothing other than a seventy-bar grid, forty feet long (with the road) and sixteen feet wide.

One advantage of the formed-steel bar cattle guard is that it can be made with a detachable "clean out"—a unit of five or six bars that folds up (or can be removed entirely) so that a man with a shovel or backhoe can easily remove the accumulated dirt and debris from the pit. Another advantage is its smoothness. Bars are usually rounded on the edges and flat on top, so that tires are not damaged, and crossing is usually no rougher than driving on a gravel road. A major disadvantage is that in order to strengthen the bars, they are made narrower at the top than at the bottom. Thus, an animal that does get one of its hooves caught experiences a traplike effect: the foot slides in easily, but cannot be pulled out.

Every type of pit-and-pole cattle guard is potentially hazardous to livestock. One of the most piteous cattle-guard accidents happened to a mare that got all four of her legs caught in a formed-steel bar guard on a national-forest road in Oregon. Tom Rice of Medford was hunting elk in 1979 when he and his companions found the mare struggling to get out, tearing her legs with every effort. They notified the rancher who owned her, and together they spent two and one-half hours with cutting torches and winches working to get her free. They had to pour water on the mare's legs in order to keep them from being burned by the cutting torches. But these efforts of four men and two women were wasted; after the mare had been extracted, they discovered that she had broken her shoulder and had to be destroyed. The frustration felt by Rice and his companions was compounded by their pity for the mare's four-month-old colt, which had neighed frantically during most of the rescue effort. Rice finished his account with a blast at what he assumed was the ultimate cause of the accident: "I do believe if the unthinking bureaucrat that designed these guards had been there at the time there would have been two bodies pulled out of there that night."

Rice's anger is understandable, but misplaced. This type of cattle guard was not designed by a bureaucrat, and livestock can get caught and hurt in almost any kind of cattle guard. Some persons, for instance, think that cattle guards made of railroad rails are safer for livestock than those made of pipe; whereas others consider rails to be extremely dangerous to animals because of their rounded tops. The Wedco Manufacturing Company, which makes many different agricultural products, has since 1960 turned out over five hundred cattle guards. These cattle guards are designed with the horse's safety in mind, for the ten bars on its grid are made of square tubing, spaced six inches apart, so that a horse can pull its foot out should it happen to step in. In addition, the square tubes, which are smoother than pipe to drive over, have no sharp edges nor do they form the hoof trap that can result from trapezoidal bars.

One of the most successful commercial producers of cattle guards in Canada is Christianson Pipe Ltd. of Calgary. According to its president, Lee Christianson, his company got into the cattle-guard business about 1970 by happenstance. They had some pipe on hand for which there was no immediate market, so they began to make some cattle guards. The earlier ones were not too strong, because of the limited contact area where a weld could be applied, but once he hit upon the idea of a gusset running between bars down each stringer, they were able to produce a guard that could stand up under the heaviest use. Christianson sent me a photograph of a cattle guard that had been installed five years earlier on a logging road in British Columbia; it showed no signs of wear. The gusset was an original idea with Christianson, so he looked into the possibility of a patent. The result was three different patents: one each in Canada, Australia, and the United States (#3,790,135, filed in 1972). All makers of cattle guards are proud of their product. Christianson is no exception; he thinks his is the finest on the market. It does have an excellent design and construction. The heavy pipe bars, solidly supported on pipe or channel-iron stringers and kept firmly in place by the gussets, are probably less tempting for an animal to try to cross than are flat-topped bars. Should an animal attempt to cross, however, the five and three-quarter inch spacing allows it to pull its foot out without injury. The entire guard—grid, stringers, and base (made of ten-and-three-quarter-inch tubing and steel side panels)—is of a single-unit weld construction that allows for easy installation and is nearly impervious to wear. Christianson Cattle Guards have been installed all over western Canada on ranch roads, mining roads, logging roads, and oil leases, and some have been sold in New Zealand and Australia as well.

A more unusual but quite successful commercial cattle guard, made of concrete, comes from the Smith Cattleguard Company. In 1960 David Smith and his son Rodney established the home office at Midland, Virginia, which franchises the manufacturing of the guards to licensees in nine states and Canada. Since its founding, more than fifteen thousand Smith Cattleguards

A Christianson Pipe
Ltd. cattle guard on a
forest road in Alberta,
Canada. (Courtesy of
Lee Christianson)

A concrete cattle guard
made by Smith Cattle-
guard Company, Mid-
land, Virginia. (Cour-
tesy of Tere Rill, Smith
Cattleguard Company)

A model of Ernest
Wells's electric cattle
guard in front of an in-
stalled guard. (Courtesy
of Ernest Wells)

(the name is copyrighted, although the guard itself is not patented) have been sold in over thirty states, and inquiries about the guard have come from as far away as India.

The Smith Cattleguard is made of steel-reinforced (each guard contains at least 350 feet of one-half-inch steel bar) precast concrete and comes in twelve-, fourteen-, and sixteen-foot lengths. All models are six and one-half feet wide and twelve inches deep with ten rounded-top bars that are three inches wide with five inch spacing between bars. The smallest guard weighs 6,000 pounds and the largest 7,200 pounds. In 1960 the Smith Company sold guards for $145 each; twenty years later the largest model cost $375 plus freight. One advantage of a concrete cattle guard is that it requires no pit. A six-inch-deep hole, one foot longer and one foot wider than the guard, is dug, and a two-inch layer of sand or gravel is put down for drainage and leveling. Then the unit is put into place. Wings usually take the form of a wooden fence panel along each end of the guard, and the road must be graded up six inches to the top of the guard. Apparently the Smith Cattleguard not only turns cattle as well as any other guard but also has a further advantage: it never wears out or breaks down. In fact, it is the only cattle guard I know of that is guaranteed to last longer than the farmer or rancher who buys it.

The original design of the Smith Cattleguard had two flat-topped cross bars running with the road to give stability to the grid bars. In the latest styles, the tops of these cross bars have been rounded so that they will not offer solid footing to any kind of livestock. A chain of convenience stores in North Carolina has put cattle guards to perhaps their most unusual use. In order to discourage persons from wheeling shopping carts home, the stores have installed thirty Smith Cattleguards at the entrances to their parking lots.

Since 1969 the Clark Materials Company of Lexington, Kentucky, has manufactured and sold a concrete cattle guard roughly comparable to the Smith Cattleguard. Clark has placed cattle guards in Kentucky, Ohio, Tennessee, Indiana, Virginia, and West Virginia. In addition, Clark makes what it calls a Blue Grass Estate Gate, which is operated by pulling a chain at the end of one of two long arms, just like the gates used on farms and rural roads in the late nineteenth century. These gates, according to Ralph Clark, are quite popular on thoroughbred-horse farms where owners do not want to chance having a race horse worth many thousands of dollars hurt itself on a regular guard or on a wire gate.

Occasionally, while driving through small rural towns from Montana to Texas, I have seen newly made cattle guards sitting outside blacksmith shops. This sight, common throughout livestock and oil-lease regions, illustrates the vitality of what might be termed the folk manufacture of cattle guards. Local blacksmiths, along with welders with portable rigs, are probably responsible for building the majority of all cattle guards.

162

Warren Godfrey putting the finishing touches on one of his cattle guards

A Godfrey cattle guard in use, Coffey County, Kansas

Thousands of these craftsmen have built cattle guards, laboring anonymously to make rural driving easier. One of these men was Lewis Newkirk, who ran the road maintainer for Sycamore Township where I was raised. Around 1960 Newkirk, who was also a mechanic and welder, created a few improved grids to replace some older, worn out ones in eastern Butler County, Kansas. Another such craftsman is W. R. Grantham, who has made scores of cattle guards in his welding shop in Marietta, Oklahoma. In the past few years, Dan Cookson has made more than 250 cattle guards for the oil fields near his home in Madison, Kansas. Mick Sage of Virgil, Kansas, is typical of many who have made cattle guards. Although he is not a cattle-guard maker by profession, he has on occasion used his welding abilities to make cattle guards both for himself and for others. One interesting variation that he was worked into some of his guards is to place the two central bars in the grid against each other for added strength. Since 1937 Frank Parsons of Susank, Kansas, has built hundreds of cattle guards in the oil fields of central Kansas for such companies as Phillips, Shell, Sunray, Skelly, and Exxon.

The most prolific producer of cattle guards I have met or heard of is Warren Godfrey of Madison, Kansas. Godfrey's reputation preceded him. Several months before I met him, I had been told about a welder in Madison who had made many cattle guards over the years. Also, when I had asked about some particularly well made cattle guards in the Flint Hills southwest of Emporia, I had been told that they had been made by Godfrey. Godfrey is a jack of all trades—farmer, pilot, hunter, implement dealer, welder. He learned welding in trade school, and when the drouth of the 1950s forced him temporarily off the farm, he began to put this skill to work. In 1956 he made his first cattle guards for various oil leases near Madison. Since then he has built hundreds of cattle guards—perhaps more than fifteen hundred.

His speciality is a portable cattle-guard deck (i.e., the grid and its underpinning, welded into a single unit) with attached triangular wings that fold inward for shipping. He first devised this design in the early 1960s for Paul Klingdon, who had come up to the Hedley Lease near Gridley as a project supervisor of a well flooding for Pure Oil Company (now Union). The company wanted a cattle guard that was transportable so that pits could be predug, with or without concrete walls. Godfrey came up with a unit that fit nicely inside a truck bed (seven and one-half feet wide); he made it in two lengths, sixteen or twenty feet. For bars he used two-and-seven-eighths-inch tubing (outside diameter) spaced seven inches from center to center (or slightly more than four inches between bars). He continues to prefer this size, he says, because, although it is not quite as strong as larger pipe, it is smoother to drive across, lighter to ship, and easier to obtain in his area. Godfrey also puts from two to four top straps of rod on each grid. These top straps give dual stability; they help to hold the pipe grid bars in place, and in wet weather they help to keep car tires from sliding off the grid, particularly if a driver hits the grid at an angle. One particular Godfrey Cattle Guard, a thirty-foot long, two-unit piece in the Flint Hills, has held loads of over fifty tons with no problems.

Although Godfrey has made many cattle guards for many different oil companies (his welding services are or have been on retainer to almost every petroleum concern operating in the southeastern section of Kansas), his biggest single customer has been the road department in Walden, Colorado. In fact, the country near Walden is full of his cattle guards. All this started in 1963, when he was deer hunting in that area. He was told by a local resident that the wooden-plank cattle guards around there were being replaced, but that the railroad-rail replacements were not working out very satisfactorily— some horses had tried walking them and had slipped off and been caught. When Godfrey found out that an eight-foot-wide rail cattle guard cost $800, he knew that he could build one for much less. He left for home with a contract to send out a truck load of seven-and-one-half-by-twenty-foot cattle guards. Within a few weeks he put ten guards on a semitrailer, which delivered the first of scores of Godfrey's cattle guards that have since been installed on Colorado roads. These first guards cost only $225 per unit plus freight. Godfrey was making money, and the Highway Department was saving over $500 per guard, even with freight expenses added in. By late 1979 the cost of cattle guards, like everything else, had risen. The last shipment of cattle guards that Godfrey sent to Colorado cost $1,500 per unit, an increase of 666 percent. Pipe that cost twelve cents per foot (for two and seven-eighths inch) and thirty-five cents per foot (for seven inch) in 1962, however, had increased in 1979 to seventy-five cents and four dollars per foot.

Godfrey has also sold his cattle guards to road departments in Texas, Oklahoma, and Kansas and to oil producers in several states. Although at one time he supplied a fence dealer, Ray Nichols of Fort Collins, Colorado, with seven-by-twelve-foot guards for ranch use, he no longer has time to custom make such guards. Godfrey has never attempted to go commercial with his cattle guards, in spite of many opportunities to do so. Sometimes he gets requests for cattle guards from people who have seen one of his guards and have gone to the trouble to make half a dozen or more phone calls in order to track down the builder. The Lone Pine Oil Company of Texas, for example, ordered some guards from him because some of its employees in Colorado had noticed a Godfrey guard on the roads there.

Godfrey has even been approached by an official from Washington State who asked him to bid on an order of several thousand cattle guards for national forests in eight of the western states. Godfrey submitted a design and a bid to make only a limited number of these cattle guards. Within a few weeks he had received a call from federal officials in Washington, D.C. His design, he was told, was superior to all others under consideration, and they wanted him to build all the cattle guards for the project. His response was to withdraw entirely from the bidding. I asked him why, and his answer was that in order to fulfill the contract, he would have had to become nothing else but a cattle-guard manufacturer. He would have had to end or neglect his other interests, and he would have had to hire a couple of dozen employees. That would have meant too much loss of freedom, too much specialization, too many federal regulations, and a possible financial squeeze if he could not locate enough pipe to build the guards at the bid price. Besides all that, when the job had been completed, he would have been trapped into trying to get more orders for cattle guards because he would have lost a large measure of flexibility.

Probably Godfrey's most interesting job was in supplying railroad cattle guards for the Wolf Creek spur, mentioned in chapter 5. In addition to the monetary factor, Godfrey had the satisfaction of creating an inexpensive cattle guard that worked — as opposed to the expensive flop that had been designed by engineers working for one of the world's largest construction companies.

Godfrey told a few anecdotes involving cattle guards. There is an extremely narrow cattle guard going into the Tom Edwards Ranch just west of Burkett in Greenwood County, Kansas, a guard barely wide enough to drive a pickup truck through. When I mentioned this particular cattle guard to Godfrey, he chuckled and said that he had built it and that it was wider now than when it had originally been installed. He had built it to order around 1960 for an official of the Glacier Oil Company, who wanted a lightweight cattle guard wide enough to drive his car through but not big enough for trucks — he was tired of beat-up, bent-down cattle guards at this particular location. The official handed to Godfrey and his assistant a sheet of paper with the dimensions written on it. When Godfrey's helper tried to point out the extreme narrowness of the guard, the official was too indignant to be corrected. So, they built the guard and set it up, but kept the original set of instructions. A couple of days later the irate oilman drove into Godfrey's place with a scraped fender, and Godfrey simply pulled out the spec sheet and offered, for a price, to add on an eighteen-inch extension. The welds of that extension are clearly visible today.

Another anecdote involved a rush order that Godfrey had gotten from Ray Nichols in Fort Collins. A rancher there needed a seven-and-one-half-by-twelve-foot cattle guard, and he needed it right away. Godfrey did not have a full load (sixteen units) ready to go to Colorado, so he contracted to deliver the single cattle guard himself. He winched the grid onto the back of his portable welding rig, chained it down, and he and his wife set out. In eastern Colorado, he was driving at the 70-mph speed limit (this was in 1971) when he was pulled over by a young state trooper, who apparently was not sure just what Godfrey was hauling. As Godfrey recounts it, the conversation went something like this:

TROOPER: What is that thing? A drag?
GODFREY: (I wanted to say, "Yeah, let's drag, man," but I didn't.) It's a cattle guard. (Then he really opened himself up.)
TROOPER: What's it doing there?
GODFREY: (I wanted to say, "Keeping cattle off — you don't see any, do you?" But I didn't.) I'm delivering it to Fort Collins.
TROOPER: Well, your license plate is obscured.
GODFREY: I've got a little farmer's friend. If you'll let me, I'll fix it.
TROOPER: You've got some what?
GODFREY: Baling wire.
TROOPER: No, go on. And if anyone else stops you, tell them I already have talked with you.
GODFREY: Okay. Now what's your name and number? (I started reading his name tag and taking down his license tag number. I tell you he got in his car in a hurry, cut a big U-turn, and headed out. I guess cattle guards not only are cow proof, but they can scare off some highway patrolmen, too.)

Godfrey's latest cattle-guard project is a contract with the Union Pacific Railroad Company to supply nearly a hundred highway cattle guards for some right-of-way fencing in northern Colorado and southern Wyoming. The tracks run through open range, but because coal trains are using them more, there is increasing danger to livestock, so the right of way is being fenced, and guards are needed at the crossings.

Surely hundreds of thousands of cattle guards have been made and then installed on roads and in gateways all over the world in the last seventy-five years. Although individual farmers and ranchers have been responsible for thousands of these and commercial manufacturers have produced many more thousands, local craftsmen — blacksmiths and welders like Warren Godfrey — have built the majority of the world's cattle guards.

10
THE ECONOMICS
OF CATTLE GUARDS

In earlier chapters I have pointed out the role that convenience played in the invention and spread of the cattle guard, often called the lazy man's gate. Often, especially in earlier years, a cattle guard was considered a sign of affluence, of a prosperous and progressive rancher. At a certain point, however, the cattle guard becomes no longer a luxury; the desire for ease and convenience is supplanted by hard-nosed practicality—a cattle guard saves (i.e., makes) money. In terms of the gross national product, the economic impact of the cattle guard is minuscule; but in terms of something like the "gross national agricultural, forestry, and mineral product," its impact increases greatly. I will not attempt to present a detailed analysis of the effects of the cattle guard on the economy but will focus attention on some of the major economic aspects of the cattle guard.

Cattle guards are used primarily in three settings—on public roads in open-range country (including forested areas), on private farms and ranches, and on oil and other mineral leases. In each of these areas, cattle guards play an important economic role. In each area the main economic feature of the cattle guard coincides with its convenience feature: it eliminates the need (and thus the time required) for opening and closing a gate. Consider, for instance, the alternatives to cattle guards on open-range roads, whether township roads in the Kansas Flint Hills, interstate highways in Wyoming, or National Forest Service roads in Idaho. If there were no cattle guards, (1) all roads would have to be fenced along both sides of the right of way, (2) gates would have to be used where a cattle guard is now placed, or (3) domestic animals would have to be kept out of pasture land through which these roads pass.

The last-mentioned possibility is absurd; were it to occur, the results would be devastating. The livestock market, for the short term, would be immediately depressed, while the long-range effect of such a massive reduction in herd size would ultimately mean much higher consumer prices.

The fencing of all right of ways is a much more reasonable solution. In fact, more and more roadways, both highway and railroad, are being fenced each year. This fencing process, however, is gradual. If all open-range roads suddenly had to be fenced, the cost of wire and of labor would create a very real hardship on ranchers and on taxpayers (much open range is on public lands). Aesthetically, the pleasures of driving through unfenced pastures are incalculable. Driving in open grassland gives one a feeling of openness, of the revitalization, even if momentary, of the frontier. Whether in the Gypsum Hills of Kansas, the Sandhills of Nebraska, the deserts of Arizona and Nevada, or the Missouri River country of the northern plains, open-range roads are a part of our heritage that should be preserved.

The other possibility—namely, gates— is the most impractical solution of all. If public roads had gates, think of the gasoline and time that would be wasted in slowing to a stop and building up speed after each gate was opened and closed, especially by freight haulers. Moreover, the expense of hiring gate openers—or fence-gap watchers—would be prohibitive. Thus, the traffic flow on open-range roads and the cash flow of open-range country are both maintained and facilitated by cattleguards.

How economical is it, however, for a small farmer or rancher to spend a thousand dollars or more to install a cattle guard on his own private road? This question has been answered forcefully by Ralph Ricketts, emeritus professor of agricultural engineering at the University of Missouri-Columbia, one of whose professional duties was farmstead planning. Professor Ricketts used to meet with farm families and help them to design the arrangement of their outbuildings, feed lots, fences, and so forth. One of his repeated contentions was that every farmstead needed at least one cattle guard to replace the gate the family used most often with its cars, pickups, and tractors. He maintained that such a cattle guard would save one week's labor per year in time spent opening and closing that gate. Ricketts once was loudly challenged on this claim, so he suggested that for one week the doubter keep track of the time he spent on one particular gate. A few weeks later the protesting farmer sent a letter saying that Ricketts was completely wrong. The farmer had counted the times he had gone through a busy gate, multiplied this number by the number of minutes it usually took to handle that gate, and determined that a cattle guard at that particular spot would save two weeks' work time in a year.

Whether that time is one's own or that of a hired hand, two weeks per year is significant to any farmer or rancher. Ricketts's conclusions are reinforced by the following anecdote told by George L. Smith, editor of *Kansas Farmer:* "About 25 years ago, when I was running cattle in Chautauqua County, I had to go through a gate at least once a day. I figured how long it took to stop the tractor or pickup, get out, open the gate, drive through, get out, close the gate, and get back into the pickup. I timed myself and as best as I can recall, it required eight, 8-hour days a year. I put in a cattle guard."

Another aspect of the economics of cattle guards is reflected in their manufacture. More than a dozen agricultural manufacturing firms make thousands of cattle guards annually, in addition to the hundreds of welders and blacksmiths throughout the country who make thousands more each year. The labor and materials involved in cattle-guard manufacturing, along with the transportation and labor involved in installing them, represent a sizable sum.

Still another economic factor concerning cattle guards deals with their role in preventing accidents. Gates are sometimes left open so that livestock get onto busy roads, resulting in accidents that cause damage to motorists, vehicles, and animals alike. Cattle guards help to prevent this type of accident and the concomitant legal actions. These legal actions were especially troublesome to railroad companies during the nineteenth century; in the twentieth century the petroleum companies have incurred some of that same trouble. The prevention of lawsuits, however, is only one part of the diversified role that cattle guards play in the production of oil.

Wages in the oil fields have always been good, so the time spent in opening and closing gates on leases translates into higher operating expenses very quickly. In fact, while no particular oil explorer or producer appears actually to have invented the cattle guard, the industry was very quick to adopt it. As early as 1912 the oil fields between Independence, Kansas, and Copan, Oklahoma, were using cattle guards. Oil producers, too, helped to spread the use of cattle guards; many rural areas got their first cattle guards in the 1920s, or even in the 1930s and 1940s, only when oil exploration and production came into the region. One advantage of the early cattle guards used by the petroleum industry was that they were usually made of used pipe or tubing rather than of wood. Thus, they were much stronger (and usually more effective) than were the wooden poles or boards used in many early cattle guards on ranches. Today many lease agreements specify the responsibility of the oil company to place cattle guards in the gateways of property containing producing oil wells, which probably explains why occasionally an unfenced wheat field will have cattle guards on the oil-well service roads running into it.

Perhaps the economic importance of cattle guards to the petroleum industry can be epitomized most effectively by taking a close look at the Burbank Oil Field near Shidler, Oklahoma. In the summer of 1978 I visited Burbank and was given a tour by Floyd D. Culver, a long-time employee of Phillips Petroleum. Culver had first drawn my attention to Burbank in a letter in which he claimed that it probably contained the heaviest concentration of cattle guards in the world.

Scholars are skeptical by nature, but I came away from Shidler convinced that indeed the thirty-six-section North Burbank Unit may well have had more cattle guards per square mile than any other area of the same size. Culver had estimated that the North Unit contained at least 400 guards. I counted twelve cattle guards per square mile on the sections we drove around and through, and if that number represents an accurate average, then there would be about 438 cattle guards in the North Unit alone, which constitutes just over half of the total field. W. F. Root, manager of Special Projects Engineering for Phillips, told me that at 1980 prices, the replacement cost for each cattle guard now in use would be $3,500, including labor — a total of over $1.5 million for the North Unit alone. A former vice-president of Phillips, now retired, L. E. Fitzjarrald of Bartlesville, estimated that each opening and closing of a gate would take five to ten minutes, and wasted gasoline would be extra. Given the fact that many employees must pass in and out of dozens of gates a day, the cattle guard means a savings of hundreds of thousands of dollars in operating costs to Phillips in all its operations. In addition, the aforementioned possibility of legal actions for damages is lessened by cattle guards; if a Phillips employee should fail to shut a gate and thus let cattle get onto the road, both motorists and livestock owners might sue the company.

How does the above example compare to usage on other oil leases? Some other leases, such as Amoco's Salt Creek Field at Midwest, Wyoming, are as saturated with cattle guards as is Burbank, while some leases have no cattle guards whatsoever. Fitzjarrald, however, estimates conservatively that at least 75 percent of the producing leases in this country have cattle guards. The American Petroleum Institute was not able to report the total number of oil leases in the United States; however, Phillips alone operates more than forty-four hundred domestic leases, including those in Alaska.

Thus, the economic impact of the cattle guard has two edges. In terms of capital outlay and installation expense, cattle guards have cost (and continue to cost) the petroleum industry, highway departments, and private owners millions of dollars. In terms of savings in labor and operational expenses, savings in livestock protected from damage and destruction, and savings in the prevention of lawsuits, however, cattle guards are an indispensable investment — a dividend rather than a liability.

11
CATTLE GUARDS
AROUND THE WORLD

The automotive cattle guard first appeared on the Great Plains about 1905; today it is found in livestock country around the world. Although I have not been able to make a definitive survey of cattle guards worldwide, I have tried to determine whether or not cattle guards are found in the major stock-raising regions of the world. In addition to traveling, I have talked to students from other countries; I have talked to people who have traveled abroad and who might reasonably have been expected to notice cattle guards; and I have contacted the appropriate personnel in the embassies of the major agricultural nations. As a result, I have learned that cattle guards are especially common in English-speaking countries or in countries that formerly were British colonies—England, Scotland, Wales, Ireland, Australia, New Zealand, South Africa, Canada, and Zimbabwe—and that they are also used in Mexico, Brazil, Venezuela, Argentina, Spain, France, Norway, West Germany, and Switzerland. Probably they are also used in countries such as Paraguay, Uruguay, Portugal, and Pakistan. Railroad cattle guards were being used in parts of India at the turn of the century, and a few years ago the Smith Cattleguard Company of Midland, Virginia, which sells franchises for the manufacture of a precast concrete cattle guard, received an inquiry from S. R. Borawake of Kopargaon, India.

Even my limited survey of the use of cattle guards in Britain suggests that a complete history of the British cattle guard would be very interesting. Cattle grids, as they are called by the English, take many unusual forms in addition to the standard pipe-bar grid. For instance, on a road in Exmoor some years ago, there was a cattle guard that had been made by setting a number of drainage tiles on end in a bed of concrete. This design and the unusual material may have been dictated by the exigencies of World War II, according to Richard Jemmett of Saffron Walden, Essex, who sent me a photograph he had taken of this guard. Jemmett thinks that this particular guard has now been replaced because of the inconvenience of cleaning the dirt and debris from the tiles.

The English tend to build unusual concrete cattle guards. During the summer of 1980, I saw numerous cattle guards all over Britain, including several made of various types of concrete building blocks set on end. I did not see, nor have I heard of, any painted-stripe cattle guards in any part of Great Britain. Cattle guards are used extensively at the entrances of stately homes and formal gardens in England, particularly those under the care of the National Trust. In Cornwall alone, cattle guards exist at such places as Lanhydrock (a Victorian manor house), Trerice (an Elizabethan manor house), and Trelissick (a landscape garden), all National Trust properties open to public view. Officials of the National Trust were not able to tell me how many cattle guards there are on properties under its control. They either lacked or did not have reasonable access to such data. In any case, all over the island, National Trust properties are well supplied with cattle guards. One of the more interesting is a seventeen-bar grid at the entrance to Charlcote Park in Warwickshire, the ancestral home of Sir Thomas Lucy. This unusually wide grid is used to keep within the park the deer, which are descendants of those allegedly poached by Shakespeare before he left Stratford-on-Avon for London. Private estates, as well as ones under the National Trust, use cattle guards extensively. An English estate was the setting for the movie *The Big Sleep,* based on a Raymond Chandler mystery and starring Robert Mitchum. Attentive watchers can observe Mitchum crossing at least one cattle guard as he drives to his client's mansion in the opening scene of the film.

Cattle guards can also be found on ordinary farms all over England, Scotland, and Wales. For example, Mr. and Mrs. Gerry Symons of Shillingford, St. George, just outside of Exeter, bought their farm at the end of World War II. They have always been progressive and innovative in their farming methods, having installed one of the first milking parlors in their section of England, for instance. Soon after buying the farm, they also installed a cattle guard which, Mrs. Symons says, has been one of their best investments. This farm is only a few miles from Dartmoor, a large open pasture area inhabited by sheep and wild ponies. The ponies are very clever, according to Symons, for they will lie down on one side of a cattle guard and roll over, then come up on the other side in order to get into a different pasture. When we crossed Dartmoor on our way to Cornwall, we saw many ponies and several

A cattle grid at the entrance to Charlcote Park, Warwickshire, England. (Courtesy of Harold Aston)

A cattle grid on Great Hewas Farm, owned by Mr. and Mrs. Frank Dymond, Grampound Road, Cornwall, England

A Combermere Ladder near Overton-on-Dee, Clwyd, Wales

cattle guards but, unfortunately, no ponies in the process of rolling across them. Some British sheep have learned to cross wingless cattle guards by lying on their sides and pushing with their feet on the fence at the side of the grid, according to B. Gallagher of the British Railways Board.

Before meeting with Symons, I had visited John V. Berryman, who operates a dairy farm on several hundred acres just outside Datchet, which is close to Windsor, which, in turn, is near London. Here, in one of the most heavily populated areas of England and one of the most cosmopolitan regions of the world, are several cattle guards on a road that runs through some small pastures where cattle and sheep roam freely in an open-range setting that exists almost literally in the shadows of Windsor Castle.

The farm that we stayed on while I was doing research on the origins and nature of the Cornish flat-stone stile was located a few miles northeast of Truro. It was equipped with two cattle guards, one at the entrance to the main road, the other protecting the yard of the farmhouse from wandering cattle, horses, and sheep. Mr. and Mrs. Frank Dymond, who have owned the farm since the late 1940s, installed the cattle guards a few years ago. Their daughter, Margaret Reed, told me that cattle guards are sometimes called "cow filters," because they let cars pass but filter out cows.

Two of the most unusual cattle guards I saw in Britain were located in Wales. One of these, on the outskirts of Monmouth, was a pitless guard that flattened out when driven over; then, after the car had passed, it was pulled back into an arch by springs housed on either side of the grid. This guard was sitting on a concrete base, and the firm footing of the concrete may well have encouraged cattle to attempt to step between the rather widely spaced bars. In any case, an extra pipe had been placed across the opening above the grid to serve as an added barrier.

Near Overton-on-Dee in northeastern Wales I was able to see perhaps the last extant Combermere Ladder (see chapter 3). In response to a query published in an English journal, Lady Ruth Lowther of Lightwood-on-Green had written to me about this unusual type of early-day cattle grid. It had been invented, patented, and sold by Sir Kenneth Crossley, son of the founder of Crossley Brothers Ltd. and himself founder of Crossley Motors Ltd. He lived at Combermere Abbey, a large rural estate near Whitchurch, in Shropshire. There, shortly after World War I, he tired of the gates on the long drive to the manor house, so he dug pits four feet deep beside the gates dividing the fields, and over each of these pits he placed two one-foot-wide iron ladders — one for each set of car wheels. Crossley was born in 1877, and he traveled widely, including hunting trips to America. Later he married a woman from Chicago. Although I do not know if these American connections had anything to do with his inventing a cattle guard, I find it intriguing that his Combermere Ladder was built on exactly the same principle as cattle guards built in the

Nebraska Sandhills and used extensively there just before Crossley built his. These Nebraska ladder guards continued to be used for decades, and even nowadays an analogous cattle guard with an open pit in the middle is used in Llano County, Texas.

When I visited Lady Lowther in June 1980, she took me to the one remaining Combermere Ladder. This old, original cattle guard is placed at the entrance to the house of an estate a few miles outside Overton-on-Dee. Modern cattle guards have been installed along the perimeter of this estate, but the Combermere Ladder has not been replaced, because the owner of the property wants to discourage motorists from driving fast as they approach his house. The sight of a gaping pit with two narrow tracks for automobile wheels is enough, Lady Lowther told me, to slow down even those callers who are used to the Combermere Ladder. First-time callers usually come to nearly a complete stop before driving over it. So this particular Combermere Ladder serves its purpose today just as well as did the first one built by Sir Kenneth Crossley about 1920.

Cattle guards are also found in most of the former Commonwealth nations. It is not surprising to find guards in Canada (from Vancouver Island to the Maritime Provinces), for the idea probably went north with American cattlemen and oilmen. (Thus, cattle guards are called "Texas gates" in western Canada.) Just how cattle guards got to South Africa or to Australia and New Zealand is not so easily determined, but get there they did — and in large numbers after World War II. Perhaps soldiers returning home, or immigrants from Britain or the States, encouraged their use.

In South Africa, cattle guards are commonly called "grid gates," "motor grids," or (as in England) "cattle grids." Leonard Thompson, currently a professor of history at Yale University, lived in South Africa from 1926 until 1937, when he turned twenty-one, then again from 1946 to 1961. He does not recall having seen any cattle guards during his earlier residency, although he admits that there may have been some. What he does remember is the "infinite tedium of opening and closing concertina barbed wire gates" while traveling secondary roads. On the more heavily traveled routes, young African boys would sometimes open and close gates in exchange for tips, but usually, as in the United States, the youngest member of the family who was capable of handling gates got the job. When Thompson returned to South Africa in 1946, he found that many cattle guards had already been or were being installed on public roads and at entrances to cattle farms.

P. Serton of the Department of Transport in Pretoria has told me that during the 1930s, grid gates began to replace public gates that had been installed for the use of motorized vehicles on public roads. These original cattle guards consisted of a concrete-lined pit some five by ten feet (depth unspecified) with two internal walls running with the road to help support the grid rails, which were usually spaced about four inches apart. These cattle guards had no approach slabs of concrete; therefore, just as in sandy regions of the United States, deep chuckholes usually formed next to the pit walls, often causing broken car springs.

G. Orczy of the Transvaal Roads Department has informed me that today's cattle guards in South Africa are often made of concrete, either precast or cast on the spot. In either case, the concrete bars are constructed so as to minimize the possibility of an animal's getting a hoof caught between the bars. Orczy also furnished me with a copy of the section of the 1933 Roads Ordinances of Transvaal that deals with fences and gates. Section 79 of chapter 8 delimits the regulations concerning by-passes for motor vehicles on public roads. These by-passes are defined in subhead 11:

> For the purposes of this section a by-pass means a track through an opening in or over a fence along or adjacent to the line of a public road designed or constructed with the object of allowing free passage for self-propelled vehicles while preventing the passage of animals. A by-pass may be constructed either by building a ramp to enable motor vehicles to be driven over the top of the fence or by way of a pit dug in or alongside the road and covered with an open grille so as to enable motor vehicles to pass over it, but to be an obstacle to the passage of animals.

Thus, cattle guards, apparently both of the arched-crossover and of the pit-and-pole types, seem to have been in use in Transvaal prior to 1933. As of 1965, when a survey was taken there, 132 cattle guards were in use on public roads, 128 of them to the side of a gate, only 4 in the middle of the road (as nearly all American cattle guards would be). Orczy estimated that this number was essentially unchanged as of 1980, but it should be noted that this survey did not include all roads in South Africa or any of the cattle guards that would be found there on privately owned farms. Orczy also pointed out that increased fencing of right of ways has lessened the need for cattle guards in some regions. Finally, Serton told me that at least one painted-stripe cattle guard was being used in his district. When the paint was well maintained, it worked as well as an ordinary grid gate.

New Zealand's sixty million sheep and eight million cattle are well guarded by what its citizens call "cattlestops." Boyd Wilson, editor of *New Zealand Farmer,* estimates that at least two-thirds of the farms in both New Zealand and Australia have at least one cattle guard. If so, then probably a greater percentage of farms use cattle guards in these two countries than anywhere else in the world.

New Zealand cattle guards, for the most part, are very much like those in the United States. They are made with bars of railroad rail or two-inch pipe spaced four or five inches apart over a pit two feet deep. Jennifer Nicol of

Christchurch told me of an amusing encounter between twenty-five or so weaned lambs and their first cattle guard. The lambs were racing down a road, and a sheep dog was vainly trying to get in front of them to turn them. The lambs did not see the barrier, and "within seconds we had a cattlestop full of very surprised woolly lambs, legs dangling between the railway irons. . . . The last of the mob had an easy getaway over the backs of those trapped! None of those stuck lambs had any injuries but I am sure they never forgot that cattlestop."

The *New Zealand Farmer* has printed two articles about cattle guards. "Cattlestop Designs," which appeared in 1976, gave building plans for the two guards that the editors judged to be the most effective and practical from among those submitted by readers in response to an appeal for suggested designs. Both designs, which are quite similar to American models, recommend using eight-inch concrete walls for the pit and either pipe or rails for bars. Some of the commentary that accompanied the building plans bears repeating: A strong grid is necessary in order to resist buckling under heavy loads. Wider cattle guards (eight to twelve feet) are necessary in pastures or pens where stock is crowded, while narrower grids (only five feet) will suffice where only an occasional animal might wander. Proper drainage for the pit is essential, although one design advocated leaving a pit two-thirds full of water so that the water would function as a visual barrier. The other design advocated a shallow pit and a four- or five-inch gap so that a cow, should it step onto the grid, could put its foot through to the pit floor and extract it without injury. A third design was appended to this article; in it the bars of the grid are laid at a twenty-five-degree angle rather than straight across the roadway. This design would permit a vehicle to "ripple" rather than to bump across. I do not know how commonly this technique is used in New Zealand, but I have encountered only one cattle guard installed in this fashion. It was on a road in the middle of the Flint Hills of northwestern Greenwood County, Kansas. It was not noticeably smoother to cross than the other guards in the area, but perhaps the angle was not the correct one.

The second article, "Ingenious Portable Electric Cattlestop," was written by the journal's editor, Boyd Wilson, in 1979. It discussed the advantages and disadvantages of a cattle guard invented by Dick Pilbrow of Oxford, New Zealand. This cattle guard looks much like a metal hospital bed frame, with charged wires running across where the innersprings would rest. The main objection to this guard is its potential danger to humans, especially children who might fall into or become entangled with the wires. Its advantages, however, are many: it stops stock, it can be made in any farm shop, it is durable, and it is easily transported, even by hand. Because it does not have a pit, it is smooth to drive over. Wilson recommended that, instead of discarding this cattle guard because of its dangers, efforts should be made to minimize the dangers. This guard, he suggested, should be used only in areas where there is no likelihood of children coming into contact with it. Also, warning signs should be erected, and, most importantly, a battery with moderate power should be used — not a high-potency energizer. The safety test that he recommended was for an adult to see if he could hold onto one of the live grid wires for thirty seconds while standing barefoot in damp grass.

I was not able to learn as much about Australian cattle guards as about those of New Zealand, although I did discover that they are called "cattle pits" if they are railroad guards, and "ramps" if they are automotive guards. Professor Russel Ward of the History Department of the University of New England in Armidale, New South Wales, said that in the 1920s, cattle pits were in use on level railroad crossings. Only after World War II did he recall having seen cattle guards on highways, At the present time in Australia, cattle guards are in common use on range roads and at entrances to farms. Ward concurred with my opinion that the automotive cattle guard developed directly from the concept of the railroad cattle guard and that both were undoubtedly American inventions. Although nothing on the subject has ever been published in Australia, he learned that railroad cattle guards, usually made by turning wooden beams on edge to make a diamond-shaped grid bar, were standard equipment on Australian railroads from the beginning of the twentieth century.

Cattle guards in Mexico, like those in Canada, can probably be considered as an extension of United States use. In some countries of Central and South America, however, fencing is at best rudimentary, and automobiles are scarce or absent, so there is little need for cattle guards. I have learned that cattle guards are being used in Argentina, Venezuela, and Brazil. According to the Reverend Carl J. Hahn, who spent nineteen years as a missionary in Brazil, the cattle guards in that country resulted, not from Brazil's Portuguese heritage, but from its economic ties with Great Britain throughout the first half of the twentieth century. Another American religious, Sister Irma Mary Grace Malaney, O.S.B., had an interesting experience with a cattle guard in Brazil. In 1972 Sister Irma wrote to Sister Anne Cawley at Mt. St. Scholastica in Atchison, Kansas, about a trip into the *fuzendas* (range country): "On our way back last week, I ran into a sort of ditch. It's really a device for containing cattle without having a fence across the road. Anyway I knocked the right front tire out of alignment, and took most of the shock out of the front shock absorber." Sister Anne told me that her colleague was from an urban background and therefore had never before seen a cattle guard.

Hahn, who married a Brazilian and has traveled extensively in the cattle regions of that country, has told me that there are many cattle guards there, most of them with grids made of wooden poles. These grids are often old, and the poles are weak and rotten. He was not surprised when I told him about

180

A cattle guard at the entrance to the thirteenth-century church at Santillana del Mar, Spain. (Courtesy of Connie Patton)

A *mato burro* (Brazilian cattle guard). (Courtesy of Sister Anne Cawley)

A *puerto ganado* (Mexican cattle guard). (Courtesy of William R. Thompson)

Sister Irma's wreck, for one of his friends had been thrown from a car and killed when the wheels had broken through a grid, wrecking the car. When Hahn was driving in Brazil, he always opened the ox gate at the side of a cattle guard and drove through there instead of going over the grid. Nowadays, when many dairy farms have been established in what was once beef-cattle country, milk trucks also must avoid the weakened grids by passing through the gates, all at great inconvenience and loss of time. What, I asked, was the point of having cattle guards if their main function was negated? His response was that the Brazilians had learned from the British (and also from some American ranchers who had holdings in Brazil) that cattle guards are an integral part of cattle country. Thus, they have them on their roads, even though some of them are unusable. When I protested to Hahn that such a situation was not practical, to put it mildly, he reminded me that, as a student of folklore, I should surely be aware of cultural differences: America is the land of Yankee ingenuity and can-do; Brazil is in the land of *mañana*.

One of my students at Emporia State University in the fall of 1980 was Enrique Alvarez-Prendes, a Venezuelan. He told me that cattle guards in his country, as in Brazil, are called *mato burros* (burro killers). Apparently burros get caught and stranded in them, then they may have to be destroyed if they have broken their legs, they may starve to death if they have been caught in a remote region, or they may be killed by jaguars and other predators. He also told me that the Indians in some remote regions use log bridges, much like those used over dry moats described in chapter 6, in order to keep livestock out of their gardens.

Cattle guards of both the railroad and the highway varieties are used in Argentina. The railroad cattle guards, similar to the surface guards used in the United States, were described to me by Victor H. Pastor, an Argentinean who practices medicine in Emporia, Kansas. Norman Schlesener, the Kingman County (Kansas) agricultural extension agent, saw highway cattle guards when he was an exchange student in Argentina in 1953. They were pit-and-pole cattle guards whose bars were made of quebracho wood, a hard, rot-resistant wood used for railroad ties in South America. Argentineans called them *guardas ganados.*

Apparently, cattle guards are not needed in many European countries because the normal practice is to drive cattle out to pasture each day and back into a barn or pen at night. I have learned of only a half-dozen cattle guards in West Germany, for instance, all near the village of Sundern in Westphalia. These cattle guards can all be traced to one man, Professor Doctor Rudolf Kaiser of Hildesheim. Sometime in the early 1950s Kaiser visited England, where, for the first time, he saw cattle guards and was struck by their simplicity and practicality. When he returned to Germany, he told his brother, who was running the family farm, about what he had seen. His brother then built three cattle guards, all of which are still in use. They measure five meters by one and two-tenths meters and have eight square wooden bars that are ten centimeters in width and are spaced ten centimeters apart. The pits are walled with concrete, and five support bars help the grid bear up under use by tractors. The reaction of his neighbors was negative at first. They were sure that either the cattle guards would fail to work or else the cattle would suffer broken legs. But none of the hundred-head herd he has maintained in the intervening years has ever escaped or been injured. Now there are three or four more guards in the village, all patterned after his.

There are cattle guards in Normandy, on the roads of the meadows of the Swiss Alps near Villars, and probably in other parts of Europe as well. From its obscure and literally pedestrian origins in moat bridges and fence stiles, through its manifestation as an essential part of railroad fencing, to the first experimental structures on the roads of the Great Plains about 1905, the cattle guard has undergone a long and interesting metamorphosis. Quietly and unassumingly it has become both a symbol of range country and a nearly indispensable tool of mechanized agrarian herding around the world.

```
┌─────────────────────────────────────────────────────────┐
│                                                           │
│                                                           │
│                    APPENDIX                               │
│                                                           │
│                                                           │
└─────────────────────────────────────────────────────────┘
```

CATTLE GUARD QUESTIONNAIRE SENT TO PROSPECTIVE INFORMANTS

The history of barbed wire is well documented, but who knows who invented the cattle guard? Its history was not recorded in the media of the times, nor is it fully recoverable from patent records. Instead, the story of the highway cattle guard (as opposed to the railroad variety) lies in the memories of those who have worked around them, who may remember early-day cattle guards and the men who built them. I am gathering material for a book on the history and lore of the cattle guard, but I need the help of those who have been a part of cattle guard country. Please respond to the items below and return to Jim Hoy, Center for Great Plains Studies, Emporia State University, Emporia, Kansas 66801. Thanks.

Your name _____ Year of Birth _____

Mailing Address_____ Phone _____

1. When and where was the first cattle guard you can remember? Who designed and/or built it?

2. Where, when, and how, in your opinion, did the cattle guard originate?

3. In your opinion, why does a cattle guard work? Which designs have worked better than others? What can be done to make a cattle guard work better?

4. What (and when and where) is the most unusual cattle guard you have ever seen?

5. What other names have you heard the cattle guard called?

6. Please list the names and addresses of people who might be able to help with this study.

7. On separate paper, please relate any interesting or unusual experiences you may have had with cattle guards, or any miscellaneous observations, comments, or lore you may have concerning them.

LETTER OF INQUIRY SENT TO NEWSPAPERS AND JOURNALS

I am seeking information about the introduction of highway cattle guards onto the roads of range country. My research thus far shows that railroad cattle guards were in use as early as 1836 and that a wooden-board guard for horse-drawn vehicles was in use near Medicine Lodge, Kansas, in the 1890s.

The earliest cattle guards intended for automotive traffic seem to date from Texas in 1913 and North Dakota in 1914. I would like to receive information on any cattle guard built before 1925.

I would also be interested in receiving stories of readers' experiences with cattle guards, of methods used to make cattle guards work more efficiently, of other kinds of devices used to replace gates, of other names by which cattle guards are known, etc. The results of my study will be published in book form.

Please send information, or names and addresses of those who might have information, to J. F. Hoy, Center for Great Plains Studies, Emporia State University, Emporia, Kansas 66801.

THE FIRST CATTLE-GUARD PATENT, GRANTED TO THOMAS J. WEST, WHITEHALL, VIRGINIA, 11 MARCH 1837

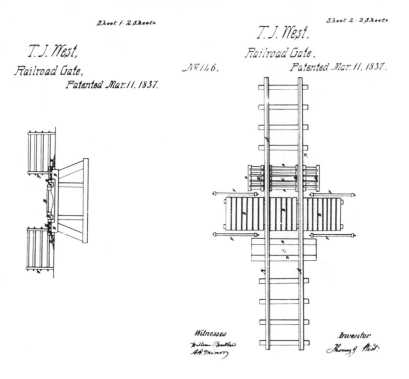

UNITED STATES PATENT OFFICE.

THOMAS J. WEST, OF WHITEHALL, VIRGINIA.

ROAD-STOP FOR PREVENTING CATTLE, &c., FROM CROSSING RAILROADS.

Specification of Letters Patent No. 146, dated March 11, 1837.

To all whom it may concern:

Be it known that I, THOMAS J. WEST, of Whitehall, in Caroline county, and State of Virginia, have invented a new and Improved mode of constructing and building that part and portion of railroads which passes over other roads and between contiguous lands and plantations; and I do hereby declare the following is a full and exact description.

The object, purpose, and value of my invention consists in this. Whereas all railroads which cross other roads, and cross contiguous lands and plantations, causes great expense to the farmers and owners of said lands, and plantations by requiring the excavation, and keeping up of constant lateral fences so as to protect the said lands from invasion and trespass of stock cattle, horses, persons, carriages &c, and whereas the proprietors of railroads are driven to great expense in paying the owners of lands, and plantations for the execution and keeping up of said lateral fences; and whereas injury is done to said railroads, by the trespass on them, of stock cattle, horses, persons, carriages &c, all of which are often necessarily destroyed, hurt, or injured. Now my invention is intended, and will necessarily prevent all these difficulties, hazards, and expenses, if used in the manner and constructed according to the principles, which I herewith set forth, and to enable others to make and use my invention, I will now proceed to describe its character, manner, and operation.

First. By constructing and building transverse open bridges or rail stops, with abutments not less than two feet perpendicular height, and as much higher as the builder may choose, the higher, the better, so that its top does not exceed the level of the rail road track, the fencing and inclosure that would otherwise run across the road to join their abutments, beginning at the top and closing at the bottom of said abutments. These abutments should be built of wood, stone, iron, and all other materials which can raise a permanent wall.

Secondly. The said transverse or open bridges, or road-stops are to be built of a width, not less than three feet from abutment to abutment, that being considered as the lowest point at which stock, cattle &c, could leap over and up—the longer the distance from abutment to abutment the better and safer, the precaution in thus preventing the leaping aforesaid transverse open bridge or road stop. The length therefore can be left to the opinion of the builder.

Thirdly. The rails are to be continued in a straight line, with the general line of the rail road across these open bridges or road-stops, which rails may be supported by the abutments, by perpendicular center supports, or by braces, the mode by which timber can be fastened and secured, will here apply. Should the rails, which cross these open bridges or road-stops be deemed of insufficient strength, others of larger dimensions, and greater strength can be used, the sides of said rails are to be sloped down in such a manner as to prevent the least possible surface, so as to prevent the hoofs of stock from hanging thereon, and affording them a foothold on the same.

Fourthly. When there are embankments on railroads the same principle will apply with equal force, and the same open bridges or road stops, by sinking them to a proper depth from the top of said embankments (on the line of the rail road track) will be of the same use and value, as set forth in the cases described. Should water settle in the bottom of the said rail road stops, or open bridges, and the land be not sufficiently porous to carry off the same, and if this effect be not produced by evaporation, then ditching, pumping, baling and other means can be used.

Fifthly. The form and shape of said open bridges, or road stops may be made in any mode which the convenience or fancy of the constructor may suggest, the petitioner claiming the principle herein set forth and its adaptation to his invention as the grounds of his prayer for a patent.

Sixthly. To prevent the difficulties, expenses, and hazards, as set forth in the specification, the builder or constructor (if he so chooses) may adopt a less perpendicular height of abutments, provided the same be guarded at or near the top, with four or more spikes of iron, metal, or wood not less than six inches long, setting in the direction of the opposite abutments. The said rods, or spikes are to be secured in a fine and durable manner (with rests if necessary) the points of the same are to be elevated, depressed or made level (as the builders may choose) provided the same do not interfere with the engine, cars &c. By this means (if the farmer or constructor choose to adopt it)

188

cattle, horses, persons, carriages, stock &c will be fully prevented from attempting to leap over, down, or up said road stops.

Seventhly. Whereas it has been specified and set forth, that in these road stops, slats, spikes &c may be used to prevent the passage on railroads, of carriages, persons, cattle, horses, hogs, &c. Now if the constructor choose, said road stops may be crossed or intersected by lattice or open work, which may run parallel or transversely. The said lattice or open work may be raised so as not to interfere with the cars, or any part thereof, and its depth, span, arch &c, may be of any character the constructor may wish, the object of this explanation being more and more to secure the principle, which your petitioner claims and sets forth for a patent.

THOMAS J. WEST.

Witnesses:

THOMAS TURNER,
ANDREW P. MINOR.

UNIVERSITY OF TENNESSEE
AGRICULTURAL EXTENSION SERVICE PLANS

- CATTLE GUARD -

JUNE 1944 ### -CONCRETE & STEEL- PLAN 5470

Guards set in a fence alongside a gate permit automobiles and trucks to pass freely, but stop cattle, hogs, sheep, and most horses and mules. However, gates are necessary for passage of animals.

The following concrete and steel design is capable of supporting a five-ton load. When possible, it is desirable to have a drain in the bottom of pit.

BILL OF MATERIAL

Concrete – 1:2½:5
  1.4 Cubic Yards

Cement	7	Bags
Sand	.65	Cubic Yards
Stone	1.25	Cubic Yards

Sills	2 Pc.	4" x 6" x 8'-0"
Rafters	6 "	2" x 4" x 8'-0"
Slats	8 "	1" x 6" x 8'-0"
Posts	2 "	5" x 5" x 8'-0"
Joists	14 "	2" diam. Pipe x 8'-0"
Bolts	4	3/8" diam. x 1'-6"
Reinforcing	4	1/2" diam Bars x 9'-0"

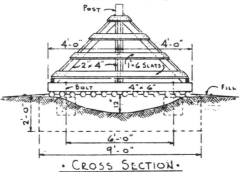

· CROSS SECTION ·

AGRICULTURAL EXTENSION SERVICE
UNIVERSITY OF TENNESSEE
KNOXVILLE

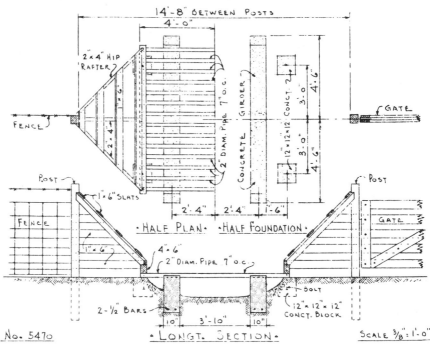

· HALF PLAN ·   · HALF FOUNDATION ·

· LONGT. SECTION ·   SCALE 3/8" : 1'-0"

SOURCES OF INFORMATION

See the List of Contributors of Information for the names, titles (where known or pertinent), and addresses of the persons who furnished information.

CHAPTER 1
THE CATTLE GUARD: AN OVERVIEW

Some of the information about the time- and energy-saving aspects of cattle guards was provided by Kenny DeDonder; Terry DeDonder; Ray Pierce; Ralph Ricketts; George L. Smith; and George R. Sollenberger.

Some of the information about the use of cattle guards in eastern states was provided by Bryan Baker; James M. Beattie; W. H. Collins; Clarence Day; Kenneth E. Felton; Danny G. Fox; Stewart Gibson; George F. Grandle; Walter A. Gross; George F. W. Haenlein; Ralph R. Harris; W. L. Harris; James F. Hentges, Jr.; Lynette S. Hoffman; Benjamin A. Jones, Jr.; Charles Kuralt; Louis A. Malkus; Edward T. Oleskie; Wiley Roger Pope; Harlan D. Ritchie; David C. Smith; Richard J. Vatthauer; and S. H. Wittwer.

Other information in this chapter was provided by Robert Clarke; Walter Eitner; and Glenn Ohrlin.

CHAPTER 2
THE NEED FOR CATTLE GUARDS

Information on fences and fencing was found in these published sources:

Duke, Cordia Sloan, and Frantz, Joe B. *6,000 Miles of Fence.* Austin: University of Texas Press, 1961, p. 6.

Fischer, John. "Barbed Wire and the Art of Stringing It." *Harper's,* July 1978, pp. 90-91.

Grant, John. "A Few Remarks on the Large Hedges and Small Enclosures of Devonshire and Adjoining Counties." *Journal of the Royal Agricultural Society* 5 (1844): 420-29.

Hartley, Dorothy. *Lost Country Life.* New York: Pantheon Books, 1979.

Hoskins, W. G. *The Making of the English Landscape.* London: Hodder & Stoughton, 1977 (originally published in 1955).

McCallum, Henry D., and McCallum, Frances T. *The Wire That Fenced the West.* Norman: University of Oklahoma Press, 1965.

Munroe, F. L. *The Practical Home Farmer.* Chicago: Interstate Publishing House, 1888, pp. 185-91, 393-94.

Pollard, E.; Hooper, M. D.; and Moore, N. W. *Hedges.* London: Collins, 1974.

Simmons, C. W. "Fences, Gates, and Cattle Guards." *Cattleman,* June 1935, p. 32.

"Thorny Theory." *Time,* 21 April 1980, pp. 76-77.

United States, Bureau of the Census. *Fourteenth Census of the United States Taken in the Year 1920.* Vol. 1: *Population 1920: Number and Distribution of Inhabitants.* Washington, D.C.: Government Printing Office, 1921.

United States, Department of Agriculture. *Report of the U.S. Agricultural Commissioner for the Year 1871.* Washington, D.C.: Government Printing Office, 1872, pp. 497-512.

Information on the development of the automobile in the United States and the importance of automotive vehicles to agriculture was found in:

Bailey, L. Scott, publ. *The American Car since 1775.* 2d ed. New York: E. P. Dutton, 1971.

Clymer, Floyd. *Treasury of Early American Automobiles, 1877-1925.* New York: McGraw-Hill, 1950.

Crabb, Richard. *Birth of a Giant.* Philadelphia: Chilton Book Co., 1969.

Eames, Hayden. "Influence of the Auto on Farm Life." *Breeder's Gazette,* 24 November 1909, p. 1472.

Freeman, Larry. *The Merry Old Mobiles.* Watkins Glen, N.Y.: Century House, 1949.

George, G. N., ed. *The Complete Encyclopedia of Motorcars, 1885-1968.* New York: E. P. Dutton, 1968.

Heeb, David. *Wheels on the Road.* New York: Collier, 1966.

"Only Two Roads in U.S. Exclusively for Autos." *Popular Mechanics,* July 1914, p. 24.

United States, Department of Agriculture. *Yearbook . . . for 1907,* pp. 257-58.

———. *Yearbook . . . for 1916,* p. 470.

———. *Yearbook . . . for 1920,* pp. 339-41, 829.

———. *Yearbook . . . for 1921,* pp. 505, 789.

Information on gates was found in:

"Evolution of the Farm Gate." *Breeder's Gazette,* 25 May 1910, p. 1235.

"Good Gates as a Factor in Farming." *Breeder's Gazette,* 7 April 1909, pp. 841-42.

"Has Anyone Seen This Gate Before?" *McKenzie County* (N.Dak.) *Farmer,* 16 February 1978, p. 11.

Hayter, Earl W. "Barbed Wire Fencing—A Prairie Invention." *Agricultural History* 13 (1939): 189-207.

Larsen, Esther Louise. "Pehr Kalm's Observations on the Fences of North America." *Agricultural History* 21 (1947): 75-78.

Martin, George A. *Fences, Gates, and Bridges: A Practical Manual.* Brattleboro, Vt.: Stephen Greene Press, 1974. Originally published in 1887.

Scientific American in the 1890s reflected the need for an easily operated gate by publishing the following articles, listed by date and the name and address of the inventor:

8 November 1890, p. 291; Charles Oesterling, Barnharts Mills, Pa.

4 February 1893, p. 73; Silas Portis, Monrovia, Ind.

24 June 1893, p. 389; John H. Williams, St. Vincent, Ky.

13 January 1894, p. 20; Levi W. Youngs, New York

16 June 1894, p. 372; Richard T. Mulcahy, Rosenburg, Tex.

9 July 1898, p. 24; Theodore Sawyer, Towanda, Ill.

17 September 1898, p. 180; Peyton B. Green, Wytheville, Va.

8 October 1898, p. 228; Benjamin F. Strange, Corvallis, Mont.

Scott, John. *The Complete Text-Book of Farm Engineering: Farm Roads, Fences, and Gates.* Vol. 3. London: Crosby Lockwood & Co., 1885, pp. 113-20.

Smith, G. B. From the *Cultivator. In* H. L. Ellsworth, *U.S. Commissioner of Patents Report for 1844,* p. 459.

Wimberley, C. G. "Gates." In *Built in Texas,* edited by Francis Edward Abernethy, pp. 191-95. Publications of the Texas Folklore Society, #42. Waco, Texas: E-Heart Press, 1979.

Information about bump gates came from Marlene Bowman; Roy ("Cap") Carpenter; O. E. ("Whitey") Cowsar; Mason Crocker; Fred B. Curry; Dudley Dobie; Dave Dodd; Kim Harsh; Dr. W. Curry Holden; Tracy King; M. H. Leining; John R. Shaw; Mrs. Corwin Trosper; C. W. Wimberley; and Viola Wyland.

Information about other types of gates was provided by George W. Altland; D. Neil Cowan; Mason Crocker; Norman Dahl; Lon J. Godley; Lyman Linger; Jim McEndree; Roy D. Mockamer; Ira ("Ike") Osteen; Carl Rauch; Elvis Riggs; Ralph R. Robinson; G. M. Sawyer; R. S. Shipman; Wilbur R. Thompson; Otis Wheat; and C. W. Wimberley.

Information on electrified gates came from brochures issued by the Farnum Co. and the Acme Manufacturing Co. James E. ("Pete") Hatch, John Ortmann, and Wilbur R. Thompson gave me information about these devices.

Information and comments on the relative merits of gates versus cattle guards came from:

Herriot, James. *The Lord God Made Them All.* New York: St. Martins Press, 1981, pp. 1-2.

McCullough, Coleen. *The Thorn Birds.* New York: Harper & Row, 1977, p. 51

Individuals who contributed information on this subject were: Helen Amsberry; Orville Burtis, Sr.; Fred B. Curry; Richard Etulain; Charles Evans; Mrs. Frank Fleck; Ray ("Turk") Harsh; William M. Jolly; Emmett LeFors; R. L. McCammon; Robert M. Magee; E. Paul Orcutt; Ira ("Ike") Osteen; Mabel Hickman Pearson; Earl E. Perkins; Lewis E. Phillips; Mrs. Ben Price, Sr.; James Rexroat; Ralph R. Robinson; L. H. Wellner; Thomas W. Winkler; and C. G. Wood.

CHAPTER 3
CATTLE-GUARD INNOVATORS, 1900 TO 1920

Information for this chapter came in part from these published sources:

Barnes, Will C. "Crossings in Fences for Autos." *Breeder's Gazette,* 29 June 1916, pp. 1349–50.

Branda, Eldon Stephen, ed. *The Handbook of Texas: A Supplement.* Vol. 3. Austin: Texas State Historical Association, 1976, p. 1033.

"Bridging a Fence for an Automobile." *Popular Mechanics,* May 1909, p. 481.

"Grooved Tracks Are Used as Automobile Bridge." *Popular Mechanics.* September 1914, p. 398.

Loftin, Jack. *Trails through Archer.* Burnet, Tex.: Nortex Press, 1979, pp. 142–43.

"Motorists Use Inclines instead of Gates." *Popular Mechanics,* November 1916, p. 865.

New Mexico. *Second Biennial Report of the State Engineer of New Mexico, 1914–1916.* Santa Fe, N.Mex.

————. *Third Biennial Report of the State Engineer of New Mexico, 1917.* Santa Fe, N.Mex., pp. 70–71.

Wimberley, C. W. "Gates." In *Built in Texas,* edited by Francis Edward Abernethy, pp. 191–95. Publications of the Texas Folklore Society, #42. Waco, Tex.: E-Heart Press, 1979.

Information on Andrew Johnston came in part from:

"Andrew Johnston: An Autobiography." *Bar North,* April 1970, pp. 6, 12. Published by the North Dakota Stockman's Association, Bismarck, N.Dak.

Cory, Robert. "Former McKenzie Cowboy Recalls How 'Reward Fund' Was Started." *Minot* (N.Dak.) *Daily News,* 7 May 1960.

Dickey, Cale. "Flood, Drought of '36 Didn't Faze Johnston." *Bismarck* (N.Dak.) *Tribune,* 20 October 1967, p. 7.

Johnston, Andrew. "The Cattle Guard." In *Looking Back down the Trail.* Boston: Meador Press, 1963, pp. 335–36. Published by the 50 Years in the Saddle Club, Watford City, N.Dak.

"Johnston Receives Swift's Centennial Award." *McKenzie County Farmer* (Watford City, N.Dak.), 9 June 1955, p. 1.

Lund, Leonard. "A Plaque Is Placed Where McKenzie County's Pioneers Wintered Cattle in 1886–87." *Minot* (N.Dak.) *Daily News,* 18 November 1972.

Obituary notices for Andrew Johnston in *Dickinson* (N.Dak.) *Press,* 5 March 1970, p. 1; and *Minot* (N.Dak.) *Daily News,* 5 March 1970.

Other information about Andrew Johnston came from Larry Adams; Joyce Byerly; Ralph Christensen; Robert Cory; C. J. Goddard; Carroll Johnston; Brooks Keogh; and Larry Remele.

Other information in this chapter was provided by Everett Anderson; Helen Bradford; Ralph H. Clark; O. E. ("Whitey") Cowsar; Frank Dieter; Dudley Dobie; John Eggen, Sr.; Charles Evans; Pollie Allen Fitch; Lon J. Godley; Dr. W. Curry Holden; Dr. Myra Ellen Jenkins; William M. Jolly; Bill King; Raymond Lauppe; Albert Lawlis; Lady Ruth K. Lowther; Jim McEndree; George McKinney; Victor Merrihew; Alfred Meyer; W. C. Mills; Ira ("Ike") Osteen; Mabel Hickman Pearson;

Earl E. Perkins; Dallas Perry; Lewis E. Phillips; Ray Purinton; Ella Reddick; Elvis Riggs; Richard Robbins, Jr.; Sarah Robbins; G. M. Sawyer; John R. Shaw; Melvin Storm; E. S. Sutton; Everett Troyer; Ona Troyer; Albert Tuttle; L. P. Wakefield; C. W. Wimberley; Thomas W. Winkler; C. G. Wood; and Green D. Wyrick.

CHAPTER 4
THE SPREAD OF CATTLE GUARDS, 1920 TO 1930

Information for this chapter came in part from:

Gentry, Raymond R. "The Old Auto Gates." *Grant County* (Nebr.) *News,* 17 August 1978.
"New Industry for Antioch." *Antioch* (Nebr.) *News,* 8 June 1922, p. 1.
"Where Cattle Graze on a Thousand Hills." *Kansas Farmer-Stockman,* 15 September 1920, pp. 10-11.

Other information came from W. D. Aeschbacher; Essie Alexander; Lawrence Alexander; K. T. Anderson; Frank Arndt; Walt Arnett; Helen Bradford; Aeola H. Brennemann; Bill Browning; Orville Burtis, Sr.; Roy ("Cap") Carpenter; Tom Case; Ralph H. Clark; O. E. ("Whitey") Cowsar; Mason Crocker; Fred B. Curry; C. E. Dauman; Mary Etta Funk Davidson; Richard Etulain; Marion Everhart; Don Fowler; Wayne Geer; Raymond R. Gentry; Lon J. Godley; W. R. Grantham; Kenneth Hoy; Mildred Jones; Emmett LeFors; Ruth Lynn; R. L. McCammon; Alfred Mercer; David Mercer; W. C. Mills; E. Paul Orcutt; Minnie Paugh; Mabel Hickman Pearson; Lewis E. Phillips; Melba Prewitt; Raymond Prewitt; Conwy Rees; Ralph L. Ricketts; Ralph R. Robinson; Sheila Robinson; Wayne Rogler; Elmer W. Sass; Lowell Scribner; John R. Shaw; David E. Smith; Everett Troyer; Ona Troyer; Albert B. Tuttle; Otis Wheat; Mrs. R. Wilkinson; Green D. Wyrick; A. G. ("Jim") Young; and "Slim" Zimmerman.

CHAPTER 5
THE RAILROAD CATTLE GUARD

Background material on railroad history was found in:

Crouch, George. *Erie under Gould and Fisk.* New York, 1870.
Dickens, Charles. *American Notes.* New York: Fawcett, 1961, p. 82.
Hayter, Earl W. "The Fencing of Western Railways." *Agricultural History* 19 (1945): 163-67.
Hofsommer, Donavan L. *Katy Northwest.* Boulder, Colo.: Pruett Publishing Co., 1976.
Hornung, Clarence P. *Wheels across America.* New York: A. S. Barnes & Co., 1959.
Noble, Joseph A. *From Cab to Caboose.* Norman: University of Oklahoma Press, 1964, pp. 90-91.
Pauly, David, et al. "Green Light on the Rails." *Newsweek,* 25 February 1980, pp. 63, 65.
Poor, Henry V. *History of the Railroads and Canals of the United States of America.* Vol. 1. New York: John H. Schultz & Co., 1860, pp. 335-37.
Waggoner, Madeline Sadler. *The Long Haul West.* New York: G. P. Putnam's Sons, 1958, pp. 282 ff.

These track manuals were consulted:

Camp, W. M. *Notes on Track.* 2d ed. rev. Chicago: W. M. Camp, 1904, pp. 832–41, 1203–4.

Huntington, William S. *The Road-Master's Assistant and Section-Master's Guide.* Revised and enlarged by Charles Latimer. 6th ed. New York: Railroad Gazette, 1881, pp. 34–35. (The section on cattle guards was unchanged from that in the original edition of 1871.)

Kirkman, Marshall M. *The Science of Railways: Financing, Constructing, and Maintaining.* Vol. 3, rev. and enl. New York and Chicago: World Railway Publishing Co., 1907, pp. 225, 256–57, 342–43. (Originally published in 1898.)

Manual for Railway Engineering (Fixed Priorities): Current to March 21, 1973. Chicago: American Railway Engineering Association, 1973, section 1-6-19.

Poor, Henry V. *Manual of Railroads.* New York: H. V. Poor, 1890, p. 1292.

Rules and Instructions for the Government of Employees of the Track, Bridge, and Building Departments. Missouri-Kansas-Texas Railroad Manual. N.p., 1911.

Track Cyclopedia. N.p.: Simmons, Boardman Publishing Co., 1978.

Tratman, E. E. Russell. *Railway Track and Track Work.* 1st ed. New York: Engineering News Publishing Co., 1897, pp. 136–41.

Descriptions of railroad cattle guards were taken from the preceding sources, from the *U.S. Patent Gazette,* and from:

"The Bush Steel Surface Cattle Guard." *Engineering News,* 21 February 1891, p. 187.

"The 'Common Sense' Cattle Guard." *Engineering News,* 28 March 1891, p. 307.

"Scaring the Cattle off the Tracks." *Scientific American,* September 1923, p. 171.

Legal material concerning railroad cattle guards came from:

Reports of the Supreme Court of the State of Iowa. New York: Banks Law Publishing Co., 1906, pp. 546.

Revised Codes of Montana, 1947, pp. 194–96.

Thornton, W. W. *The Law of Railroad Fences and Private Crossings.* Indianapolis: Bowen-Merrill Co., 1892, passim.

Comments on James Hill were made by Joel Overholser. Hill's attitude toward the upgrading of livestock was reported in:

"Farming and Railroads." *Breeder's Gazette,* 15 June 1916, p. 1255.

Other information in this chapter was taken in part from these published sources:

Craigie, Sir William, and Hubert, James R., eds. *A Dictionary of American English on Historical Principles.* Chicago: University of Chicago Press, 1938. (The entry on cattle guards includes the references to the *Chicago Times* story and James Dana's book.)

Franck, Ron. "Ranchers Feud with Railroad." *Laramie* (Wyo.) *Boomerang,* 24 February 1980, pp. 1, 10.

Greer, Larry. "'Gator' Post." *International Barbed Wire Gazette,* July 1981.

Longrigg, Paul. "Railroad-Highway Vehicular Movement Warning Devices at Grade Crossings." *IEEE Transactions on Industry Applications.* Vol. 1A-2, no. 2, March/April 1975, pp. 211–21.

"Railroad Cattle Guard Used in India." *Popular Mechanics,* March 1913, p. 392.

Material on Thomas J. West, the name West, and the Cornish in Virginia came from Patricia L. Taylor, Mabel Apple Talley, and Rebecca E. Bordwine and from the following published sources. Those marked with an asterisk were provided by Mrs. Talley.

Matthews, C. M. *English Surnames*. New York: Charles Scribner's Sons, 1966, p. 300.
*Murphy. *Guardian Bonds: Albemarle County, Virginia*.
Rowe, John. *The Hard-Rock Men: Cornish Immigrants and the North American Mining Frontier*. New York: Barnes & Noble, 1974, pp. 39, 197.
Rowse, A. L. *The Cousin Jacks: The Cornish in America*. New York: Charles Scribner's Sons, 1969, pp. 37–41.
Virginia Magazine of History and Biography 23:87.
William and Mary College Quarterly, ser. 1, vol. 8, p. 194.

These persons from railroad companies, railroad historical societies, and the U.S. Patent Office provided information for this chapter: Bill Armstrong, engineer of buildings, Chicago & North Western Railway Co.; Anne O. Bennof, manager, Education and Information Services, Association of American Railroads; Harriette C. Black, librarian and curator, Newcomen Society in North America; Bill Burk, vice-president for public relations, Atchison, Topeka & Santa Fe Railroad Co; Louis T. Cerny, acting executive director, American Railway Engineering Association; Barry B. Combs, director of public relations, Union Pacific Railroad Co.; commissioner of patents, Ottawa, Canada; P. Allen Copeland, Pacific Southwest Railway Museum; B. Gallagher, British Railways Board, London; Donald W. Ginter, curator, Mid-Continent Railway Historical Society; Howard F. Greene, president, Railway and Locomotive Historical Society; D. E. Hoadley, principal engineer-staff, Delaware & Hudson Railway Co.; Nick Kallas, general manager, Illinois Railway Museum; W. A. McKenzie, director of information services, Burlington Northern Railroad Co.; Robert A. Matthews, vice-president, Railway Progress Institute; David J. Neubauer, publicity director, Wabash, Frisco & Pacific Association; Mrs. J. A. Sullivan, examiner, Classification Section, Patent Office, London; Richard Teeter, advertising and technical publications supervisor, Tamper Division, Canron Corp.; and V. Allan Vaughn, president, National Railway Historical Society.

Other information in this chapter was provided by B. G. Baker; Mary Baker; Edwin H. Bredemeier; J. Warren Brinkman; W. J. Campbell; J. G. Côté; D. Neil Cowan, Mrs. Donald B. Crane; John Davis; Cecil Farthing; Warren Godfrey; W. C. Gordon; Gene M. Gressley; Clay Hardy; Keith Hayes; Bud Hills; Adam Horst; Melvin L. Johnson; Jesse Jordan; Tom L. Kern, Jr.; Tracy King; James Kiser; Karen Laughlin; Raymond Lauppe; M. H. Leining; Marcus Lind; R. L. McCammon; F. B. McCann; Otto Michetti; Rex C. Myers; Joseph A. Noble; E. Paul Orcutt; Joel F. Overholser; Victor H. Pastor; Dallas Perry; Lewis E. Phillips; W. C. Phillips; Wayne Rogler; Richard Smith; Mabel Apple Talley; Patricia L. Taylor; Jerry Underwood; Wayne Wangsness; C. G. Wood; and A. F. Young.

CHAPTER 6
CORNISH STILES, LICH GATES, AND CATTLE GUARDS

Information for this chapter came in part from these published sources:

Angove, Richard. "Cornwall's Granite Stiles." *Cornish Life*, vol. 5, no. 5 (1978), pp. 9, 11.

Burl, Aubrey. *The Stone Circles of the British Isles.* New Haven, Conn.: Yale University Press, 1976, pp. 119, 127–28.

"Chysauster." *Treasures of Britain.* New York: Norton, 1969, pp. 141.

Courtney, M. A. *Cornish Feasts and Folk-Lore.* Penzance: Beare & Son, 1890.

Cox, J. Charles. *County Churches: Cornwall.* London: George Allen & Co. Ltd., 1912, p. 130.

D'Argenville, A. J. Dezallier. *La Theorie et la pratique du jardinage.* Paris, 1709. Trans. by John James, 1712. Reprinted in *The Genius of Place: The English Landscape Garden, 1620–1820,* ed. John Dixon Hunt and Peter Willis, pp. 125–31. New York: Harper & Row, 1976.

Fiennes, Celia. *Through England on a Side Saddle: In the Time of William and Mary: Being the Diary of Celia Fiennes.* London: Field & Tuer, 1888.

"Ha-ha." *Encyclopedia of Gardening.* Vol. 6. New York: Marshal Cavendish Corp., 1970, p. 826.

Hartley, Dorothy. *Lost Country Life.* New York: Pantheon Books, 1979, p. 24.

Henderson, C. G. "Note on the History of St. Ives." *St. Ives Times,* 13 March 1925, pp. 3–4.

Hoskins, W. G. *The Making of the English Landscape.* London: Houghton & Stoddard, 1977 (first published in 1955), pp. 20–32.

Hunt, John Dixon, and Willis, Peter, eds. *The Genius of Place: The English Landscape Garden, 1620–1820.* New York: Harper & Row, 1976, pp. 11–12.

Matthews, J. H. *A History of St. Ives, Lelant, Towednack, and Zennor.* London: Elliot Stock, 1892, pp. 55–57, 90, 102.

Olivey, Hugh P. *Notes on the Parish of Mylor Cornwall.* Taunton: Barnicott & Pearce, Athenaeum Press, 1907.

Pollard, E.; Hooper, M. D.; and Moore, N. W. *Hedges.* London: Collins, 1974, p. 28.

St. Just-in-Roseland Church. St. Ives: Beric Tempest & Co. Ltd., n.d., 16 pp.

Shorter, A. H.; Ravenhill, W. L. D.; and Gregory, K. J. *Southwest England.* London: Thomas Nelson & Sons Ltd., 1969, p. 89 and pl. 5.

Silis, Ivars. "Wild in the Streets." *Geo,* October 1980, pp. 86–99.

Sloane, Eric. *Our Vanishing Landscape.* New York: Wilfred Funk, Inc., 1955, p. 101.

"Thorny Theory." *Time,* 21 April 1980, pp. 76–77.

Information on dry moats and ha-has was given to me by Richard Eversole; Donald Perry; Ray Purinton; and Eric Sloane.

Letters about Cornish stiles have been published in these British journals:

Country Life, 19 April 1941 — about St. Just-in-Roseland.
Field, 10 July 1958, by J.C.D.S. of Bristol — about St Levan; 15 January 1959, by K.F. of Whipton, Exeter — about St. Just-in-Roseland; and 2 July 1966, by M. H. Hadfield of Ledbury, Herefordshire — about St. Just-in-Roseland.

In response to my queries about Cornish stiles in *Country Life, Farmer's Weekly,* and *Field,* I received letters from W. F. H. Ansell, Trendrine, St. Ives, Cornwall; Harold H. Aston, Warley, West Midlands; John V. Berryman, Datchet, Slough, Berkshire; S. G. Bryant, Henley-on-Thames, Oxfordshire; T. R. Faull, Bude, Cornwall; William W. Gilroy, Looe, Cornwall; Thomas Frederick Gwennap, St. Buryan, Cornwall; Dennis Jeffreys, Crawley, Sussex; Richard Jemmett, Saffron Walden, Essex;

Donald A. Levy, Leighton Buzzard, Bedfordshire; John C. Lyall, Gweek, Cornwall; Gerry Symons, Shillingford St. George, Exeter, Devon; Mrs. James Vanstone, Clovelly, Devon; and David J. Vellam, Beaminster, Dorset.

Although I spoke with many Cornish men and women whose names I did not record, some with whom I corresponded or spoke to about Cornish stiles are Canon J. B. D. Cotter, vicar of Zennor, Cornwall; John S. Creasey, librarian and information officer, Museum of Rural Life, University of Reading; H. L. Douch, curator, County Museum, Truro, Cornwall; Mrs. Frank Dymond, Great Hewas Farm, Cornwall; Alan Gailey, secretary, Society for Folk Life Studies, Ulster Folk Museum, County Down, Northern Ireland; Miles H. Hadfield, Ledbury, Herefordshire; Mrs. Enid V. Malec, secretary, Isles of Scilly Museum Association, Hugh Town, St. Mary's, Isles of Scilly; L. W. Mitchell, acting council clerk, Hugh Town, St. Mary's, Isles of Scilly; Mr. and Mrs. Lawrence S. Powell, St. Just-in-Roseland, Cornwall; Margaret Reed, Great Hewas Farm, Cornwall; Rosemary Robertson, Institute of Cornish Studies, University of Exeter, Trevenson House, Pool, Redruth, Cornwall; Dr. John Rowe, School of History, University of Liverpool; Ian Smith, Mabe, Cornwall; and Professor Charles Thomas, Institute of Cornish Studies, University of Exeter, Trevenson House, Pool, Redruth, Cornwall.

CHAPTER 7
LORE ABOUT CATTLE GUARDS

Information for this chapter came in part from these published sources:

Abbey, Edward. *The Monkey Wrench Gang.* New York: J. B. Lippincott Co., 1975, pp. 119-20.
Alleman, Roy. "The Barbed Wire Gate." *American Cattle Producer* 39 (1957): 26-27.
Bone, Jack. "After Deadline." *Minot* (N.Dak.) *Daily News,* 19 January 1980, p. 3.
Brunvand, Jan Harold. *The Study of American Folklore.* Rev. ed. New York: Norton, 1978, pp. 5 (definition of folklore) and 313 (log-cabin building techniques).
Femling, Charlie. "Remnants of Ramblings: Old Inner Tubes Guard Cattle." *Billings* (Mont.) *Gazette,* 17 November 1979, p. 14-A
Gentry, Raymond R. "The Old Auto Gates." *Grant County* (Nebr.) *News,* 17 August 1978.
Hall, Lynn. *Wild Mustang.* New York: Scholastic Books, 1971, pp. 71-73.
McDonough, Doug. "Farm Scene." *Plainview* (Tex.) *Daily Herald,* 22 October 1978, p. 8-B.
McMurtry, Larry. *Hud* (original title *Horseman, Pass By*). New York: Popular Library, 1961, pp. 41, 68, 122.
O'Hara, Mary. *My Friend Flicka.* New York: J. B. Lippincott Co., 1941, p. 118.
Nethaway, Rowland. "Close Calls." *Austin* (Tex.) *American Statesman,* 21 February 1980.
Nichols, John. *The Milagro Beanfield War.* New York: Holt, Rinehart, & Winston, 1974, pp. 30, 164.
Reid, Herbert L., ed. *California Mining Journal,* September 1979, p. 1.
Swaffer, Paul. *Look What I Stepped In.* Kansas City, Mo.: Lowell Press, 1972, pp. 48-49.
Weberg, Mary. "Honey, You Get the Gate." *Farm Journal,* September 1959, p. 87.

In addition to material gleaned from reference works such as the *Oxford English Dictionary* and *Dictionary of Americanisms,* information about names for cattle guards came from Helen Amsberry; Steven A. Bealby; Don Bell; Aeola H. Brennemann; Howard C. Brown; Mrs. Burton Buchman; W. J. Campbell; Arthur Carmody; Roy ("Cap") Carpenter; Elmer Cooper; D. Neil Cowan; Dennis W. Cowan; Bill Dale; William Delinger; Thelma Diffey; W. H. Dorris; Virgil E. Enfield; Charles Evans; Mrs. Frank Fleck; Mrs. Paul Frey; Wayne Geer; Raymond R. Gentry; Jack Glover; W. C. Gordon; Dr. W. Curry Holden; Raymond Hull; Alex Johnston; Bill King; Gloria Krueger; George W. McKinney; Victor H. Merrihew; David Miller; Earl H. Monahan; D. J. Newberry; Jennifer Nicol; E. Paul Orcutt; Ira ("Ike") Osteen; Margaret Reed; A. D. Ridge; Ralph R. Robinson; Robert L. Rothwell; Elmer W. Sass; G. M. Sawyer; Norman Schlesener; "Lucky" Simpson; Matthew M. Syler; Kaye Y. Turner; Leland J. Turner; Bud Winger; DeEtta Winger; Thomas W. Winkler; C. G. Wood; and Charles L. Wood.

Information and opinions about the effectiveness of cattle guards and improvement of them were provided by Lawrence Alexander; Arthur Carmody; Roy ("Cap") Carpenter; Don Coldsmith; George M. Constantino; Elmer Cooper; Dennis W. Cowan; Charles Evans; Robert F. Fankhauser; Cecil Farthing; James Fisher; Mabel Fletchall; Jack Glover; Warren Godfrey; W. R. Grantham; Ray ("Turk") Harsh; Clair Houseman; Mildred Jones; Christina Kemper; Bill King; Tracy King; Tom Mc-Crea; George W. McKinney; David Mercer; David Miller; Earl H. Monahan; John Ortman; Ira ("Ike") Osteen; Frank Parsons; Melba Prewitt; Raymond Prewitt; Elmer Priefert; Ray Purinton; James Rexroat; Tom Rice; Ralph L. Ricketts; Sheila Robinson; Robert L. Rothwell; John Sautter; "Lucky" Simpson; David E. Smith; E. A. Stephenson; Elmore Stout; Floyd Thompson; Everett Troyer; L. H. Wellner; Larry Whitmer; William J. Williams; C. W. Wimberley; Thomas W. Winkler; and C. G. Wood.

Information about the use of cowhides with cattle guards came from Louie W. Attebery; Riley R. Chambers; C. O. Dobbins; Mrs. Paul Frey; Alex Johnston; Tom L. Kern, Jr.; Bill King; E. C. Lesher; Tom McCrea; Victor H. Merrihew; Mrs. James Murphy; Raymond Prewitt; Tom Quirk; Ralph R. Robinson; Penni Signs; "Lucky" Simpson; and Jay Taylor.

Information about unusual variations and materials in cattle guards came from Reuben Albaugh; Don Bell; Art Dorsett; Charlie Femling; Don Fowler; Wayne Geer; Lon J. Godley; Brenda Heins Heller; Richard Jemmett; Lyman Linger; John Miller; Merle New; Ray Purinton; Dorey Schmidt; "Lucky" Simpson; Mrs. Tom Wyse; and "Slim" Zimmerman.

Information about cattle-guard humor came from Rosemarie Blundell; Alice Bullock; Ralph D. Falconer; Charlie Femling; Tracy King; Doug McDonough; Yvonne J. Milspaw; Rowland Nethaway; Raymond Prewitt; "Ace" Reid; Britton Thompson; Donald Thompson; and Merle Walker.

Other information in this chapter was provided by Marlene Bowman; Carole Cookson; Fred B. Curry; Patricia Diness; T. Elwess; Margaret Hailey; Arlene Larson; Carolyn Logan; Archie Shepard; Linny Teter; Kaye Y. Turner; and Linda Voights.

CHAPTER 8
UNUSUAL CATTLE GUARDS

Printed source materials for this chapter include the *U.S. Patent Gazette;* advertising brochures from the Smith Cattleguard Co., the U.S. Cattle Guard Corp., the Smith Fencer Corp., and the Parker-McCrory Manufacturing Co.; newspaper clippings (from Oregon and Northwest newspapers) sent by Ernest Wells; specification sheets from state highway departments in the western states; University of Missouri Extension Service Bulletin #6-778-C1; and the following books and articles:

DeForest, S. S. "Fences and Gates." *Successful Farming,* March 1956, pp. 41–48.

Fisher, James J. "It May Be Ugly, but It Works." *Kansas City* (Mo.) *Times,* 24 September 1981, sect. D, pp. 1, 8.

"Gates, Gates, Gates." *Successful Farming,* October 1952, pp. 34–35.

Gibson, Eleanor J., and Walk, Richard D. "The 'Visual Cliff.'" *Scientific American,* April 1960, pp. 67–71 (about depth perception in animals).

Nichols, John. *The Milagro Beanfield War.* New York: Holt, Rinehart, & Winston, 1974, pp. 30, 164.

Watson, Chick. "You Can Tell a Cattle Guard Crossing by Its Stripes." *Cattleman,* February 1972, p. 56.

Wilson, Boyd. "Ingenious Portable Electric Cattlestop." *New Zealand Farmer,* 12 April 1979, pp. 17–19.

Highway-department officials from the following states sent information about painted-stripe cattle guards: Arizona, Arkansas (Lawrence Fletcher), California (E. B. Thomas), Colorado, Idaho, Iowa (Dwight L. Stevens), Kansas (LeRoy Pitt and Glenn Anschutz), Louisiana (S. N. Whitthorne and Gorman S. Pounders), Minnesota (R. A. Adolfson), Missouri (Robert N. Hunter), Montana (Stephen C. Kologi and H. J. Anderson), Nebraska (Fred B. Nelson and A. H. Dederman), Nevada (Frank Smyth), New Mexico (Ronald F. Ripley), North Dakota (Floyd Robb), Oklahoma (Max J. Hinderliter), Oregon (R. P. Hamilton), South Dakota (Marlin Larson), Texas (Byron C. Blaschke and B. L. DeBerry), Utah (J. Q. Adair), Washington (D. D. Ernst), and Wyoming (Jeffrey W. Couch).

Information, questions, and comments about painted-stripe cattle guards came from John W. Aldrich; Ted Baehr; T. Lindsay Baker; John B. Curtis; Mary Etta Funk Davidson; Mrs. Nicholas DeLollis; Steven K. Disch; C. O. ("Pete") Erwin; G. Ward Fenley; Gordon W. Fleming; James T. Forrest; Jackie Glenn; James Glenn; Raymond Hull; Virgil Johnson; Mrs. Virgil Johnson; John A. Kennedy; Bill King; Charles E. Lacey; Lyman Linger; Mrs. H. R. Luster; Richard G. Marek; Ken Martin; Victor H. Merrihew; Louise Miller; Jerald W. Pereto; Dallas Perry; Della Oldham Phillips; Don Reese; Tom Rice; Henry Rozier; Sandy Schulz; "Lucky" Simpson; Charlene Slagowski; M. K. Swingle; Karen Swoyer; Matthew M. Syler; Elizabeth Triplett; Bob Wade; Connie Wade; Richard Walk; Chick Watson; John M. White; Mrs. R. Wilkinson; C. W. Wimberley; and C. G. Wood.

Other material in this chapter was provided by Roger Anderson; Steven A. Bealby; Kay Calvert; Duane Cross; Kenneth Hoy; Paul Kottman; Karen Krause; Norman V. Lanquist; J. U. Morris; Jennifer Nicol; Lynn Pearson; Dale Remsberg; Ralph L. Ricketts; Tere Rill; Richard Robbins, Jr.; Stanley Stout; Fred Vahshotz; Ernest Wells; and Otis Wheat.

CHAPTER 9
MAKERS OF CATTLE GUARDS

Brochures provided by these manufacturers of cattle guards were used in gathering information for this chapter: Christianson Pipe, Ltd., Calgary, Alberta; Clark Materials Co., Lexington, Ky.; Goshute Enterprises, Ibapah, Utah; Northland Steel Co., Billings, Mont.; Powder River Enterprises, Provo, Utah; Smith Cattleguard Co., Midland, Va.; Wedco Manufacturing Co., Jackson, Wyo.; and Wikco Industries, Inc., Broken Bow, Nebr.

Other information in this chapter was provided by Lee H. Christianson; Ralph D. Clark; Dan Cookson; James H. Ebbinghaus; Paul K. Edmunds; Darrel Godfrey; Warren Godfrey; W. R. Grantham; Harold B. Halter; Vickie Homfeld; Adam N. Horst; Jackson M. Ideen; Melvin L. Johnson; Frank Parsons; Lynn Pearson; Tom Rice; Tere Rill; Mick Sage; Robert K. Schnell; and Meredith Spencer.

CHAPTER 10
THE ECONOMICS OF CATTLE GUARDS

Information for this chapter was provided by G. R. Brainard, Jr.; Floyd D. Culver; E. G. ("Ty") Dahlgren; L. E. Fitzgarrald; James O. Kemm; Fred H. Lester; Richard L. Manning; Ralph L. Ricketts; Hailey A. Roberts; W. F. Root; William J. Sallans; Lois Schuermann; Sam F. Shakely, Jr.; E. A. Smith; George L. Smith; and Howard Upton.

CHAPTER 11
CATTLE GUARDS AROUND THE WORLD

Information for this chapter came in part from:

"Cattle Grids for Private Roads." *Fixed Equipment of the Farm.* Leaflet #7. London: Ministry of Agriculture, Fisheries, and Food, 1969, 11 pp.
"Cattlestop Designs." *New Zealand Farmer,* 13 May 1976, pp. 26–27.
Herriot, James. *The Lord God Made Them All.* New York: St. Martins Press, 1981, pp. 1–2.
"Fencing and Gates." *The Roads Ordinance, 1933, Province of Transvaal,* chap. 8, pp. 33–36.
"Fencing and Gates." *Road Ordinance and Resolutions, 1957, Province of Transvaal,* chap. 8, pp. 30–32.
Four cattle-grid specification sheets from Transvaal.
"Sir Kenneth Crossley." *Who's Who,* 1911–57.
Wilson, Boyd. "Ingenious Portable Electric Cattlestop." *New Zealand Farmer,* 12 April 1979, pp. 17–19.

These correspondents and informants provided information about the use of cattle guards in other countries: Argentina — Victor H. Pastor and Norman Schlesener; Australia — C. M. H. Clark, James R. Smith, Russel Ward, and Boyd Wilson; Brazil — Sister Anne Cawley, Luiz Felipe de Seixas Corrêa, and the Reverend Carl J. Hahn; Canada — Lindsay Barnham, W. J. Campbell, W. C. Gordon, Alex Johnston, Dian Latiff, Omer Lavallée, John P. Miska, Agnes K. Rice, A. D. Ridge, "Lucky"

Simpson, David C. Smith, and Leland J. Turner; Germany—Prof. Dr. Rudolf Kaiser and Prof. Dr. Gunter Moltmann; Great Britain—Harold H. Aston, John Berryman, D. Bingham, S. G. Bryant, John S. Creasey, Patricia A. Diness, Frank Dymond, Mrs. Frank Dymond, B. Gallagher, Miles Hadfield, Dennis Jeffreys, Richard Jemmett, C. King, William H. Longenecker, Lady Ruth K. Lowther, Margaret Reed, A. M. Robathan, Gerry Symons, Mrs. Gerry Symons, Irene M. Smith, J. D. A. Widdowson, Michael Wright, and Nigel E. Young; India—Tere Rill and Ravi Sheorey; Mexico—E. C. Lesher, William R. Thompson, and Anna Vaughn; New Zealand—T. Hughes, Jennifer Nicol, and Boyd Wilson; Norway—Hanne Henriksen; South Africa—J. E. Nel, G. Orczy, John E. Peterson, P. Serton, and Leonard Thompson; Spain—Roberto Bermúdez, Connie Patton, and Jerri Pennington; Switzerland—J. Warren Brinkman and Chuck Thompson; Venezuela—Enrique Alvarez-Prendes; and Zimbabwe—an embassy spokesman in Washington, D.C.

Other information for this chapter was provided by E. Denig, James Lee Garver, Ed Grimwood, Walter Overstreet, David C. Smith, and C. W. Wimberley.

LIST OF CONTRIBUTORS OF INFORMATION

This list contains the names, titles (where known or pertinent), and addresses of about six hundred and fifty persons who have helped me as I gathered information for this book. The names of many others cannot be listed because their contributions were made anonymously—persons who sent suggestions or bibliographical items by mail or persons who talked with me but whose names I did not record.

The letters in parentheses that follow each entry indicate the nature of the assistance offered:

B   bibliographical material such as newspaper clippings, references to books or articles, technical publications, and advertising brochures
I   interview
L   letter
P   photograph
Q   questionnaire
S   specification sheet or blueprint or construction plan
T   telephone interview

This book could not have been written without the help of these contributors. I am grateful to every one of them.

Abernethy, F. E., secretary, Texas Folklore Soc., Nacogdoches, Tex. (L, P)
Adair, J. Q., Dept. of Transportation, Salt Lake City, Utah (Q, S)
Adams, Jay, lead interpreter, Old Sturbridge Village, Sturbridge, Mass. (L)
Adams, Larry, ed., *North Dakota Stockman,* Bismarck, N.Dak. (L, P)
Adolfson, R. A., design standards engineer, Dept. of Highways, St. Paul, Minn. (Q)
Aeschbacher, W. D., prof. of history, Univ. of Cincinnati, Cincinnati, Ohio (L)
Albaugh, Reuben, extension animal scientist emeritus, Univ. of California, Davis, Calif. (L, P)

Aldrich, John W., Fort Collins, Colo. (L)

Alexander, Essie, Riverton, Nebr. (L)

Alexander, Lawrence, Platte City, Mo. (L)

Allen, James A., ed., *Herald and News,* Klamath Falls, Oreg. (B, L)

Altland, George W., Vici, Okla. (L, P)

Alvarez-Prendes, Enrique, Valencia, Venezuela (I)

Alysmeyer, Henry, librarian, Hendrix Coll., Conway, Ark. (I, L)

Amsberry, Helen, Mullen, Nebr. (Q)

Anderson, Everett, Torrington, Wyo. (L)

Anderson, H. J., director of highways, Helena, Mont. (L)

Anderson, K. T., Emporia, Kans. (Q)

Anderson, Roger, Americus, Kans. (I)

Andre, Paul D., ed., *Beef,* St. Paul, Minn. (L)

Anschutz, Glenn, engineer of design, Dept. of Transportation, Topeka, Kans. (L)

Ansell, W. F. H., Trendrine, Cornwall, England (L)

Armstrong, John B., managing ed., *Northwest Unit Farm Magazines,* Spokane, Wash. (L)

Armstrong, W. F. ("Bill"), engineer of buildings, Chicago & North Western Railway, Chicago, Ill. (L, S)

Arndt, Frank, Emporia, Kans. (I)

Arnett, Walt, Matfield Green, Kans. (I)

Aston, Harold H., Oldbury, West Midlands, England (L, P)

Attebery, Louis W., chairman, Dept. of English, Coll. of Idaho, Caldwell, Idaho (L)

Baehr, Ted, Scottsdale, Ariz. (I, P)

Baker, Bryan, Jr., head, Dept. of Animal Science, Mississippi State Univ., Mississippi State, Miss. (L)

Baker, Mary, Saginaw, Mich. (L to Don Coldsmith)

Baker, T. Lindsay, assoc. curator, Panhandle-Plains Historical Museum, Canyon, Tex. (L, Q)

Bald, Prof. Dr. W. D., Institut für Anglistik, Technischen Hochschule, Aachen, West Germany (L)

Balgooyen, Warren, director-naturalist, Teatown Lake Reservation, Ossining, N.Y. (L)

Barker, S. Omar, Las Vegas, N.Mex. (L)

Bauer, Frederick E., Jr., assoc. librarian, American Antiquarian Soc., Worcester, Mass. (L)

Bealby, Steven A., Russell, Kans. (L)

Beattie, James M., Agricultural Experiment Sta., Pennsylvania State Univ., University Park, Pa. (L)

Beedle, Grace, Bazaar, Kans. (L)

Bell, Don, Byron, Wyo. (Q)

Bell, Elbert L., Long Bell Farms, Fort Scott, Kans. (L)

Bennett, Sharon, office manager, Dept. of Agriculture, Topeka, Kans. (L)

Bennof, Anne O., manager, Educational and Informational Services, Assn. of American Railroads, Washington, D.C. (L)

Bermudez, Roberto, minister for cultural affairs, Spanish Embassy, Washington, D.C. (L)

Bern, Enid, Mott, N.Dak. (L to Larry Remele)

Berryman, John V., Southlea Farm, Datchet, Berkshire, England (I, L)

Bingham, D., ed., *Field*, London, England (L)

Black, Harriette C., librarian and curator, Newcomen Soc. in North America, Downington, Pa. (L)

Blaschke, Byron C., chief engineer of maintenance operations, Dept. of Highways, Austin, Tex. (Q)

Bliss, Lee, Story, Wyo. (I)

Blundell, Mrs. Rosemarie, Chadron, Nebr. (L)

Bohannon, J. R., Knights Landing, Calif. (L)

Boling, L. K., North Platte, Nebr. (I)

Boling, Nellie R., North Platte, Nebr. (B, L)

Bone, Jack, *Minot Daily News*, Minot, N.Dak. (B, L)

Bordwine, Rebecca E., archives librarian, Winchester-Frederick County Historical Soc., Winchester, Va. (B, L)

Bowman, Marlene, Emporia, Kans. (I)

Bradford, Helen, Greenwood County Historical Soc., Eureka, Kans. (L, P)

Brainard, G. R., Jr., Broken Arrow, Okla. (L)

Bredemeier, Edwin H., Steinauer, Nebr. (L, P)

Brenneman, Aeola (Mrs. K. W.), Hyannis, Nebr. (L, Q)

Brewster, Lyman, Radersburg, Mont. (L)

Bridgewater, Jim, Calgary, Alberta, Canada (I by W. J. Campbell)

Brinkman, J. Warren, dean of academic services, Emporia State Univ., Emporia, Kans. (I, P)

Brown, Howard C., dean, School of Agriculture and Natural Resources, California Polytechnic State Univ., San Luis Obispo, Calif. (L)

Browning, Bill, Madison, Kans. (L)

Bryant, S. G., Henley-on-Thames, Oxfordshire, England (L)

Buchman, Mrs. Burton, Hymer, Kans. (I)

Bullock, Alice, Santa Fe, N.Mex. (L)

Burk, Bill, vice-president of public relations, Atchison, Topeka & Santa Fe Railway, Chicago, Ill. (L)

Burnham, Lindsay, Glenbow-Alberta Inst., Calgary, Alberta, Canada (L)

Burtis, Orville, Sr., Manhattan, Kans. (Q)

Byerly, Joyce, secretary, McKenzie County Grazing Assn., Watford City, N.Dak. (I)

Calvert, Kay, Emporia, Kans. (B)

Campbell, Jack W., ed., *Fence Rider*, Armco Steel Corp., Kansas City, Mo. (B)

Campbell, W. J., manager, Heritage Park, Calgary, Alberta, Canada (B, L)

Carmody, Arthur, Trenton, Nebr. (Q)

Carpenter, Roy ("Cap"), San Angelo, Tex. (L, P, Q)

Case, Tom, Platte City, Mo. (I, P)

Cawley, Sister Anne, O.S.B., coordinator, Friends of Brazil, Atchison, Kans. (L, P)

Cerny, Louis T., acting executive director, American Railway Engineering Assn., Chicago, Ill. (L)

Chambers, Riley R., Mountain City, Nev. (Q)

Christensen, Ralph M., Watford City, N.Dak. (L)

Christianson, Lee H., pres., Christianson Pipe Ltd., Calgary, Alberta, Canada (L, P, S, T)

Clark, C. M. H., prof. of Australian history, Australian National Univ., Canberra, Australia (L)

Clark, Ralph D., Clark Materials Co., Lexington, Ky. (B, L)

Clark, Ralph H., WaKeeney, Kans. (L)

Clarke, Robert, prof. of biology, Emporia State Univ., Emporia, Kans. (I, P)

Clayton, Lawrence, chairman, Dept. of English, Hardin-Simmons Univ., Abilene, Tex. (L)

Coldsmith, Don, M.D., Emporia, Kans. (I)

Collins, W. H., extension specialist, agricultural engineering, Virginia Polytechnic Inst., Blacksburg, Va. (L)

Combs, Barry B., director of public relations, Union Pacific Railroad, Omaha, Nebr. (L, S)

Constantino, George M., acting refuge manager, Wichita Mountains Wildlife Refuge, Indiahoma, Okla. (L)

Cookson, Carole, Madison, Kans. (I)

Cooper, Elmer, Saffordville, Kans. (Q)

Copeland, P. Allen, Pacific Southwest Railway Museum Assn. Inc., San Diego, Calif. (L)

Correa, Luiz Felipe de Seixas, counselor for cultural affairs, Brazilian Embassy, Washington, D.C. (L)

Cory, Robert, *Daily News,* Minot, N.Dak. (B, L)

Côté, J. G., Canadian National Railways, Edmonton, Alberta, Canada (L)

Cotter, Canon J. B. D., vicar of Zennor, Zennor, Cornwall, England (I, L)

Couch, Jeffrey W., highway engineering designer II, Highway Dept., Cheyenne, Wyo. (Q, S)

Cowan, D. Neil, Mosca, Colo. (L)

Cowan, Dennis W., Ellinwood, Kans. (Q, T)

Cowsar, O. E. ("Whitey"), New London, Tex. (I)

Crane, Mrs. Donald B., Broad Brook, Conn. (L)

Creasey, John S., information officer, Museum of English Rural Life, Univ. of Reading, Reading, England (L)

Crisler, Robert M., secretary-treasurer, Louisiana Historical Assn., Lafayette, La. (L)

Criss, Lloyd, Emporia, Kans. (I)

Crocker, Mason, Brady, Tex. (B, I)

Cross, Duane, Cross Machinery & Manufacturing Co., Mindenmines, Mo. (T)

Crosson, David, research historian, Western History Research Center, Univ. of Wyoming, Laramie, Wyo. (L)

Culver, Floyd D., Ponca City, Okla. (I, L)

Curry, Fred B., New Braunfels, Tex. (L)

Curtis, John B., Santa Fe, N.Mex. (L)

Dahl, Norman, Watford City, N.Dak. (B, L, P)

Dahlgren, E. G. ("Ty"), Oklahoma City, Okla. (L)

Daily, Rose Marie, Kenne, Wash. (Q)

Dale, Bill, Protection, Kans. (I by Cynthia Dale)

Dale, Cynthia, Protection, Kans. (I)

Dallas, Jean C., director/curator, Riley County Historical Soc. and Museum, Manhattan, Kans. (L)

Dauman, C. E., Ponca City, Okla. (T)

Davidson, Mary Etta Funk (Mrs. F. A.), Craig, Colo. (L)

Davis, Barbara Hillyer, director, Women's Studies Program, Univ. of Oklahoma, Norman, Okla. (L)

Davis, John, farm ed., *Pittsburg Sun,* Pittsburg, Kans. (T)

Day, Clarence, Orono, Maine (L)

DeBerry, B. L., engineer-director, Dept. of Highways, Austin, Tex. (L)

Dederman, A. H., maintenance engineer, Nebraska Dept. of Roads, Lincoln, Nebr. (Q, S)

DeDonder, Kenny, Reading, Kans. (I)

DeDonder, Terry, Reading, Kans. (I)

Delay, L. G., historian, Nebraska State Historical Soc., Lincoln, Nebr. (L)

Delinger, William, Physics Dept., Northern Arizona Univ., Flagstaff, Ariz. (B, L, T)

DeLollis, Mrs. Nicholas J., Albuquerque, N.Mex. (L)

Denig, E., agricultural counselor, Royal Netherlands Embassy, Washington, D.C. (L)

Devine, Marge, scribe, National Cartoonists Soc., Brooklyn, N.Y. (L)

Dieter, Frank H., Longford, Kans. (L)

Diffey, Thelma, Capitola, Calif. (L)

Diness, Mrs. Patricia A., Middletown, N.Y. (L)

Disch, Steven K., public relations, Henderson Mine, AMAX, Inc., Empire, Colo. (L)

Dixon, Thomas W., Jr., pres., Chesapeake & Ohio Historical Soc., Alderson, W.Va. (B, L)

Dobbins, C. O., Coffeyville, Kans. (L)

Dobie, Dudley, San Marcos, Tex. (I by C. W. Wimberley)

Dodd, Dave, Flagstaff, Ariz. (L)

Dorris, W. H., Arthur, Nebr. (Q)

Dorsett, Art, Vestring Ranch, Olpe, Kans. (I)

Douch, H. L., curator, County Museum and Art Gallery, Truro, Cornwall, England (I, L)

Durst, Harold, dean of graduate studies, Emporia State Univ., Emporia, Kans. (I)

Dymond, Frank, Great Hewas Farm, Cornwall, England (I)

Dymond, Mrs. Frank, Great Hewas Farm, Cornwall, England (I)

Earl, Phillip I., curator of exhibits, Nevada Historical Soc., Reno, Nev. (L)

Ebbinghaus, James H., Farm and Industrial Equipment Inst., Chicago, Ill. (L)

Edmunds, Paul K., program director, Cooperative Extension Service, Utah State Univ., Logan, Utah (L)

Edwards, G. P., senior curator, Gilcrease Inst., Tulsa, Okla. (L)

Eger, Stephany, librarian, Museum of New Mexico History Library, Santa Fe, N.Mex. (L)

Eggen, John, Sr., Sedan, Kans. (I by Linda Musgrave Hull)

Eggleston, Urie, Cassville, Mo. (I by Brenda Heins)

Eitner, Walter H., Dept. of English, Kansas State Univ., Manhattan, Kans. (T)

Elkins, Charles J., director, Membership Service, National Cattlemen's Assn., Denver, Colo. (L)

Ellis, L. Tuffly, director, Texas State Historical Assn., Austin, Tex. (L)

Elwess, T., Chadron, Nebr. (L)

Enfield, Virgil E., Arthur, Nebr. (Q)

Engel, Catherine T., reference librarian, State Historical Soc. of Colorado, Denver, Colo. (L)

Ernst, D. D., highway maintenance engineer, Dept. of Transportation, Olympia, Wash. (L, S)

Erwin, C. O. ("Pete"), former chief state highway engineer, Highway Dept., Santa Fe, N.Mex. (I by John B. Curtis)

Etulain, Dick, Dept. of History, Univ. of New Mexico, Albuquerque, N.Mex. (L)

Evans, Charles M., H O Ranch, North Platte, Nebr. (Q)

Everhart, Marion E., Scottsdale, Ariz. (B, L)

Eversole, Richard, Dept. of English, Univ. of Kansas, Lawrence, Kans. (L)

Falconer, Ralph D., Grand Junction, Colo. (B)

Fankhouser, Robert F., Madison, Kans. (Q)

Farthing, Cecil, Olpe, Kans. (T)

Faulk, Odie B., chairman, Dept. of History, Oklahoma State Univ., Stillwater, Okla. (L)

Faull, T. R., Glcombe Cottage, Bude, Cornwall, England (L)

Felton, Kenneth E., extension agricultural engineer, Univ. of Maryland, College Park, Md. (L)

Femling, Charles F. ("Charlie"), farm and ranch ed., *Billings Gazette*, Billings, Mont. (B, L)

Fenley, G. Ward, *Albuquerque Journal*, Albuquerque, N.Mex. (L)

Fife, Austin E., Fife Western Folklore Archive and Research Center, Utah State Univ., Logan, Utah (L)

Fisher, James, *Kansas City Star* and *Times*, Kansas City, Mo. (I)

Fitch, Mrs. Pollie Allen, Rexburg, Idaho (B, L, P)

Fitzjarrald, L. E., vice-pres. (retired), Phillips Petroleum, Bartlesville, Okla. (L)

Fleck, Mrs. Frank, Grassy Butte, N.Dak. (Q)

Fleming, Gordon W., Kirkland, Wash. (L)

Fletchall, Mabel, Kansas City, Kans. (I by Mary Kemper)

Fletcher, Lawrence, Dept. of Highways, Little Rock, Ark. (Q)

Florida, Bob, National Forest Service, Cody, Wyo. (T)

Foris, Gladys R., program manager, Educational Standards, Dept. of Education, Juneau, Alaska (L)

Forrest, James T., Laramie, Wyo. (Q)

Fowler, Don, Wiley, Colo. (L)

Fox, Danny G., assoc. prof. of animal sciences, Cornell Univ., Ithaca, N.Y. (L)

Fox, Frank, Montezuma, Kans. (L)

Fox, Linda, Montezuma, Kans. (L)

Fredericks, Kenneth J., acting director, Office of Trust Responsibilities, BIA, Interior Dept., Washington, D.C. (L)

French, Robert M., Okanogan, Wash. (L)

Frey, Mrs. Paul, Hay Springs, Nebr. (L)

Gailey, Alan, secretary, Soc. for Folk Life Studies, Ulster Folk and Transport Museum, County Down, Ulster, Northern Ireland (L)

Gallagher, B., British Railways Board, London, England (B, L)

Garnett, Ruth E., Roswell, N.Mex. (B)

Garver, James Lee, Emporia, Kans. (I)

Geer, Wayne, Walden, Colo. (Q)

Geil, Bonnie, communications director, *Western Farmer*, Seattle, Wash. (L)

Gentry, Raymond R., Alliance, Nebr. (B, L)

Gibson, Arrell Morgan, Dept. of History, Univ. of Oklahoma, Norman, Okla. (L)

Gibson, Eleanor J., Susan Linn Sage Professor of Psychology, Cornell Univ., Ithaca, N.Y. (L)

Gibson, Stewart, extension dairyman, Animal Sciences, Univ. of Vermont, Burlington, Vt. (L)

Gililland, Lois M., director, Deaf Smith County Museum, Hereford, Tex. (L)
Gilroy, William W., Looe, Cornwall, England (L)
Ginter, Donald W., curator, Mid-Continent Railway Historical Soc., North Freedom, Wis. (L)
Glenn, Jackie, Emporia, Kans. (I)
Glenn, James, Emporia, Kans. (I)
Glover, Ellen E., research asst., Wyoming State Archives and Historical Dept., Cheyenne, Wyo. (L)
Glover, Jack, Sunset, Tex. (Q)
Goddard, C. J., V H Ranch, Watford City, N.Dak. (B, L)
Godfrey, Darrell, Eureka, Kans. (I)
Godfrey, Warren, Madison, Kans. (I, L)
Godley, Lon J., Hardesty, Okla. (L)
Gordon, W. C., director, Animal Industry Div., *Agriculture Week*, Edmonton, Alberta, Canada (L)
Gouley, Bob A., publications ed., *California Sheepman's Quarterly*, Sacramento, Calif. (L)
Grandle, George F., instructor, Agricultural Engineering, Univ. of Tennessee Inst. of Agriculture, Knoxville, Tenn. (L)
Grantham, W. R., Marietta, Okla. (L)
Grassham, John W., archivist, State Records Center and Archives, Santa Fe, N.Mex. (L, P)
Gray, J. Rufus, Pratt, Kans. (L, Q)
Graybill, Lyle S., Friend, Nebr. (L)
Green, Frank L., librarian, Washington State Historical Soc., Tacoma, Wash. (L)
Greene, Howard F., pres., Railway and Locomotive Historical Soc. Inc., Harvard Business School, Boston, Mass. (L)
Greer, Larry, Emporia, Kans. (I, L)
Gressley, Gene M., director, Western History Research Center, Univ. of Wyoming, Laramie, Wyo. (L)
Griggs, William C., director, Panhandle-Plains Historical Museum, Canyon, Tex. (L)
Grimwood, Ed, Burns, Kans. (I, L)
Gross, Walter A., cooperative extension specialist, dairy/livestock/horse, Univ. of Rhode Island, Kingston, R.I. (L)
Gwennap, F., Pendrea Farm, St. Buryan, Cornwall, England (L, P)
Hadfield, Miles, Ledbury, Herefordshire, England (L)
Haenlein, George F. W., prof. and extension dairyman, Coll. of Agricultural Science, Univ. of Delaware, Newark, Del. (L)
Hahn, The Reverend Carl J., Emporia, Kans. (I)
Hahn, Henry, Modesto, Calif. (L)
Hailey, Margaret, Phoenix, Ariz. (L)
Hall, Mrs. Ralph, Coffeyville, Kans. (L)
Halter, Harold B., Farm Equipment Manufacturers Assn., St. Louis, Mo. (L)
Hamilton, R. P., director of permits, Highway Div., Salem, Oreg. (Q, S)
Hanson, Charles E., director, Museum of the Fur Trade, Chadron, Nebr. (L)
Hardy, Clay, Las Vegas, Nev. (L, Q)
Harris, Mac R., Oklahoma Historical Soc., Oklahoma City, Okla. (L)
Harris, Ralph R., prof. of animal and dairy science, Auburn Univ., Auburn, Ala. (L)

Harris, W. L., director, Agricultural Experiment Sta., Univ. of Maryland, College Park, Md. (L)

Harsh, Kim, Cassoday, Kans. (I)

Harsh, Marie, Cassoday, Kans. (L)

Harsh, Ray ("Turk"), Cassoday, Kans. (L, Q)

Hart, Arthur A., director, Idaho State Historical Soc., Boise, Idaho (L)

Hartley, Dorothy, Llangollen, Clwyd, Wales (L)

Hatch, Ivan, Meriden, Kans. (L)

Hatch, James E. ("Pete"), Hilltop Ranch, Roswell, N.Mex. (B, L)

Hayes, Keith, Hutchinson, Kans. (Q)

Heilstine, Viola, Clark County Highway Dept., Ashland, Kans. (L)

Heller, Brenda Heins, Bartlesville, Okla. (I)

Hemy, Peter, public relations officer, Great Western Soc. Ltd., Didcot, Oxfordshire, England (L)

Henriksen, Hanne, Skagen, Denmark (I)

Hentges, James F., Jr., prof. of animal science, Univ. of Florida, Gainesville, Fla. (L)

Henthorne, Marilyn, former director, Instructional Television, Emporia State Univ., Emporia, Kans. (I)

Hess, Jerry N., National Archives and Records Service, Washington, D.C. (L)

Hickey, Joe, assoc. prof. of sociology/anthropology, Emporia State Univ., Emporia, Kans. (I)

Hills, Bud, Mankato, Kans. (T)

Hills, Henry G., WaKeeney, Kans. (Q)

Hinderliter, Max J., maintenance engineer, Dept. of Transportation, Oklahoma City, Okla. (Q)

Hoadley, D. E., principal engineer-staff, Delaware & Hudson Railway Co., Albany, N.Y. (L)

Hoffman, Lynette S., Agricultural Experiment Sta., Kansas State Univ., Manhattan, Kans. (L)

Hofsommer, Donovan L., head, Dept. of History, Wayland Baptist College, Plainview, Tex. (L)

Holden, Dr. W. Curry, prof. emeritus of history, Texas Tech Univ., Lubbock, Tex. (L)

Holder, Ruth, Wichita, Kans. (B, L)

Holland, Bonnie, Moses Lake, Wash. (L)

Homfeld, Vickie, secretary, Farm Equipment Manufacturers Assn., St. Louis, Mo. (L)

Horst, Adam, Yates Center, Kans. (L, T)

Houseman, Claire, Aberdeen, S.Dak. (I, L)

Hoy, Benjamin Franklin, Aspermont, Tex. (L)

Hoy, Kenneth, Flying H Ranch, Cassoday, Kans. (I)

Hoy, Orville, B., Sweet Home, Oreg. (L)

Hubbell, Chloe, Severy, Kans. (Q)

Hughes, T., information officer, New Zealand Embassy, Washington, D.C. (L)

Hull, Linda Musgrave, Emporia, Kans. (I)

Hull, Raymond, Lake City, Kans. (L, Q)

Hunter, Robert N., chief engineer, Highway and Transportation Commission, Jefferson City, Mo. (L)

Huseman, Virgil, Kansas Livestock Assn., Topeka, Kans. (L)

Ideen, Jackson M., pres., Wikco Industries Inc., Broken Bow, Nebr. (L, Q)

Jacobs, Jim, Anchor Park, Alaska (L)

James, Benjamin A., Jr., assoc. director, Coll. of Agriculture, Univ. of Illinois, Urbana, Ill. (L)

Jeffreys, Dennis, Crawley, Sussex, England (L)

Jemmett, Richard, Saffron Walden, Essex, England (L, P)

Jenkins, Dr. Myra Ellen, state historian, State Records Center and Archives, Santa Fe, N.Mex. (B, L, P)

Johnson, Melvin L., manager nuclear plant engineering, K G & E Co., Wichita, Kans. (L, S)

Johnson, Mrs. Virgil, Crowell, Tex. (L)

Johnston, Alex, range management specialist, Agriculture Canada, Lethbridge, Alberta, Canada (L)

Johnston, Carroll, Watford City, N.Dak. (I)

Jolly, William M., Clifton, Tex. (L)

Jones, Benjamin A., Jr., assoc. director, Agricultural Experiment Sta., Univ. of Illinois, Urbana, Ill. (L)

Jones, Mildred, Cathlamet, Wash. (L)

Jordan, Jesse, curator, Western Trails Museum, Clinton, Okla. (L)

Jutzi, Alan, Rare Book Dept., Huntington Library, San Marino, Calif. (L)

Kachel, Harold S., curator, No Man's Land Historical Museum, Panhandle State Univ., Goodwell, Okla. (L)

Kaiser, Prof. Dr. Rudolf, Hochschule Hildesheim, Hildesheim, Germany (I, L, P)

Kallas, Nick, general manager, Illinois Railway Museum, Union, Ill. (L)

Kemm, James O., executive manager, Oklahoma Petroleum Council, Tulsa, Okla. (L)

Kemper, Christina, Kansas City, Kans. (I by Mary Kemper)

Kemper, Mary, Kansas City, Kans. (I)

Kennedy, Jane F., general manager, Library Div., U.S. Postal Service, Washington, D.C. (L)

Kennedy, John A., Albuquerque, N.Mex. (L)

Keough, Brooks, Keene, N.Dak. (L)

Kern, Tom L., Jr., Laramie, Wyo. (Q)

King, Bill, Kim, Colo. (L, Q)

King, C., National Trust, London, England (L)

King, C. Richard, prof. of journalism, Univ. of Texas, Austin, Tex. (L)

King, Scottie, assoc. ed., *New Mexico Magazine*, Santa Fe, N.Mex. (L)

King, Tracy, Roby, Tex. (L, Q)

Kiser, James, Chanute, Kans. (B, I)

Koch, Mary Ann, regional ed., *North Platte Telegraph*, North Platte, Nebr. (L, P)

Koch, William E., prof. emeritus of folklore, Kansas State Univ., Manhattan, Kans. (I, L, P)

Kologi, Stephen C., preconstruction bureau chief, Dept. of Highways, Helena, Mont. (Q, S)

Kordick, Alexander M., Sr., Seymour, Conn. (L)

Kottman, Paul, Ellsworth, Kans. (T)

Krause, Karen, Overland Park, Kans. (I)

Krueger, Gloria, Missoula, Mont. (L)

Kuehn, Claire R., archivist-librarian, Panhandle-Plains Historical Museum, Canyon, Tex. (L)

Kuralt, Charles, CBS-TV News, New York, N.Y. (T)

Lacey, Charles E., Lawrence, Kans. (L)

Langley, John, director (retired), Regents Press of Kansas, Lawrence, Kans. (B)

Lanquist, Norman V., prof. of English, Eastern Arizona Coll., Thatcher, Ariz. (I, L)

Larrimore, Irl E., Jr., Dept. of Highways and Public Transportation, Austin, Tex. (L, Q, S)

Larson, Arlene, English Dept., Casper Coll., Casper, Wyo. (I)

Larson, Marlin, senior engineer, Secondary Roads Program, Dept. of Transportation, Pierre, S.Dak. (Q, S)

Latiff, Dian, *Alberta Farm Life*, Edmonton, Alberta, Canada (L)

Laughlin, Karen, librarian, Iowa State Historical Dept., Iowa City, Iowa (L, P)

Lauppe, Raymond E., Arbuckle, Calif. (L,Q)

Lavallee, Omer, corporate archivist, Canadian Pacific Railway, Montreal, Quebec, Canada (L)

Lawlis, Albert, Broken Bow, Nebr. (L, P)

Lawson, David, Dept. of English, Univ. of Wyoming, Laramie, Wyo. (L)

Leagley, C. Y., works general engineer, British Railways Board, London, England (L)

Lee, Edna Marie, ed., *Kanhistique: Kansas History and Antiques,* Ellsworth, Kans. (L)

Lefors, Emmett, Pampa, Tex. (Q, T)

Leining, M. H., Alta Loma, Tex. (L)

Leon, Pam, editorial asst., *Brangus Journal,* San Antonio, Tex. (L)

Lesher, E. C., Del Rio, Tex. (L)

Lester, Fred H., chief of police, Midwest, Wyo. (B, L)

Lester, Margaret, Utah State Historical Soc., Salt Lake City, Utah (L)

Levy, Donald A., Leighton Buzzard, Bedfordshire, England (L)

Lind, Marcus, Salem, Oreg. (L)

Linger, Lyman, Loveland, Colo. (I by Marilyn Henthorne)

Loftin, Jack, Archer County Historical Commission, Windhorst, Tex. (B, L)

Long, Esther, librarian, National Cowboy Hall of Fame and Western Heritage Center, Oklahoma City, Okla. (L)

Longenecker, William H., Reference Div., National Agricultural Library, Beltsville, Md. (B, L)

Loomis, Faith M., El Dorado, Kans. (Q)

Lowther, Lady Ruth K., Lightwood Green, Overton-on-Dee, Clwyd, Wales (I, L)

Luster, Mrs. H. R., Palisade, Colo. (L)

Lyall, John C., Bonallack Barton, Gweek, Cornwall, England (L, P)

Lynn, Ruth (Mrs. Fred), Emporia, Kans. (T)

McCammon, R. L., Hillsboro, Oreg. (L)

McCann, F. B., McCann's Polled Hereford Ranch, Culbertson, Mont. (L, Q)

McCormick, Dewey Z., Manhattan, Kans. (L, Q)

McCrea, Tom, Plains, Mont. (L)

McDonough, Doug, farm ed., *Plainview Daily Herald,* Plainview, Tex. (B, L)

McEndree, Jim, Springfield, Colo. (L, Q)

McKenzie, W. A., director, Information Services, Burlington Northern, St. Paul, Minn. (B, L, S)

McKinney, George W., Englewood, Kans. (L, Q, T)

MacKinnon, Charlie, Calgary, Alberta, Canada (I by W. J. Campbell)

Magee, Robert M., Rock Island, Ill. (L)
Maguire, Jack R., executive director, Inst. of Texan Cultures, San Antonio, Tex. (L)
Malec, Enid V., Isles of Scilly Museum Assn., Hughtown, St. Mary's, Isles of Scilly, United Kingdom (L)
Malkus, Louis A., extension livestock specialist, Univ. of Connecticut, Storrs, Conn. (L)
Manly, Will, Hymer, Kans. (T)
Manning, Gordon, asst. librarian, Oregon Historical Soc., Portland, Oreg. (L)
Manning, Richard L., public affairs manager, Western Gas & Oil Assn., Los Angeles, Calif. (L)
Marek, Richard G., National Assn. of County Agricultural Agents, Carlsbad, N.Mex. (L)
Martin, Ken, Jacksonville, Oreg. (L)
Matthews, Robert A., vice-pres., Railway Progress Inst., Alexandria, Va. (L)
Mercer, Alfred, Matfield Green, Kans. (T)
Mercer, David, Cedar Point, Kans. (I, T)
Merrihew, Victor H., Ashby, Nebr. (L, Q)
Meyer, Alfred, Wellfleet, Nebr. (L)
Michetti, Otto, Edmonton, Alberta, Canada (L, S)
Miller, David, Albert, Kans. (Q)
Miller, Jack, range management, U.S. Dept. of Agriculture, Forest Service, Washington, D.C. (L)
Miller, John, Bryan, Tex. (L)
Miller, Louise, "Action Line," *Albuquerque Journal,* Albuquerque, N.Mex. (B, L)
Mills, Jack, manager, Goshute Enterprises, Ibapah, Utah (B, Q, S)
Mills, W. C., Lake City, Kans. (I, L)
Milspaw, Yvonne J., Pennsylvania State Univ. (Capitol), Middleton, Pa. (I)
Miska, John P., library area coordinator, Agricultural Canada, Lethbridge, Alberta, Canada (L)
Mitchell, L. W., acting secretary to the Council of the Isles of Scilly, St. Mary's, Isles of Scilly, United Kingdom (L)
Mockamer, Roy D., Osage City, Kans. (I)
Moltman, Prof. Dr. Gunter, German Assn. for American Studies, Cologne, West Germany (L)
Monahan, Earl H., Hyannis, Nebr. (Q)
Moore, R. A., director, Agricultural Experiment Sta., South Dakota State Univ., Brookings, S.Dak. (L)
Morris, J. U., Columbia, Mo. (L, S)
Murphy, Michael, Conifer, Colo. (L)
Murphy, Mrs. T. James, Z C Ranch, Livingston, Mont. (L)
Myers, Rex C., reference librarian, Montana Historical Soc., Helena, Mont. (B, L)
Mzorek, Don, Dept. of History, Kansas State Univ., Manhattan, Kans. (L)
Neal, Tom Y., Las Vegas, Nev. (L)
Nel, J. E., agricultural-scientific counselor, Embassy of South Africa, Washington, D.C. (L)
Nelson, Fred B., public information manager, Dept. of Roads, Lincoln, Nebr. (L)
Nethaway, Rowland, assoc. ed., *Austin American Statesman,* Austin, Tex. (B, T)
Neubauer, David J., publicity director, Wabash, Frisco, & Pacific Assn. Inc., Hazelwood, Mo. (L)

215

New, Merle, Magdalena, N.Mex. (I)
Newberry, D. J., Grand Island, Nebr. (L)
Nicol, Jennifer, Christchurch, New Zealand (B, L)
Noble, Joseph A., Amarillo, Tex. (L, Q)
Oakham, Elizabeth, Citrus Heights, Calif. (L)
Ohrlin, Glenn, Mountain View, Ark. (L)
Oleskie, Edward T., extension specialist, dairy science, Rutgers Univ., New Bruns-
wick, N.J. (L)
Oliphant, J. Orin, Salem, Oreg. (L)
Orcutt, E. Paul, Bozeman, Mont. (L)
Orczy, G., director of roads, Transvaal Roads Dept., Pretoria, South Africa (B, L)
Ortmann, John, staff writer, *York News-Times*, York, Nebr. (L)
Osteen, Ira ("Ike"), Springfield, Colo. (L, Q)
Overholser, Joel F., ed., *The River Press*, Fort Benton, Mont. (L)
Overstreet, Walter, Lone Grove, Tex. (P, Q)
Pacholik, Louise, Chicago Historical Soc., Chicago, Ill. (B, L)
Parsons, Frank, Susank, Kans. (L)
Pastor, Victor H., M.D., Emporia, Kans. (T)
Patton, Connie, assoc. prof. of foreign languages, Emporia State Univ., Emporia,
Kans. (I, P)
Paugh, Minnie, special collections librarian, Montana State Univ., Bozeman,
Mont. (L)
Pearson, Lynn, Ad Design Ltd., Midland, Va. (L)
Pearson, Mabel Hickman (Mrs. George), Valentine, Nebr. (L, Q)
Pendergraft, Clarence, Emporia, Kans. (I, Q)
Pennington, Jerri, acquisitions librarian, William Allen White Library, Emporia
State Univ., Emporia, Kans. (I)
Pereto, Jerald W., Orange, Tex. (L)
Perkins, Doug, editorial director, *Cattleman,* Fort Worth, Tex. (L)
Perkins, Earl E., Howard, Kans. (Q)
Perry, Dallas W., Kimball, Nebr. (I, L)
Perry, Donald, chairman, Dept. of Art, Emporia State Univ., Emporia, Kans. (I)
Peterson, Dorothy, Douglas, Wyo. (L)
Peterson, John E., dean of liberal arts & sciences, Emporia State Univ., Emporia,
Kans. (I)
Phillips, Della Oldham, Tuscarora, Nev. (Q)
Phillips, Lewis E., Kimball, Nebr. (L)
Phillips, Vicki, documents librarian, Oklahoma State Univ., Stillwater, Okla. (L)
Phillips, W. C., Reading, Kans. (L to Don Coldsmith)
Pierce, Ray, ed., *High Plains Journal,* Dodge City, Kans. (L)
Pitt, LeRoy, road engineer, Dept. of Transportation, Topeka, Kans. (Q, S)
Pontrelli, Jeanny, Univ. of Nevada-Reno, Reno, Nev. (I, L)
Pope, Wiley Roger, asst. reference librarian, Minnesota Historical Soc., St. Paul,
Minn. (L)
Porras, Edmundo, editorial director, *World Farming,* Overland Park, Kans. (L)
Pounders, Gorman S., chief maintenance & operations engineer, Dept. of Trans-
portation and Development, Baton Rouge, La. (L, S)
Powell, Lawrence S., St. Just-in-Roseland, Cornwall, England (L)
Powell, Mrs. Lawrence S., St. Just-in-Roseland, Cornwall, England (I)
Prewitt, Melba, P L Ranch, Cassoday, Kans. (I, L)

Prewitt, Raymond, P L Ranch, Cassoday, Kans. (I)

Price, Gladys (Mrs. Ben, Sr.), Reading, Kans. (L)

Priefert, Elmer, Fairmont, Nebr. (L)

Purinton, Ray, Quinter, Kans. (I)

Quirk, Tom, Dept. of English, Univ. of Missouri-Columbia, Columbia, Mo. (I)

Rasmussen, Wayne D., executive secretary-treasurer, Agricultural History Soc., Washington, D.C. (L)

Rauch, Carl, Coffeyville, Kans. (B, L)

Reddick, Ella, Wood Lake, Nebr. (L)

Reed, Margaret, Great Hewas Farm, Cornwall, England (I)

Rees, Conwy, Emporia, Kans. (I)

Reese, Don, Turin, Iowa (L)

Reid, "Ace," Kerrville, Tex. (T)

Remele, Larry, managing ed., *North Dakota History*, Bismarck, N.Dak. (B, L, P)

Remsberg, Dale, Cassoday, Kans. (I)

Rexroat, James, Hoisington, Kans. (Q)

Rexroat, Walker, Downs, Kans. (Q)

Rice, Agnes K., Ladysmith, British Columbia, Canada (L, P)

Rice, Tom, Medford, Oreg. (L)

Richards, Opal, Severy, Kans. (L)

Richmond, Robert W., asst. secretary, Kansas State Historical Soc., Topeka, Kans. (L)

Ricketts, Ralph L., prof. emeritus of agricultural engineering, Univ. of Missouri, Columbia, Mo. (L, S)

Ridge, A. D., provincial archivist, Edmonton, Alberta, Canada (L)

Riggs, Elvis, Stephenville, Tex. (I)

Rill, Tere, administrative asst., Smith Cattleguard Co., Midland, Va. (B, L, S)

Ripley, Ronald F., Public Affairs Office, Highway Dept., Santa Fe, N.Mex. (Q, S)

Ritchie, Harlan D., prof. of animal husbandry, Michigan State Univ., East Lansing, Mich. (L)

Robathan, A. M., county secretary, National Farmers' Union, Cornwall County Branch, Truro, Cornwall, England (L)

Robb, Floyd, Highway Dept., Bismarck, N.Dak. (Q)

Robbins, Richard W., Jr., Pratt, Kans. (Q)

Robbins, Sarah, Aptos, Calif. (L)

Roberts, F. W., Austin, Tex. (B)

Roberts, Hailey A., managing director, Pipe Line Contractors Assn., Dallas, Tex. (L)

Robertson, Rosemary, Inst. of Cornish Studies, Univ. of Exeter, Redruth, Cornwall, England (L)

Robinson, Ralph R., Franklin, Nebr. (L, Q)

Robinson, Sheila (Mrs. Dave), Coleharbor Stock Farm, Coleharbor, N.Dak. (L, P)

Rodenberger, Lou, English Dept., Texas A & M Univ., College Station, Tex. (I)

Rodgers, Warren, educational director, Stuhr Museum of the Prairie Pioneer, Grand Island, Nebr. (B, L)

Rogler, Wayne, Matfield Green, Kans. (I, Q)

Root, W. F., manager, Special Projects Engineering, Phillips Petroleum Co., Bartlesville, Okla. (L)

Rothwell, Robert L., Hyannis, Nebr. (Q)

Rowe, Dr. John, School of History, Univ. of Liverpool, Liverpool, England (L)

Rowe, William S., D.V.M., Helotes, Tex. (L)

Rozier, Henry, Riverton, Wyo. (L)

Rupp, Robert G., ed., *Farmer,* St. Paul, Minn. (L)

Ryons, Debi, Information Service, *Los Angeles Times,* Los Angeles, Calif. (L)

Sage, Mick, Virgil, Kans. (I)

Sakugawa, James, Maui, Hawaii (L)

Sallans, William J., executive vice-pres., Petroleum Equipment Suppliers Assn., Houston, Tex. (L)

Sass, Elmer W., Nevada, Mo. (L)

Sautter, John H., Mullen, Nebr. (Q)

Sawyer, G. M., Valentine, Nebr. (L, Q)

Schatz, Mrs. Gail, *Grant County News,* Elgin, N.Dak. (L)

Schlebecker, John T., curator of agriculture, Smithsonian Inst., Washington, D.C. (L)

Schlesener, Norman, Kingman County agricultural extension agent, Kingman, Kans. (I, T)

Schmidt, Dorey, Pan American Univ., Edinburg, Tex. (I)

Schnell, Robert K,, director of membership services and convention manager, Farm Equipment Manufacturers Assn., St. Louis, Mo. (L)

Schuermann, Lois, asst. librarian, American Petroleum Inst., Washington, D.C. (L)

Schultz, Sandy, field technician, U.S. Geological Survey, Santa Cruz, Calif. (L)

Schultz, Walter F., Midwest, Wyo. (Q)

Scribner, Lowell, T Z Ranch, El Dorado, Kans. (I)

Seihold, Clark, Mid-Continent Oil & Gas, Tulsa, Okla. (B)

Serton, P., Dept. of Transport, Pretoria, South Africa (L)

Shakely, Sam F., Jr., Interstate Oil Compact Commission, Oklahoma City, Okla. (L)

Shaw, Collins, Dallas, Tex. (L)

Shaw, John R., Dallas, Tex. (L)

Shell, Thelma A., Story, Wyo. (L)

Sheorey, Ravi, Dept. of English, Oklahoma State Univ., Stillwater, Okla. (I)

Shepard, Archie, Shepard Gallery of Landscape Paintings, Greensburg, Kans. (I)

Sheppard, Burt, O H Ranch, Longview, Alberta, Canada (I by W. J. Campbell)

Shideler, James H., ed., *Agricultural History,* Univ. of California, Davis, Calif. (L)

Shipman, R. S., *McKenzie County Farmer,* Watford City, N.Dak. (B)

Shonley, Tom, Wessington Springs, S.Dak. (L)

Signs, Penni, Amarillo, Tex. (L)

Simpson, "Lucky," Hanna, Alberta, Canada (L)

Skaggs, J. M., prof. of American studies, Wichita State Univ., Wichita, Kans. (L)

Slagowski, Charlene, Carlin, Nev. (L, Q)

Slease, Robert P., director of public information, Dept. of Transportation, Topeka, Kans. (L)

Sloan, Jay C., Georgetown, Tex. (L)

Sloane, Eric, Warren, Conn. (L)

Smallwood, Charles M., dean, School of Agriculture, West Texas State Univ., Canyon, Tex. (L)

Smith, David C., prof. and chairman, Dept. of History, Univ. of Maine, Orono, Maine (L)

Smith, David E., Olathe, Kans. (I, L, P, Q)

Smith, E. A., chairman, Service Drilling Co., Tulsa, Okla. (L)

Smith, George L., ed., *Kansas Farmer,* Topeka, Kans. (L)

Smith, Ian, Mabe, Cornwall, England (I)

Smith, Irene M., Willowdale, Ontario, Canada (L)

Smith, James R., agricultural counselor, Australian Embassy, Washington, D.C. (L)

Smith, Max B., D.V.M., Livestock Disease Control Branch, Dept. of Agriculture, Honolulu, Hawaii (L)

Smith, Richard, Deerhead Ranch, Laramie, Wyo. (L)

Smyth, Frank, public information officer, Dept. of Highways, Carson City, Nev. (B, Q, S)

Snoddy, Donald D., asst. state archivist, Nebraska State Historical Soc., Lincoln, Nebr. (B, L)

Socolofsky, Homer E., Dept. of History, Kansas State Univ., Manhattan, Kans. (I by Don Mzorek)

Sollenberger, George R., ed., *Furrow,* Moline, Ill. (L)

Southcombe, John W., Blanchester, Ohio (L)

Spade, Grayson, Reading, Kans. (I)

Spencer, Meredith, Powder River Enterprises, Provo, Utah (B, L, Q, S)

Stansbury, Olin, Butler County Historical Soc., El Dorado, Kans. (T)

Stenberg, Christian, Watford City, N.Dak. (L)

Stephenson, E. A., Bucklin, Kans. (Q)

Stevens, Dwight L., Dept. of Highways, Des Moines, Iowa (Q)

Stone, Bill, Piedmont, S.C. (L)

Storm, Melvin G., assoc. prof. of English, Emporia State Univ., Emporia, Kans. (I)

Stout, Elmore, T S Ranch, Bazaar, Kans. (I)

Stout, Stanley E., Lenexa, Kans. (L)

Strain, Anthony James, staff photographer, *Sheridan Press,* Sheridan, Wyo. (L, P)

Sullivan, Mrs. J. A., examiner, Classification Section, Patent Office, London, England (B, L)

Sutton, E. S., Benkelman, Nebr. (L, Q)

Swingle, M. K., California Historical Soc., San Francisco, Calif. (L)

Swoyer, Karen, Westmoreland, Kans. (I)

Syler, Matthew M., Burton, Tex. (Q)

Symons, Gerry, New Barn Farm, Exeter, Devon, England (I, L)

Symons, Mrs. Gerry, New Barn Farm, Exeter, Devon, England (I)

Talley, Mabel Apple, Albemarle County Historical Soc. Library, Charlottesville, Va. (B, L, T)

Taylor, Jay, Amarillo, Tex. (L, P, Q)

Taylor, Patricia L., reference librarian, Virginia State Library, Richmond, Va. (L, T)

Teeter, Richard, advertising and technical publications supervisor, Tamper Division, Canron Corp., West Columbia, S.C. (B, L)

Teter, Linny, Thrall, Kans. (I)

Thomas, Prof. Charles, Inst. of Cornish Studies, Univ. of Exeter, Redruth, Cornwall, England (L)

Thomas, E. B., Dept. of Transportation, Sacramento, Calif. (Q)

Thompson, Britton, Chanute, Kans. (L, P)

Thompson, Chuck, Dept. of Art, Long Beach State Univ., Long Beach, Calif. (L)

Thompson, Donald, Arlington, Tex. (I)
Thompson, Floyd, McCracken, Kans. (L, P)
Thompson, Leonard, prof. of history, Yale Univ., New Haven, Conn. (Q)
Thompson, Wilbur R., Chanute, Kans. (B, I)
Thompson, William R., Lawrence, Kans. (I, P)
Tindall, Elizabeth, reference asst., Missouri Historical Soc. Library, St. Louis, Mo. (L)
Todd, Doug, Rexford, Kans. (I)
Todd, Joan, Rexford, Kans. (I)
Tracy, R. J., commissioner of patents, Ottawa, Canada (B, L)
Triplett, Elizabeth, Evans, Wash. (L)
Trosper, Mrs. Corwin, Higgins, Tex. (L)
Troyer, Everett, North Platte, Nebr. (L)
Troyer, Ona, North Platte, Nebr. (L)
Turner, Kaye Y., Pocatello, Idaho (L)
Turner, Leland J., Roberts, Mont. (L)
Tuttle, Albert, Quinter, Kans. (Q)
Tyson, Pat, U.S. General Accounting Office, Washington, D.C. (L)
Underwood, Jerry, *Emporia Gazette,* Emporia, Kans. (B, L)
Upton, Howard, executive vice-pres., Petroleum Equipment Inst., Tulsa, Okla. (L)
Vahshotz, Fred, Abilene, Kans. (T)
Vanstone, Janet M. (Mrs. James), Clovelly, Devon, England (L)
Vatthauer, Richard J., extension livestock specialist, Univ. of Wisconsin, Madison, Wis. (L)
Vaughan, Margot C., registrar, Shelburne Museum, Shelburne, Vt. (L)
Vaughn, Anna, Grand Junction, Colo. (L, P)
Vaughn, V. Allan, pres., National Railway Historical Soc., Oak Park, Ill. (L)
Vellam, David J., Beaminster, Dorset, England (L)
Vestwebber, Jerry, D.V.M., School of Veterinary Medicine, Kansas State Univ., Manhattan, Kans. (T)
Vise, Yvonne, Library Dept., *Minot Daily News,* Minot, N.Dak. (B, L)
Voights, Linda, Dept. of English, Univ. of Missouri, Kansas City, Mo. (I)
Wade, Bob, Grand Island, Nebr. (L)
Wade, Connie, Grand Island, Nebr. (L)
Wagner, B. J., Dept. of English, National Coll. of Education, Evanston, Ill. (L)
Wakefield, L. P., Stephenville, Tex. (I, L, P)
Walk, Richard, prof. of psychology, George Washington Univ., Washington, D.C. (T)
Walker, Merle, Ellis County Historical Soc., Hays, Kans. (L)
Wangsness, Wayne R., Decorah, Iowa (L)
Ward, Russel, prof. of history, Univ. of New England, Armidale, New South Wales, Australia (L)
Washington, Mary A., Utah State Univ., Logan, Utah (L, P)
Watson, Chick, Belmont, Calif. (L)
Watson, Lloyd, Sublette, Kans. (L)
Weiner, P. B., reference specialist, State Historical Soc. of Missouri, Columbia, Mo. (L)
Welch, John, assoc. director of policy development, National Cattlemens Assn., Denver, Colo. (L)
Wellner, L. H., Virgil, Kans. (L, Q)

Wells, Ernest R., Elgin, Oreg. (B, L, P, S)

Wendeln, Leo N., sales manager, Pax Distributing Co., Coldwater, Ohio (L)

Wheat, Otis, Alva, Okla. (L)

White, John H., Jr., curator, Div. of Transportation, Smithsonian Inst., Washington, D.C. (L)

White, John M., Las Cruces, N.Mex. (L, P)

Whiteley, Tommie, assoc. archivist, Southwest Collection, Texas Tech Univ., Lubbock, Tex. (B, L)

Whitmer, Larry, Zenda, Kans. (I)

Whitten, Ronnie, Killeen, Tex. (L)

Whitthorne, S. N., asst. road maintenance engineer, Louisiana Dept. of Transportation and Development, Baton Rouge, La. (Q)

Widdowson, J. D. A., director, Centre for English Cultural Tradition and Language, Univ. of Sheffield, Sheffield, England (L)

Wilkerson, Olvin, patent search advisor, U.S. Patent & Trademark Office, Washington, D.C. (B, L)

Wilkinson, Mrs. R., Henderson, Nev. (L)

Willard, Bruce, Homer, Alaska (L)

Williams, William J., Emporia, Kans. (I)

Wilson, Boyd, ed., *New Zealand Farmer,* Auckland, New Zealand (B, L)

Wimberley, C. W., San Marcos, Tex. (L, P, Q)

Wing, Kenneth E., director, Agricultural Experiment Sta., Univ. of Maine, Orono, Maine (L)

Winger, Bud, Yuma, Colo. (I by Cynthia Dale)

Winger, DeEtta, Johnson, Kans. (I by Cynthia Dale)

Winkler, Thomas W., Wichita, Kans. (L, Q)

Wittwer, S. H., asst. dean, Coll. of Agriculture & Natural Resources, Michigan State Univ., East Lansing, Mich. (L)

Wolin, Ron, executive director, Cartoonists Guild Inc., New York, N.Y. (L)

Wood, C. G., Floresville, Tex. (L, Q)

Wood, Charles L., prof. of history, Texas Tech Univ., Lubbock, Tex. (L)

Wood, J. Roy, Trousdale, Kans. (I)

Wright, David G., chief, Office of Park Planning and Environmental Quality, National Park Service, Washington, D.C. (L)

Wright, Linda S., Maryo River Ranch, Deeth, Nev. (L)

Wright, Michael, ed., *Country Life,* London, England (L)

Wyland, Mrs. Viola F., Mulberry, Kans. (L)

Wyrick, Green D., Emporia, Kans. (I)

Wyse, Mrs. Tom, Lindsay, Mont. (L)

Yamamoto, Tom T., acting county extension chairman, Cooperative Extension Service, Hilo, Hawaii (L)

Yost, Nellie Snyder, North Platte, Nebr. (L)

Young, A. F., Riley, Kans. (L)

Young, A. G. ("Jim"), T Z Ranch, Cassoday, Kans. (I)

Young, Nigel E., Grassland Research Inst., Hurley Maidenhead, Berkshire, England (L)

Young, Richard, Dickinson, N.Dak. (L, P)

Zimmerman, "Slim," Afton, Wyo. (L)

INDEX